BASIC
TENT CAMPING

BASIC
TENT CAMPING

• •

FRAZIER M. DOUGLASS IV

BASIC TENT CAMPING

iUniverse books may be ordered through booksellers or by contacting:

iUniverse
1663 Liberty Drive
Bloomington, IN 47403
www.iuniverse.com
1-800-Authors (1-800-288-4677)

Because of the dynamic nature of the Internet, any web addresses or links contained in this book may have changed since publication and may no longer be valid. The views expressed in this work are solely those of the author and do not necessarily reflect the views of the publisher, and the publisher hereby disclaims any responsibility for them.

Any people depicted in stock imagery provided by Thinkstock are models, and such images are being used for illustrative purposes only. Certain stock imagery © Thinkstock.

ISBN: 978-1-4917-7941-5 (sc)
ISBN: 978-1-4917-7942-2 (e)

Library of Congress Control Number: 2015916925

Print information available on the last page.

iUniverse rev. date: 10/12/2015

CONTENTS

Other Books by Frazier Douglass

Lightweight Camping for Motorcycle Travel: Revised Edition

The Tent Camper's Handbook

The Family Camping Guide to Wisconsin, Michigan, Illinois & Indiana

To the three women who have joined me on many past camping trips:
Eva Garcia Noveron Douglass,
Robin Elizabeth Fain (Douglass) Moore, and
Peggie Katherine Weese (Douglass) Tucker

And to basic tent campers who reject the
artificial extravagance of RV living
and want to learn better ways to travel comfortably with small tents.

A man who gets his two weeks' salary while he is on vacation should be able to put those two weeks in fishing and camping and be able to save one week's salary clear. He ought to be able to sleep comfortably every night, to eat well every day and to return to the city rested and in good condition.

—Ernest Hemmingway (1920)

PREFACE

In 1967, my new bride and I bought an old canvas tent from an army surplus store and began camping in state and federal campgrounds around the country. We realized that camping allowed us to visit many popular attractions for a fraction of the cost of staying in motels and eating in restaurants. One night camping in St. Andrews State Park in Panama City, Florida, allowed us to visit the beach for less than ten dollars a day, whereas staying in a motel on the Florida Gulf Coast cost sixty dollars or more in those days. Most of our camping trips were in the southeastern states, but a few ventured farther away. We enjoyed glorious camping trips to the Grand Canyon, the Colorado Rockies, the Great Plains of Kansas, Northern Utah, and Lake Manitoba in Canada. Today, the financial savings of camping over motel-based vacations amounts to over $1,000 per week. Although the marriage did not survive, my love of camping did. Over the next half decade, I came to enjoy camping as a recreational activity that provided many personal benefits in addition to the financial ones.

Given the enormous financial savings of tent camping in public campgrounds, one might wonder why more people do not choose tent camping as their vacation travel strategy. Based upon conversations with family members and acquaintances, I have concluded that one reason is that many noncampers hold irrational fears that tent camping is an uncomfortable and even dangerous activity. Unfortunately, many modern camping books and articles do not allay these fears and, in some cases, further reinforce common irrational fears. Survival books and articles, in particular, describe broken bones, hypothermia, dehydration, and near-death experiences with bears or cougars that most basic tent campers will never encounter. Backpacking, mountaineering, and canoe camping books describe blisters, strained muscles, dehydrated meals, dirt, contaminated drinking water, and other discomforts associated with backcountry travel. In short, most camping books fail to provide an accurate overview of basic camping equipment and procedures that can enhance comfort when camping in public campgrounds. People's unrealistic fears are further reinforced when they attempt poorly planned camping trips and experience predictable discomforts or when they hear exaggerated stories about other people's unpleasant camping experiences. Scary campfire stories about bears and other wild animals help to transmit these irrational fears to children.

Regardless of the cause, many noncampers believe that sleeping on the ground must be cold and uncomfortable, that the weather will be unbearably hot or cold, that food cannot be properly cooked, that cleanliness and personal hygiene cannot be maintained, that toilets will be nasty or unavailable, that mosquitoes and other bugs will make life miserable, that life in the woods without a TV and computer will be painfully boring, that dangerous critters or people will attack them, and that other serious problems will befall them.

A second reason why many people do not take advantage of the financial savings of camping-based travel is that they lack practical knowledge about modern equipment and strategies that can make camping trips more comfortable and mobile—and do not know where to acquire this information. Although many books have been written about camping, few provide the practical information that noncamping families need to acquire.

I first became aware of the limitations of modern camping books back in 1999. I had attempted a few short motorcycle camping trips with old bulky equipment and found that I had difficulty packing everything on my motorcycle and living comfortably in the campsite. After returning home from one trip, I bought a motorcycle camping book to learn what specific tents, sleeping bags, and kitchen gear were best suited for motorcycle travel and where to find them. Unfortunately, the book failed to answer my questions. Instead, it displayed photos of old, bulky cabin tents, kitchen shelving units, and stoves that could never be packed on a motorcycle, and focused upon general travel topics.

Over the next several months, I attempted more motorcycle and lightweight camping trips and identified more problems. To find solutions to these problems, I bought several car camping, family camping, wilderness camping, backpacking, and mountaineering books only to discover that not one of them answered my specific questions, such as, What are the best tents for basic tent camping? Where can you buy them? How much do they cost? How do you acquire firewood? How can you split it? Why is some firewood easy to split while other firewood is difficult?

In general, these camping books suggested that camping was fun and provided a few basic tips, but not one of them provided a complete overview of basic tent camping. In general, they featured outdated equipment; provided little information about current model names, features, and prices; ignored typical campground regulations regarding firewood, quiet hours, speed limits, and campsite setup; gave questionable advice based upon little, if any, objective rationale; ignored the dangers associated with camping in small, remote campgrounds; overlooked several common camping tasks, such as setting up kitchen canopies and safeguarding food from animal scavengers; ignored many common camping problems, such as thunderstorms and disorderly neighbors; and failed to mention the need to reserve campsites in popular campgrounds months before a trip.

After realizing that current books failed to answer many important questions about basic tent camping, I began reading store catalogues; online product descriptions; old camping books, such as the ones by Thomas H. Holding (1908) and Horace Kephart (1917); and modern backpacking books, such as those by Rick Curtis (2005) and Ryan Jordan (2005). Although none of these resources answered all my questions, each one provided some useful information plus a framework for finding solutions to common camping problems. Using these resources as general guides and personal experience to fill in details, I developed a familiarity with modern equipment and practical solutions to dozens of common camping problems. Over the next nine years, my reading and practical experiences led to three books.

In 2009, I published some of this information in *Lightweight Camping for Motorcycle Travel*. Three years later, I described general tent-camping equipment and procedures in *The Tent Camper's Handbook*. After publishing these two books, I began taking more-challenging camping trips and testing better ways to improve my overall mobility and comfort. I also began reading about the history of tent camping and looking for nuggets of information that have been lost over the past one hundred years. I spent a considerable amount of time testing various pieces of modern lightweight camping equipment and learning about their strengths and limitations. These efforts have helped me see many more omissions of modern camping books and the limitations of many commonly repeated camping tips.

By 2013, I realized that *The Tent Camper's Handbook* still omitted a lot of useful information, and so I decided to revise it and include information about motorcycle camping, resulting in this book. As the revisions were extensive, I decided to rename the book *Basic Tent Camping*. This updated book organizes camping-related observations, information, and insights that I have acquired over the past fifty years. It explains, in great detail, how to plan and execute economical and comfortable basic-tent-camping vacation trips to developed state and federal campgrounds located many miles away from one's home. Furthermore, it provides considerable information about the history of camping equipment and critically examines common misconceptions.

The book is organized into eighteen chapters. The first chapter presents a brief history of basic tent camping. The next eight chapters present detailed information about modern camping equipment and important features to consider before purchasing major items such as tents, sleeping bags, stoves, kitchen sets, hatchets, and clothing. In these chapters, specific product names and retailers are cited so that readers can go to the Internet and view pictures, compare specifications, read consumer reviews, and determine current prices. Although some models may be discontinued after a year or two, new models may be introduced, and prices fluctuate during the year, details presented in this section should provide a solid foundation for evaluating camping equipment for many years to come. The opinions expressed in this section are based upon my own personal experiences and readings and are not influenced by manufacturer payments or incentives.

Subsequent chapters of this book describe how to plan basic-tent-camping vacations to state, federal, county, or municipal campgrounds around the country; how to quickly set up comfortable camping quarters in different types of campsites; how to stay dry and warm in a wide range of weather conditions; how to live comfortably in a small campsite for several days or weeks; how to prepare a variety of simple but great-tasting meals with a camp stove or campfire; and how to maintain and upgrade camping equipment for many years to come.

In sum, this book presents important information about basic tent camping that can be found in no other book. It describes modern equipment that can enhance both comfort and mobility. It describes simple procedures that can resolve most common camping problems. It also clarifies many misconceptions and undocumented opinions that are commonly voiced in other books. Regardless of past camping experience, all readers will discover useful strategies that will make their future camping vacations more enjoyable.

ACKNOWLEDGMENTS

I want to express my deep appreciation to my wife, Eva Noveron Douglass, who has joined me on dozens of camping trips since 2010. Although she never camped before we met, she immediately fell in love with it and learned the routine quickly. She enjoys camping because it reminds her of her childhood growing up in Tierra Caliente, Mexico. She has joined me on several multiday trips to Florida and Alabama Gulf Coast beaches; Elkmont Campground in Great Smoky Mountains National Park; Peninsula State Park near Fish Creek, Wisconsin; West Michigan's beaches; and other destinations throughout the southeastern and upper-midwestern United States.

I would like to express appreciation to my family members who have joined me on various trips over the past fifty years. I am grateful to my father, Frazier Michel Douglass III, and stepmother, Kitty Douglass Whitehurst, for introducing me to camping when I was a child. They took me on several camping trips to Cheaha State Park near Gadsden, Alabama; Monte Sano State Park in Huntsville, Alabama; and Wind Creek Park in Alexander City, Alabama. Despite being in her late eighties, Kitty recently joined me and my sisters for a weekend camp at F. D. Roosevelt State Park in Georgia. My sister Carla also joined us on that trip. My two sons, Shel and Lyle Douglass, have joined me on several camping trips over the past thirty years. My sisters Jean Douglass Baswell and Cecelia Douglass Herndon have provided friendship and support over the past sixty years and have accompanied me on a few past camping trips. My stepson, Leonardo Diaz; his wife, Maria; and their two older sons, Cristian and Eric Ochoa, have joined us on several recent trips. In fact, Cristian and Eric have joined us on trips to Joe Wheeler State Park in Alabama; Elkmont Campground in Great Smoky Mountains National Park in Tennessee; Gulf Islands National Seashore in Pensacola, Florida; and Holland State Park in West Michigan. A few months ago, Leonardo and Maria's youngest son (little Leonardo) joined us for his first camping trip to Wind Creek State Park in Alabama. He was just eighteen months old. I am especially grateful to my sister Jean Douglass Baswell, who has been a regular camping companion, a critical editor, and a major source of support and inspiration.

I want to thank all my friends who have joined me on camping trips over the last fifty-five years. This list includes Garret and Mary Deckert, who introduced Peggie (my first wife) and me to great camping destinations in southeastern Wisconsin and dispersed camping in the Black River State Forest near Black River Falls, Wisconsin. More recently, Forest and Celeste Bedingfield joined me and Robin (my second wife) on two cold, rainy fall trips to Smoky Mountains National Park and Cheaha State Park near Gadsden, Alabama. Carey Cooper was a longtime lunch companion who listened to my camping stories and suggested many new destinations. Regina Anderton and her husband, David, survived violent storms with me at Raccoon Mountain in Tennessee. Gail Worthy and Kay Tersigni accompanied me on a few trips during the late 1990s. Jim Kerner tried motorcycle camping with me at the 29 Dreams Motorcycle Only Campground near Birmingham. Richard and Bonnie Webb joined me for a week in Door County, Wisconsin. Linda Voitle Bozeman joined my family on trips to Cades Cove; Helen, Georgia; and Stone Mountain, Georgia. Gene Tiser joined Eva and me during a short trip to the Northern Highland–American Legion State Forest in Wisconsin.

Finally, I would like to thank the friends who have provided special support over the past twenty-five years, including Al Elmore, Harry Joiner, Randy McIntosh, Tim Jones, Bruce Thomas, Ron Fritze, Celeste Bedingfield, Debbie Kelley, Mary Simpson, Betty Marks, Steve Clark, Damon Lares, and Tracy Hicks. I am especially grateful to James Gadberry and Connie Alred, who have been good friends and regular lunch companions over the past eleven years. They first encouraged me to write a book on camping one morning while eating breakfast at Waffle House. They have listened to many stories from past camping trips, read several parts of the manuscript, offered advice when I could not see the best way to proceed, and watched Eva's and my house while we were away on several trips.

INTRODUCTION

The terms *car camping* and *family camping* are frequently used in many camping books to refer to a wide range of camping equipment that could not possibly be transported in most cars and a wide range of procedures that may not apply in many typical camp settings. After pondering these inconsistencies for several years, I have concluded that the term *car camping* should be divided into two specific, clearly defined camping approaches.

Basic tent camping is a car-camping approach practiced by thousands of American families—including my family. It emphasizes a balance between economy, comfort, and mobility. Basic-tent-camping families typically buy small four- to six-person tents and compact camping equipment that can be packed into small, fuel-efficient vehicles. They travel to developed state and federal campgrounds that have defined campsites, parking areas, picnic tables, fire rings, potable water, and clean toilets. Larger campgrounds may also have electrical outlets for charging cell phones, hot showers, Laundromats, swimming areas, and convenience stores. Couples without children can pack all their equipment in the trunks of their vehicles while couples with children usually need to add rooftop carriers. Since this approach uses relatively few well-chosen and well-organized pieces of equipment, it requires little time to pack, little time to set up camp, and little time to break camp—thus facilitating mobility. As a result, these families are able to take more trips, travel farther, camp overnight along the way, visit more attractions, and have more fun. After setting up camp, these families can enjoy a wide variety of activities, including swimming, fishing, visiting historic sites, attending nature programs, and enjoying local festivals.

Luxury tent camping, on the other hand, is a very different approach that emphasizes extravagance. Families that practice this approach typically need large trucks and trailers to haul a massive amount of equipment, including large eight- to twelve-person cabin tents (or small pop-up camping trailers) that would completely fill many small campsites. After setting up the tent, these families typically set up large screen rooms and unpack large grills, huge tubs of kitchen equipment, huge bags of clothing, and a variety of recreational equipment. Because this type of camping requires considerable effort to pack, set up camp, and break camp, these families usually take fewer trips each year, travel shorter distances, and frequently stay in the same old campgrounds every year. Walk-in campsites would be out of the question. After setting up camp, they spend most of the time relaxing in their campsites, preparing elaborate meals, visiting with neighbors, and swimming in lakes within walking distance of their campsites.

In addition to basic tent camping and luxury tent camping, several other camping approaches have been identified over the past twenty years. These approaches include classic tent camping, backpacking, mountaineering, canoe camping, equestrian camping, motorcycle camping, and bicycle camping. (Some people include RV living, but I contend that this is not camping.) While all these approaches share a few commonalities, each approach requires specific equipment and specific procedures that may not be appropriate for other approaches. For example, basic tent campers can pack a lot of clothing and personal items because they do not need to pack much water or food. They can usually find potable water in most public campgrounds and food in nearby grocery stores or restaurants. Backpackers, on the other hand, often only have room to pack a change of underwear and socks because they must pack water, water-purification equipment, and dehydrated food for the entire length of their trip.

One of the first tasks of any camping approach is to assemble all the equipment and clothing needed to live comfortably in different weather conditions and locations. To help campers select the equipment they will likely need, several camping books offer checklists. Some of these lists include hundreds of items, and the authors expect each family to select the specific items they will need—but these checklists are of little value for inexperienced families who may not know what they will need in certain situations. Other books offer short lists of "essential items," suggesting that campers can live comfortably with just those few items.

Although most early books and magazine articles included lists of essential items, the concept of essential items was popularized by the *Mountaineers' Handbook*, published in the 1930s by a Seattle, Washington, hiking and mountain-climbing club. This book, now titled *Mountaineering: Freedom of the Hills*, became the bible of mountain-climbing enthusiasts and included a list of ten items needed for any mountaineering trip to survive emergencies, such as sudden snowstorms or getting lost in the wilderness. The ten essential items were map, compass, sunglasses and sunscreen, extra food and water, extra clothes, headlamp or flashlight, first aid kit, fire starter, matches, and knife.

Over the next several years, other camping and hiking groups adopted the concept of ten essentials and modified the list to fit particular geographic areas and recreational activities. REI, for example, recently published a list of ten essential gear categories for hikers. The REI list includes gear needed for navigation, sun protection, insulation, illumination, first aid supplies, fire, repair kit and tools, nutrition, hydration, and emergency shelter.

While these ten-essentials lists may at first appear to offer helpful guidance, further consideration quickly reveals that these lists do not include dozens of specific items, such as toothbrush, sleeping bag, bath towel, and cord, needed by most basic tent campers for extended camping trips. Furthermore, these essential-gear lists include other items, such as a compass and water-purification equipment, that most basic-tent-camping families would never need. None of these lists mention kitchen shelters despite the fact that early pioneer campers considered them to be essential and that many contemporary tent campers routinely set them up in their campsites.

For many years, I used first one published list and then another to guide my gear-packing decisions but repeatedly was disappointed because each one failed to include items I needed for specific camping situations and included other items that I never needed and that repeatedly got in the way. After several years of disappointing experiences, I concluded these lists did not emphasize the items that I believed to be essential. Consequently, I developed my own system for classifying and listing camping equipment.

My system begins by defining ten general equipment categories and then lists essential and optional items in each category. Currently, the system includes over eighty essential items, but most of these items are small and can be packed in a small space. In fact, all of the essential items plus one or two optional items can be packed in motorcycle saddlebags and a T-Bag.

To organize this equipment so that any item can be easily found, items in each category should be packed together in a special container. For example, tents should be packed in duffel bags; kitchen equipment should be packed in milk crates; and small personal items should be packed in small day packs. More details about the equipment in each category and how it should be packed are presented in chapters 2 through 9. The complete packing guide is provided at the end of this book.

Many of the essential and optional items introduced in the following chapters can be purchased from local department stores and sporting goods stores. Champion sportswear garments sold in Target stores, for example, are economically priced and make excellent camping and recreational garments. Good-quality tents, sleeping bags, air mattresses, kitchen equipment, and clothing can be purchased in Bass Pro Shops, Cabela's, and Gander Mountain stores. But the best-quality camping clothing and equipment is only available at camping outfitters such as REI, Campmor, Backcountry.com, MountainGear.com, Moosejaw, and Sierra Trading Post.

This campsite in the Platte River Campground in the Sleeping Bear Dunes National Lakeshore in Michigan shows my wife's and my ideal camp setup. Our tent is on an elevated, crushed-stone tent pad, and our kitchen canopy is directly in front of the tent. Nearby trees and understory vegetation provide shade and privacy plus places to hang our clothesline and hammocks. A nice shower building with flush toilets is located a few yards away, and dozens of recreational opportunities are available within a few miles.

This was our camp in Waterloo State Recreation Area's Big Portage Lake Campground in Michigan.

In hilly terrain, such as that found at Lake Lurleen State Park in Alabama, our setup can be modified.

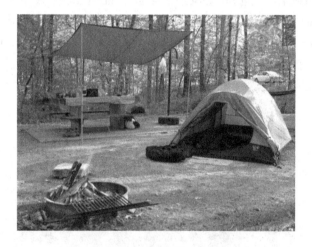

This campsite at Cedars of Lebanon State Park in Tennessee shows essential equipment that was packed on a motorcycle.

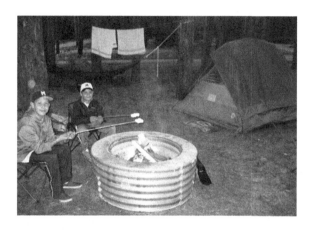

Campfires allow families to cook meals, make s'mores, warm up on cool days, and enjoy many relaxing hours staring into the flickering flames.

1

HISTORY

Basic tent camping has been a popular recreational activity for over one hundred years. During the early years, ordinary families typically prepared their camping kits by making some items, collecting a few cooking supplies from their kitchens, selecting a few garments from their closets, and buying a few modern items from retailers such as the former outfitter Abercrombie & Fitch. They packed this equipment and clothing in or on horse-drawn wagons, bicycles, motorcycles, or automobiles and traveled to destinations that permitted overnight camping. After setting up camp, they typically lived in their camp for several days or weeks. They hunted or fished and ate many simple, tasty meals.

During these early years, basic tent camping was supported by many social institutions. State and federal governments established hundreds of state and federal parks with developed campgrounds. Several companies began developing improved technology and equipment. And several accomplished woodsmen wrote inspiring books and magazine articles featuring glorious descriptions of camping techniques and exciting destinations. This chapter will summarize specific developments that have stimulated the growth of basic tent camping as a travel strategy and recreational activity.

Late 1800s

Early seeds of interest in basic tent camping as a recreational activity were sown in the late 1800s when state and federal governments claimed several scenic areas across the country as protected public properties. For example, the federal government claimed Yosemite Valley and the Mariposa Grove and granted the land to the state of California in 1864 to be managed as a state park. A few years later, Yellowstone was established as the first national park in 1872. In 1885, Niagara Falls Reservation was established by the state of New York as a state preserve, and in the same year Yosemite was deeded back to the federal government to be managed as a national park. Each of these events opened attractive vacation and camping destinations.

In 1891, the Forest Reserve Act established national forest preserves that would later become national forests. In 1892, the Sierra Club was established to help conserve scenic lands in the West. Noted American conservationists and outdoor enthusiasts, including Ralph Waldo Emerson, Henry David Thoreau, John Muir, and President Theodore Roosevelt traveled to remote wilderness areas during the late 1800s and described these beautiful places in popular magazines and books. In these articles, the authors argued that the unique beauty of these properties should be preserved for all Americans, including future generations, to enjoy. Although these places could only be accessed by rail and horseback at the time, they inspired many Americans to dream about future trips to exotic camping and vacation destinations across America.

1900–1946

After the turn of the century, economic prosperity plus the availability of motorcycles, automobiles, improved highways, and more public parks stimulated interest in camping vacations. The American Antiques Act, passed in 1906, authorized the president to designate unique scenic places as national landmarks to protect them from commercial development, and these landmarks offered additional camping destinations. The National Park Service was established in 1916, and several parks, including Rocky Mountain (1915), Grand Canyon (1919), and Smoky Mountains (1925) offered more camping opportunities. At the same time, many states created their own state parks with camping opportunities. For example, Wisconsin established Interstate, Peninsula, Devil's Lake, Wyalusing, Perrot, Tower Hill, Rib Mountain, and Terry Andrae as state parks before 1930. Newly constructed national roads and highways allowed ordinary families to easily travel to these new public camping and vacation destinations within a day or two.

During this same time, several books and magazine articles described how to assemble comfortable camping kits, cook good-tasting meals on campfires, and travel by car, motorcycle, bicycle, or canoe to distant camping destinations. One such book was *The Camper's Handbook* published by Thomas Hiram Holding in 1908. Holding, who is now called the Father of Modern Recreational Camping, helped establish the Association of Cycle Campers (a.k.a. the Camping and Caravanning Club) that currently claims over half a million members in Great Britain. His interest in camping began in 1853 when, as a child, he and his father crossed the American frontier on a wagon trip to California. After returning to the British Isles, Holding began taking canoe and bicycle camping trips through England and Ireland and writing about his adventures. *The Camper's Handbook* is generally considered to be his best work. It provides lengthy discussions about making tents, packing compact camping kits, preparing meals, selecting clothing, and avoiding problems. Like other early camping publications, most of the gear and food products described in his book are now outdated, but his discussion identified common camping problems and provided a foundation for evaluating future camping equipment and procedures.

Another detailed camping book was written by Horace "Kep" Kephart. Initially titled *Book of Camping and Woodcraft*, it was expanded and republished in two volumes in 1917 as *Camping and Woodcraft*. Kephart, who is now called the Dean of American Campers, lived in the mountains of North Carolina near the current Great Smoky Mountains National Park. The first volume, *Camping*, described tents, bedding, clothing, personal kits, food, and other items needed for short camping vacation trips. The second volume, *Woodcraft*, described skills needed for comfortable forest living for months at a time. Some of the skills discussed in this volume include pathfinding, marksmanship, axmanship, cabin building, skin tanning, cave exploration, and bee hunting. Although the equipment described in these volumes has been outdated for many years, the book offers a framework for describing camping equipment and procedures plus dozens of practical suggestions and insights that continue to hold value one hundred years later.

Several other books and magazine articles published during the early 1900s described camping gear and procedures. For example, "Camping Out with an Automobile" was published in *Outing* magazine in 1905. The *Boy Scouts Handbook* was first published in 1911. "The Sine Qua Non of Motorcycle Camping" was published in *Outing* magazine in 1913, "Camping Trips with a Motorcycle" was published in *Recreation* magazine in 1916, and Nessmuk's [George W. Sears's] *Woodcraft and Camping* was published in 1920. Recently, David Wescott (2009) described the early 1900s as the "golden age of camping."

The thing I like most about these early camping books and magazine articles is that they, in contrast with contemporary camping books, recognized common camping problems, offered practical solutions, and described how to prepare and execute camping trips from the start to the end. The authors of these books and articles described specific items that should be packed for camping trips, where to find them, and how to pack them. They also offered opinions about strengths and limitations of available camping gear and the best ways to use these items to achieve maximum comfort in the woods. Furthermore, they addressed dozens of common mistakes made by inexperienced campers. In other words, these early publications presented comprehensive and thoughtful discussions of tent-camping strategies rather than collections of random, poorly organized, and insufficiently justified facts and opinions.

From 1930 to 1946, interest in recreational camping continued to grow but was limited by World War I, the Great Depression, and World War II. In 1933, President Franklin D. Roosevelt founded the Civilian Conservation Corps (CCC), which built roads, dams, buildings, campgrounds, and other improvements that continue to provide the infrastructure for many state and national parks today. The Mountaineers Club of Seattle formulated a list of ten essential survival items to be packed for every mountaineering or wilderness trip and published this list in the book *Mountaineering: Freedom of the Hills*. Small camping trailers emerged during the 1930s as supplementary equipment that could add a little more comfort for tent-camping trips. Ansel Adams published breathtaking photographs of scenic vistas and unique places in Yosemite National Park and throughout the American West. And dozens of auto camps were established along newly built national highways as economical places for families to camp overnight while traveling to distant destinations.

For more information about this golden age of camping, check out *Camping in the Old Style* by David Wescott and watch YouTube videos by Steve Watts.

1947–1999

After World War II, interest in recreational camping blossomed. The country enjoyed a long period of economic prosperity. Many families had extra money and extended vacation leave. The Coleman Company began manufacturing gas lanterns, portable stoves, and other equipment suited for family camping trips. Eureka and other companies began making ready-made tents. In the 1950s, congress created national seashores and lakeshores to preserve fragile shoreline and provide water recreation and camping opportunities for American families living across the country. In 1964, the Wilderness Act created large national wilderness areas that were ideally suited for backpacking, canoe camping, and equestrian camping. Later the same year, Congress created national recreation areas, such as Land Between the Lakes in Kentucky and Tennessee and Grand Island in Michigan. Most of these recreation areas built developed and semideveloped camping areas. And thousands of families assembled camping kits and embarked upon camping vacation trips to hundreds of state and national parks around the country.

It was during this time that I first experienced the pleasure of tent camping at the age of ten. In 1955, my father bought a Volkswagen van and a small motorboat with a 35 hp motor so that he could take our family on economical waterskiing vacations to various lakes around central Alabama. Our first trip was to Wind Creek Park on Lake Martin. My father and his wife slept in the van along with my sister while my younger brother and I slept on cots in a small tent. We spent one glorious week waterskiing, swimming, hanging out with other youth, napping in our hammocks, and eating great home-cooked meals. After entering Auburn University in 1963, I bought an army surplus canvas wall tent with no floor so that I could continue taking economical weekend trips around the southeastern United States. Since then I have taken hundreds of basic-tent-camping vacation trips to over two hundred different campgrounds in twenty different states and one Canadian province.

During the 1960s and 1970s, camping blossomed, and many park officials and conservation-minded citizens began to realize that the growing numbers of people visiting state and national parks every year were gradually destroying many of the resources that the parks were created to protect. These conservationists also realized that rules and regulations were not sufficient for preventing this destruction. People were coming by the thousands year after year, hiking through forests, throwing litter on the ground, cutting vegetation, carving initials into wooden structures, killing wildlife, making fires on bare soil, and removing souvenirs. In the early 1960s, leaders in the US Forest Service in the Department of Agriculture introduced the no-trace concept for preserving national forest properties for future generations. Over the next twenty years, the US Forest Service developed this concept into a formalized no-trace program emphasizing wilderness ethics for hiking and camping.

In 1994, the Center for Outdoor Ethics assumed the leadership for this program and incorporated Leave No Trace as the primary organization for developing a general ethical code for all public-land usage. To promote this ethical code, Leave No Trace has developed a variety of educational programs and materials for park visitors of all ages. The goal of these programs and materials is to teach regular park users seven general ethical guidelines for wilderness enjoyment and encourage park users to teach others and set good examples for them to follow. These seven guidelines will be discussed in chapter 17, "Ethics."

2000–Present

After 2000, basic tent camping flourished as a popular recreational and vacation activity for thousands of American families. This growth has been partially stimulated by the development of new materials such as Lexan, titanium, nylon, and polyester and by innovative improvements to tents, mattresses, sleeping bags, cookware, clothing, and other camping equipment. It has also been stimulated by the development of dozens of public campgrounds in every state. Every year, more American families have discovered that basic tent camping offers an economical way to travel and vacation plus provides opportunities to learn about history, ecology, biology, and self-sufficiency. Families can pack a tent, some bedding, a little food, and a few kitchen items into a small car and save thousands of dollars on weeklong vacations.

The popularity of basic tent camping as a vacation activity can be seen in many parts of the country. For example, longtime campers like me have noticed that getting good campsites in popular state and federal campgrounds in Wisconsin, Michigan, and other states has become much more difficult over the past twenty years. The best campsites are now claimed months in advance. Thus, trips must be planned, and campsites must be reserved as much as six to twelve months ahead. During the month of July, campers will frequently see No Vacancy signs posted at the entrance of many popular campgrounds—even those with over a hundred campsites. Upon entering most campgrounds, campers will notice many more vehicles, tents, people, and children playing in the playgrounds than were seen twenty years ago.

Indeed, many state and federal parks have become extremely overcrowded during the camping season. Great Smoky Mountains National Park, for example, had more than 9.4 million visitors in 2010, and many of these visitors camped in one of the nine developed campgrounds in the park. Four of these campgrounds (Cades Cove, Elkmont, Smokemont, and Deep Creek), having a combined total of over 550 campsites, have been filled to capacity every summer weekend for the past five years. Anyone who visited this park during past summer-fall camping seasons found crowded campgrounds, insufficient toilets, frequent traffic jams, and difficulty obtaining parking places near popular attractions. In the same year, the Grand Canyon had approximately four million visitors, and Yellowstone had approximately three million visitors.

More evidence demonstrating the growing popularity of basic tent camping can be found in the *2014 American Camper* Report published by the Coleman Company, Inc. and Outdoor Foundation. Based upon communications with park officials and online interviews of 19,240 individuals or households chosen by a random sampling of the US population, the report estimated that 40.1 million people went camping in 2013, 2.5 million more than in 2010. Campers responding to the surveys took an average of 5.4 trips during the year, drove an average of 180 miles to their campground destinations, and spent an average of 14.9 days on camping trips, and most of them (76 percent) slept in tents. A previous study published in 2012 reported that campgrounds in the north-central region of the United States (including Michigan and Wisconsin) had one of the larger increases in total campsite occupancy from 2010 to 2011 (4.9 percent).

Other studies also demonstrate the growing popularity of camping. For example, a study by the Sporting Goods Manufacturers Association and the Outdoor Industry Association concluded that 53 million Americans camped out at least once in 2003 and over 51 million took more than one camping trip (Tilton and Hostetter 2006). A report entitled *Parks in Transition* by the Property and Environmental Research Center concluded that visitors to state parks across the United States increased from 193 million in 1980 to 750 million in 1997. And a recent *National Park Service Report* concluded that visitors to national parks increased from 220.5 million in 1980 to 277.6 million in 2006.

Future

The future of basic tent camping is hard to predict. In some states, such as Wisconsin and Michigan, it appears to be growing stronger and stronger every year. But in other states, such as Indiana and Alabama, it seems to be on the decline. Growing personal debt, a shrinking middle class, higher entrance and camping fees, youth sports programs, advertising and political pressures from the RV and hotel industry, and several other social factors seem to be impacting the number of ordinary families who take tent-camping vacations each year. In many states few families have the time, money, or inclination to spend a week or two in the woods. In these states, very few tent-camping families are seen during the weeks and weekends after school starts in August.

In fact, some public campgrounds in Indiana, Alabama, and Florida are being redeveloped to accommodate large motor homes and fifth wheels owned by retired upper-class couples rather than tents that are typically used by young families with children. In Alabama, for example, Gulf State Park's campground and a few other state park campgrounds have been converted into large trailer parks with small, closely spaced, paved parking spaces and few acceptable tent-camping sites. To accommodate more of these large motor homes and fifth wheels, parks typically cut trees, widen roads, crowd small sites together, pave large amounts of ground space, install 50-amp electrical service, install underground water and sewer connections for each site, and generally destroy the old forest campgrounds that our forefathers worked so hard to create.

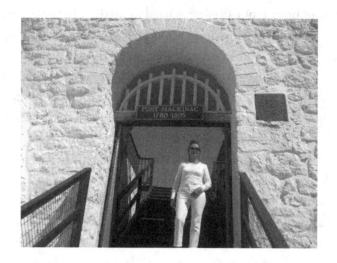

Fort Mackinac was established as America's second national park in 1875 and rededicated as Michigan's first state park in 1895.

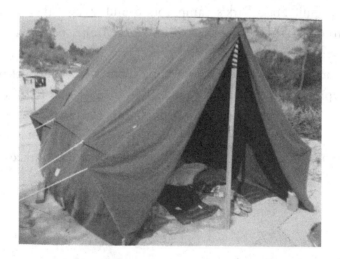

I purchased this military-style canvas tent from an army surplus store in 1965. Notice that it had no floor. Photo was taken in St. Andrews State Park in Florida.

This was my 1969 campsite in the South Rim campground of the Grand Canyon National Park in Arizona. The park was initially established as a forest reserve in 1893 and subsequently rededicated as a national park in 1919.

Great Smoky Mountains National Park in Tennessee and North Carolina was established in 1934. This church and other historic buildings are scattered around the Cades Cove loop.

2

SHELTER

In the early 1900s, very few companies sold ready-made tents. Typically, campers found suitable patterns in books such as *The Camper's Handbook* (Holding 1908) or *Camping and Woodcraft* (Kephart 1917); purchased material such as cotton duck, heavy wigan, oiled calico, linen, or silk; cut sheets according to the selected pattern; and sewed these sheets together. After making the tent body, campers had to make poles and pegs from hickory or cut them from saplings after arriving at a campsite. Some early tent patterns described in *The Camper's Handbook* included the army bell, cabin, Canadian, Gypsy, tepee, and brigand. A few outdoorsmen, who could afford it, ordered ready-made tents from Abercrombie & Fitch or another outfitter. Since these tents did not have sewn-in floors, many campers sewed a twelve-inch sod cloth around the bottom edges that could be folded inward and used with straw or a canvas tarp to make a weatherproof tent floor.

As camping became more popular during the early 1900s, several companies began selling ready-made tents. The Eureka Tent & Awning Company, founded in 1895 in Binghamton, New York, was one of the first. Their tents, made from natural white cotton duck cloth, quickly developed a reputation for quality and durability. During World War II, Eureka developed a nationwide reputation by making tents for the military. After the war, the company began producing several different styles for recreational camping.

The Coleman Company, headquartered in Wichita, Kansas, and Racine, Wisconsin, was founded in 1905 after W. C. Coleman purchased the rights to make an unusually bright gas lamp that he'd seen displayed in a store window in Brocton, Alabama. During World War II, the company began making gas stoves for the military and established a name for quality outdoor-recreation products. After the war, the Coleman Company responded to the increasing popularity of recreational camping by making folding camping stoves and subsequently added tents and steel-clad coolers to its product line.

Recreational Equipment Inc. (REI), founded in 1938 in Seattle, Washington, as an equipment co-op making economical ice axes for mountain climbers, subsequently began buying outdoor equipment from various manufacturers at wholesale prices and selling this equipment to co-op members at lower-than-retail prices. Within a couple of decades, the co-op began making its own tents for recreational camping. An early tent model available in 1972, called the High-Light, had huge screened side windows and became a popular design.

Today, dozens of companies make a wide range of ready-made tents and kitchen canopies, eliminating the need for campers to make their own tents. Eureka, Coleman, and REI have been joined by the North Face, Kelty, Sierra Designs, Mountain Hardwear, Marmot, Big Agnes, and several other tent-making companies. Wenzel and Slumberjack have established reputations for making economically priced tents while outdoor clothing companies such as L.L.Bean, Field & Stream, Cabela's, and Columbia have added tents to their product lines. Several chain department and sporting goods stores, such as Walmart, Kmart, Dick's Sporting Goods, Bass Pro Shops, Gander Mountain, and Academy Sports, also sell tents made exclusively for their stores. Most tent makers offer several different patterns and sizes to meet a wide range of individual and family needs. And these tents range in size from tiny one-person backpacking tents to spacious ten- and twelve-person family and base-camp tents.

When shopping for a tent, I suggest that most couples and small families purchase a four-person family tent. The tent should be sturdy enough to provide shelter from wind, rain, dewfall, dust, dirt, insects, critters, and other occasional environmental inconveniences. To facilitate maximum mobility, it should be compact enough to pack in a small space, easy to set up, and easy to take down. In addition, it should be large enough so that users can conveniently store all their bedding, clothing, and personal items and arrange these items so that they can easily find anything they need when needed.

After purchasing a tent, basic tent campers should also consider purchasing or making a kitchen canopy. A kitchen canopy provides shade from the sun, protection from rain, and a comfortable place to prepare food, eat meals, wash dishes, play games, and relax during the day. My family uses two eight-by-ten-foot tarps as our kitchen canopy, but other campers prefer commercial screen rooms and freestanding canopies.

Tent Designs

Since the late 1800s, tents have been made in several shapes, and each shape had certain strengths and limitations. *A-frame tents* (formerly known as *wedge tents*) were introduced in the late 1890s and periodically updated over the past one hundred years. They are called A-frames because they look like the capital letter *A* from the front or back—with a high center ridge and sloping sides pulled out and down to the ground. In 1972, the Eureka Tent & Awning company offered a two-person model called the Mount Marcy that became very popular. Today, very few companies offer this design, but Eureka has continued to make A-frame tents for the past forty years. Their A-frame tent, now called the Timberline, is designed with inverted-V pole structures at each end with a center ridge or spanner pole that connects the two. In 2014, Eureka offered the standard Timberline, the Sequoia (SQ) with a few upgraded features, and the Outfitter with more-durable materials. Each model is available in two-person, four-person, and six-person sizes.

Cabin tents (previously known as *wall tents*) were popularized in the early 1900s. A cabin tent typically has vertical sidewalls that allow campers to stand and place cots inside the tent. Older cabin tents simply used three or four heavy wooden or steel poles positioned along each wall to hold it upright. Newer cabin tents use innovative designs with fewer aluminum poles to secure the top edge of each wall. PahaQue, for example, makes several comfortable cabin tent models.

In 2006, the Coleman Company introduced a series of *Instant Cabin Tents* that have become very popular with tent-camping families and are commonly seen in many campgrounds. Originally, these tents were called Instant Tents, but in 2014, they were redesigned and renamed Instant Cabins. They are made with preattached, telescoping steel poles that can be easily extended and locked into place. They are available in three sizes and are sold in many department stores and sporting goods stores. The older Instant Tent 4 initially sold for $130 but has been replaced by the Instant Cabin 4 ($185). The Instant Cabin 6 now costs $235, and the Instant Cabin 8 costs $310. These tents have been marketed as requiring only one minute to set up, but this claim is misleading for at least two reasons. First, their setup procedure does not include deploying a ground cloth, staking the tent to the ground, staking guy lines to the ground, or deploying the rain fly—all of which should be done before spending the night in one of these tents. Second, their one-minute setup procedure was performed by two experienced company employees rather than an ordinary couple who recently bought the tent and only take a few camping trips a year. Other tents could also be set up in less than a minute by two experienced campers, but all tents I discuss in this chapter typically require fifteen to twenty minutes by ordinary families who may not be as organized or practiced as the experts. Furthermore, these tents reportedly leak and have other limitations reported on the Web.

Umbrella tents are similar to cabin tents but have a top center hub where four or more side poles can be attached. Each side pole extends out across the roof and down its respective tent corner to the ground. The Eureka Headquarters is a good example of an umbrella tent.

Today, many experienced camping families prefer either dome or tunnel tents because these tents require less packing space, are easy to carry to walk-in campsites, are easy to set up in any campsite, are easy to take down, and are easy to store. *Dome tents* were first introduced by the North Face in 1975 and were subsequently copied by several other companies over the next thirty years. These tents are typically designed with two or three long, flexible poles that cross over the tent from one corner to its diagonal opposite corner. Some models require the poles to be inserted through sleeves at the top of the canopy body before attaching them to their respective corners, while other models simply require the poles to be clipped to the canopy after they're attached to the corners. Regardless of the attachment method, once the tent body or canopy is attached to the two poles, the tent looks like a small, freestanding dome—hence its name—with steeply sloped walls. Although the sloped walls deflect wind, they also cut living space inside the tent to much less room than the floor dimensions. To increase living space, several makers have recently added additional poles and pullout tabs to pull the tent walls out to a more vertical position, but these modifications typically add about $100 more to the tent's price tag.

Tunnel (or hoop) tents have recently emerged as a popular tent design. They are small, lightweight, nonfreestanding tents that have short poles that bend over and across the tent. For several years, ultralight one-, two-, and three-person hoop tents were especially popular with backpackers and bicycle campers because they offered the best space-to-weight ratio. They were also excellent choices for motorcycle campers because they required less packing space than similar-sized cabin and dome tents. Around 2012, other makers began to enlarge this design and add more models. The Coleman Coastline 4, MSR Dragontail 2, and Hilleberg Keron 4 are examples of small tunnel tents. The Sierra Designs Flash 4 and GoLite Imogene 3 are examples of small modified tunnel tents. The REI Kingdom 4, 6, and 8 are larger modified tunnel tents.

Freestanding tents. Before 1960, campers had to stake the edges and corners of tents to the ground before inserting supporting poles to hold the tent bodies upright. But in 1960, Eureka Tent & Awning Company introduced the Draw-Tite tent with an external frame that could hold the tent body upright without having to drive stakes into the ground. Subsequently, other tent makers began developing variations of this Draw-Tite tent and called these variations freestanding tents.

Today, many modern camping books seem to favor freestanding tents over nonfreestanding tents because the former can be set up on concrete pads or flat rocks and do not require ground stakes to keep them upright. Furthermore, these books suggest that being able to move freestanding tents from one location to another without having to disassemble them is a great feature. Examples of modern freestanding tents include dome tents with rain hoods such as the Coleman Sundome, Big Agnes Rabbit Ears 4, the REI Family Dome, and the Eureka Timberline.

On the other hand, a few modern tents, especially tunnel and hoop tents, continue to be nonfreestanding designs. Their edges and corners must be staked to the ground before their poles will support them. To move this type of tent to another location, campers must first remove the poles and then the stakes to allow the tent to completely collapse. Although nonfreestanding tents require a little more effort to set up, some backpackers and motorcycle campers prefer them because they have shorter and/or fewer poles and thus require less packing space. Examples of modern nonfreestanding tents include the Exped Aries Mesh, Mountain Hardwear Lightpath, Kelty Crestone, and several Hilleberg tents.

Most modern three- and four-person backpacking dome tents with full-coverage rain flies fall between these two extremes. While other camping books typically call them freestanding tents, they should be called semifreestanding. They have an inner tent canopy that is freestanding but also have an outer rain fly that must be staked to the ground to provide full ventilated weather protection. Many of these semifreestanding tents actually require six or more stakes to be completely set up. And once set up, they cannot be moved to another location until all the ground stakes have been removed. Examples of modern semifreestanding tents include the Kelty Salida 4, Marmot Den 4, and Mountain Hardwear Lightwedge 3.

In the final analysis, the distinction between freestanding and nonfreestanding may be moot. All tents should be staked to the ground to prevent them from being damaged by gusty winds. Some must be staked before inserting poles, while others can be staked after inserting the poles. Thus, the presumed advantages of freestanding tents (i.e., stability and mobility) are not as great as other books and magazine articles suggest.

Seasonal categories. A common practice is to classify all tents into one of three or four seasonal categories. Large, economically priced tents designed for short, mild-weather camping trips are frequently called *summer tents.* These tents are usually made with thin fiberglass poles, small rain hoods (or no hoods at all), and economically priced nylon and polyester materials. They will protect campers from sun, bugs, and light rain but frequently leak and occasionally collapse in windy and rainy weather. They will most likely collapse under the weight of light ice or snow. Typically, summer tents are sold in chain stores as entry-level tents for less than $100. These tents are made by Coleman, Ozark Trail (Walmart), Northwest Territory (Kmart), Guide Series (Gander Mountain), Swiss Gear (Target), Stansport (Target), Wenzel, and Columbia. They are very popular and can be seen in large numbers throughout most state and federal park campgrounds. Occasionally, more-luxurious and more-expensive PahaQue summer cabin tents can be seen in some campgrounds.

Smaller, one- to four-person tents designed for spring, summer, and fall camping trips—the seasons that most people like to camp—are called *three-season tents.* These three-season tents frequently have low ceilings but are often ideally suited for basic tent camping. They are easy to set up, made to withstand moderate wind and rainfall, and easy to pack up. In warm southern states, these tents could be used all year long since this region gets little frozen participation. Within this category, family tents with rain hoods covering the top and sides of the tent offer greater mobility than backpacking tents that have full-coverage rain flies. The price of a three-season tent typically varies from $150 to $500 and depends primarily upon its size-to-weight ratio.

Backpackers consider the weight of a tent to be one of the most important, if not *the* most important, factors when purchasing a tent. For backcountry hikers, every extra ounce of weight carried on their backs reduces their long-distance hiking endurance. Because of this fact, most tent makers specify the tent's actual weight or minimum weight, which includes the tent body, rain fly, and poles but not the ground cloth, stakes, and doormat. Basic tent campers should also consider a tent's weight before purchase because the weight of a tent is directly related to packing space. Heavier tents typically require more packing space, while lighter tents require less. Four-person tents that weigh less than twelve pounds will be easy to pack in small cars and will be easy to set up. Two- and three-person tents that weigh less than seven pounds will be relatively easy to pack on motorcycles. When investigating a tent's weight, be warned that some manufacturers may give the fast weight or trail weight (which may not include the inner canopy) or the packed weight (which includes the packing box and instruction manual).

Four-season tents, also called *mountaineering tents* or *expedition tents*, are heavier, more-expensive shelters ranging in price from $500 to $2,000. They are designed for harsh winter weather and typically have several poles, pole sleeves, thicker fabrics, and less mesh than three-season tents. Examples of four-season tents include the North Face VE 25, Sierra Designs Mountain Meteor, Black Diamond Bombshelter, Nemo Alti Storm, and Hilleberg Saitaris. *Convertible tents* are four-season tents that have optional poles that could be removed to approximate the weight of a three-season tent. The Sierra Designs Alpha 3 is one of these convertible tents. Prices of these tents are comparable to those of four-season tents. Because of their expense and weight, four-season and convertible tents are poorly suited for basic tent camping.

Size. The size of a tent is usually expressed in terms of the number of small adults who could lie flat on their backs on the floor of the tent. For example, a one-person tent, such as the Eureka Backcountry 1, is a very small tent that is only large enough for one person to lie flat on the floor. Its floor measures ninety-six inches (eight feet) long by thirty-six inches (three feet) wide and has only twenty-four square feet of floor space. In general, tents with thirty-five to forty-five square feet of floor space are called two-person tents, tents with forty-five to fifty-five square feet are called three-person tents, and tents with fifty-five to sixty-five square feet are called four-person tents. Although backpacking books typically recommend that campers buy the smallest and lightest tent possible, basic tent campers can easily pack and live comfortably in larger tents rated for two more people than the number of adults sleeping in the tent. In other words, most couples should buy four-person tents.

Although the height of a tent is rarely considered when discussing the size of a tent, this feature is important for several reasons. For example, low-profile tents, such as the Eureka Backcountry 1 (38 inches or 3.17 feet high), have lower doors that make entry and exit more difficult. In other words, older, heavier, and less-mobile campers, like me, will have considerable difficulty entering and exiting the tent. Low profile tents also provide less interior space, making it harder to move around inside or set up cots. Finally, low-profile tents tend to have more condensation problems. On the other hand, high-profile family tents, such as the Big Agnes Rabbit Ears 4 (5 feet) or Big House 4 (5.67 feet), are easier to enter and exit and provide space for cots but require more packing space and are more likely to fail in strong storms.

Regardless of the particular tent style, campers should practice setting up a new tent at home before taking it out on a trip so that they can become familiar with the setup procedure. If they do not understand how some parts fit, they can read the manual in leisure or call a technical expert at the store where they bought it. Setting the tent up at home before the first trip will also allow campers to make sure all the parts were included in the package and that they are undamaged. Furthermore, setting it up will allow campers to repack the tent to include its ground cloth, or footprint, and a doormat.

Tent Features

Modern tents have a variety of features that make them more or less comfortable. Basic tent campers should become familiar with these features so they can select the particular tent that best fits their families' needs.

Fabric. The materials used to make tents have evolved over the past one hundred years. In the early 1900s, silk, cotton duck, canvas, linen, lawn, calico, and wigan were common tent-making materials. Today, most tents are made with ripstop nylon and polyester. Typically, five pieces are cut and sewn together: floor, sides, zippered doors, mesh, and fly or hood. These fabrics are usually treated with waterproof coatings. The thickness of these fabrics varies from one tent to another and is expressed in denier units, abbreviated as D. A 75 D wall on a four-season mountain tent, for example, would be thicker and heavier than a 68 D rain fly on the Marmot Halo tent. Economically priced tents may use some polyethylene tarp material while mid-priced tents are typically made with combinations of nylon and polyester. Some high-priced tents may be made with silnylon—an ultrathin nylon that has been impregnated with silicone.

Poles. Tent poles have also evolved over the past one hundred years. In the early 1900s, they were made from hickory or some other type of wood. Sometimes they were cut from saplings growing near the planned campsite. In subsequent years, poles were made from heavy steel and then large-diameter aluminum stock. Today, poles for most three- and four-person tents are made from thin fiberglass or aluminum. They vary in diameter from about six to fifteen millimeters. Larger-diameter poles provide better storm protection but add more weight and cost to the tent. The type of poles used to make a tent and how they attach to the tent play important roles in determining the tent's ability to provide protection from stormy weather.

Fiberglass poles are typically used to make economically priced summer tents. Although these poles can last up to five years or longer with careful handling, they can easily break under the pressure of moderately strong wind or accidental misuse, especially in cool weather. Often poles break when campers accidentally step on them while setting up or breaking down their campsites.

Aluminum poles, compared with fiberglass poles of comparable diameter, are lighter and provide greater strength for stormy weather. These poles are less likely to break in cold and windy weather. If they are damaged, they can be patched with a pole repair tube until permanent repairs can be made. Aluminum poles used for most tents are made by one of two companies: Dongah Aluminum Corporation (DAC) Featherlite poles, made using an eco-friendly process, are used for Kelty, REI, Sierra Designs, and the North Face tents, and Yunan Aluminum Company's Atlas Scandium aluminum poles are used for Mountain Hardwear and some other brands of tents. Recently, several companies have been experimenting with ultralight carbon fiber and other types of materials.

Floor. Older tents typically had no floors. Campers sometimes added a twelve-inch sod cloth around the floor edges and placed straw, tarps, or some other material on the ground to reduce the dirt and debris inside the tent. Modern tents, on the other hand, typically have waterproof floors made with durable nylon or polyester sheeting sewn onto the tent walls. Economy tents sometime sew the floor and wall together at ground level, but this method of construction facilitates the seepage of moisture through the seams into the tent. When rain hits the side of the tent, it runs down the side and accumulates at the bottom where the floor and side are sewn together. When the water remains on the seam, it will eventually seep through the seam and into the tent. In heavy rain, this water could soak anything near the edge of the tent, such as your sleeping bag, pillow, and clothing.

Most good-quality tents have *bathtub floors* made with a single piece of waterproof material that forms the floor and lower walls of the tent. The floor is sewn to the upper wall or mesh approximately five to ten inches above the ground. Rain rolls down the walls and past the seam to the ground and thus does not have the opportunity to soak through a seam. The Marmot tent company uses a similar method of construction called a *catenary floor*.

Tent stakes (pegs). In the early 1900s, most campers used wooden pegs to secure their tents to the ground. Sometimes these early campers waited until they arrived at their campsite and then used a machete or hatchet to cut a small sapling into six to eight pegs. Today, most tents come with about ten thin stainless steel stakes, but these stakes are unsuited for most campsite surfaces. They work well when setting up the tent on soft black soil—just push the stakes into the soil. But they cannot be pushed into rocky limestone soil or crushed-stone tent pads found in many developed campgrounds. If campers attempt to drive them into rocky soil, the stakes bend and become useless. Furthermore, they will not hold in sandy soil found along the Florida Gulf Coast and western desert areas.

Camping outfitters sell a variety of replacement tent stakes, but most of them also have serious limitations. For example, most stores sell yellow plastic stakes, but these stakes only work well in soft soil or sandy soil where they can be gently driven into the ground. They will shatter when driven into rocky soil—even when a plastic mallet is used. Longer V-shaped metal stakes can be used in gravel soil, but they require excessive packing space and frequently are difficult to remove from the ground when the time comes to pack up. Backpackers use ultralight six-inch aluminum and titanium stakes, but these stakes are expensive.

Perhaps the best replacement stakes are ten-inch nail-type stakes with plastic tips, but twenty of these stakes (six to ten for the tent, eight more for a kitchen canopy, and a few extras just in case) require considerable packing space that may not be available in small cars or on motorcycles. Removing the plastic tips can help to reduce bulk but not enough for motorcycle travel. A few years ago, I discovered six-inch galvanized nails sold in building supply stores. They can be easily driven into gravel tent pads, hold well in strong wind, can be easily removed from the ground with a pair of channel lock pliers when ready to pack up, and twenty of them pack into a small space. Additional information about tent stakes will be presented in chapter 4, "Tools."

Rain hood or fly. Most modern three-season dome and A-frame tents are constructed as two separate parts. They have an interior canopy made with lots of mesh and an exterior waterproof rain hood or rain fly. Because of these two parts, these tents are sometimes called *double-wall tents*. Typically, the mesh canopy is set up with poles and stakes, and then the rain hood or fly is deployed over the erect canopy. A *rain hood* is a smaller waterproof sheet that only covers the top and sometimes sides of the tent. These hoods are effective for shedding light rain but vary in terms of their ability to protect tent occupants and contents from strong winds and blowing rain. Examples of tents with large rain hoods include the Eureka Timberline 4 and REI Family Dome 4. Tents with smaller rain hoods, such as the Coleman Sundome 4, are typically sold in chain department and sporting goods stores.

A *rain fly* is a much-larger waterproof sheet that completely covers the top, sides, and doors of the canopy, thereby offering greater weather protection than tents with smaller hoods. Most small three-season backpacking dome tents are designed with full-coverage rain flies that cover the entire inner canopy and protect the occupants and contents from rain and wind. These rain flies extend down to the ground all the way around the tent—covering all sides, ends, and doors. They have zippered doors adjacent to each canopy door so that campers can enter the tent. The North Face Flint 3 and Mountain Hardwear Lightwedge 3 are two examples of tents with full-coverage rain flies.

Most four-season dome tents and many cabin tents are designed to provide complete weather protection without a rain fly or hood. These tents are frequently called *single-wall tents*. Four-season and convertible tents are able to provide weather protection without rain flies or hoods because they are made with thick, durable waterproof fabrics and multiple poles. Two examples of good-quality single-wall tents are the Black Diamond Bombshelter 4 and Marmot Alpinist 2. A few economy tents designed as single-wall tents will leak and require a separate tarp to provide complete protection from heavy rain.

Vestibule. Most modern backpacking tents have a large full-coverage rain fly that covers a small inner mesh canopy and extends several feet away from the doors, creating a covered area of ground in front and back of the tent. Backpackers need these covered areas, called vestibules, to store backpacks and boots from rain and dewfall because their tents are too small to accommodate these items inside. In addition to providing extra storage space, tents with full-coverage vestibules presumably provide more protection from stronger winds than tents without vestibules.

Over the past ten years, many books and sales associates have argued that tents with full-coverage vestibules are generally better than tents without vestibules—for all types of camping. I disagree with these popular arguments and suggest that basic-tent-camping families should purchase family tents with large rain hoods rather than full-coverage rain flies. To support this position, I offer several arguments. Most importantly, basic tent campers do not need vestibules to protect boots and backpacks, because they can buy larger tents that have extra interior space. Furthermore, tents with vestibules

- require larger ground area to set up, potentially exceeding the defined limits of some tent pads;
- require more time to set up and more time to take down, thus reducing mobility;
- have lower doors that make it more difficult for older and larger people to enter and exit;
- require unzipping and rezipping two doors (rain fly and inner canopy) every time a person enters or exits the tent, making it a hassle to get anything inside the tent;
- accumulate much more condensation than tents with large rain hoods;
- are hotter on summer nights;
- provide storm protection that will be rarely, if ever, be needed;
- do not protect shoes and other gear in the vestibule from spiders, scorpions, mice, or porcupines.

My advice for most couples is to buy a four-person tent with a large rain fly, such as the Eureka Timberline, REI Family Dome, or Big Agnes Big House, and leave sweaty shoes and clothing in the car.

Ventilation, heat retention, and condensation. Some tents seem to cool quickly after hot days, while other tents seem to hold the heat in several hours after sunset. If a tent holds heat, vestibule doors and fabric window covers can be opened and rain flies can be removed, but frequently this does not provide relief. In this situation, mesh doors can be opened, but this step allows mosquitoes to enter.

On cool nights, especially when the overnight temperature drops several degrees, many tents develop condensation (or water droplets) on the inside surface of their rain fly or hood. Warm, humid air from breathing, sweaty clothing, and ground moisture rises to the top and sides of the tent and is trapped by the waterproof material. When the moisture is cooled by the cool tent wall, the steam turns into water droplets. Condensation is especially heavy when cool fronts with rain showers pass through the area after warm, humid days. This condensation can be aggravating because movement in the tent or wind gusts can shake the rain fly and release these droplets to shower tent occupants trying to stay dry. Frequently this moisture will soak sleeping bags and clothing, making life miserable until these items can be dried out. When exiting or entering the tent, campers can accidentally soak their clothing by brushing against the wet fly.

Strategies for reducing condensation are essentially the same as those for reducing heat retention. Windows and doors should be opened as much as possible. However, tents with full-coverage rain flies are difficult to ventilate as long as the rain fly covers the tent. Regardless of what other camping books may say, condensation is virtually certain when camping in tents with full-coverage rain flies on cool nights. Family tents with rain hoods, such as the Eureka Timberline 4, on the other hand, are much easier to ventilate.

Sleeves, clips, and Velcro strips. Each tent employs a unique method for attaching the inner tent canopy and the outer rain fly to the poles. Many three-season dome tents employ plastic clips. To set these tents up, campers just insert the pole tips into their respective seats and then clip the tent canopy to the poles. Other tents require the poles to be inserted through sleeves before erecting the canopy and inserting the pole tips into their respective seats. In general, tents with sleeves are stronger and lighter while tents with clips are easier to set up and take down. Economy tents made with thin fiberglass poles need sleeves to add overall structural strength and stability. More-expensive mountaineering tents use sleeves with stronger poles to support the possible weight of ice or snow. Several backpacking tents use sleeves in combination with clips to add strength while reducing weight. Regardless of the particular method for attaching the inner canopy to the poles, most tents also use Velcro or hook-and-loop strips to attach the outer rain fly or hood to the poles.

Guy-out loops. Two to four loops are sewn into each sidewall of a tent or rain fly about two feet above the ground. These loops are typically sewn opposite to the Velcro strips used to attach the fly to the tent poles. These loops provide attachment points for guy lines to hold the tent down to the ground in moderate wind. Sometimes these loops will be made from reflective materials so campers can easily see their tents in the dark. People who plan to camp one night in good weather may be able to forgo staking these extra guy lines, but campers planning to set up a base camp for a few days should stake at least one guy line on each side to prevent accidental damage from unexpected wind gusts. Procedures for rigging these guy lines will be described in chapter 14, "Ropes and Knots."

Doors. The size, placement, and design of tent doors are important, but often overlooked, considerations. Young, athletic backpackers may not be concerned about door size and placement, but older, less agile campers like me would probably appreciate larger tents with one or two high doors on the front (and perhaps back) since moving into and out of small tent doors can require excessive stooping, squatting, kneeling, crawling, and twisting. Backpackers typically prefer small dome tents with two small doors—one on either side—because having two doors allows each occupant to enter and exit the cramped tent without having to crawl over his or her partner. Recreational campers may also appreciate tents with two doors because a door on each side allows campers to set up their tent according to the terrain and still have a door where needed. Furthermore, having two doors allows each occupant to retrieve his or her personal items, such as headlamps or keys, without having to crawl into the tent.

Tents with one door on the front end typically have a higher door that is easy to enter and exit. Examples of tents with large doors on the front end include the Eureka Timberline 4 and the Mountain Hardwear Lightwedge 3. Tents with large D-shaped doors, such as the Big Agnes Rabbit Ears 4, are preferable to tents with upside-down-U doors because D-shaped doors hang to the side when open and permit easy entry and exit. Upside-down-U doors, such as those found on the Marmot Den 4, typically fall on the floor or outside ground when open and are easily stepped on when people are in a hurry. Tents with full-coverage rain flies will typically have smaller doors than tents with large rain hoods. Before purchasing a tent, campers should examine photos on the web and consider the tent's height and determine the relative ease of entry and exit.

Footprint (ground cloth). Most camping books recommend that tent campers spread an extra sheet of waterproof material on the ground under the tent floor to provide an extra layer of protection from sharp rocks or twigs and to block ground moisture from penetrating the tent floor. Some tent makers sell custom-made protective sheets, called footprints, to fit each tent model for an extra thirty to fifty dollars. Campers who do not want to pay this extra expense frequently make protective sheets (ground cloths), from polyethylene tarps or polyester sheeting. When making a ground cloth for a particular tent, the ground cloth should be cut a few inches smaller than the tent's floor dimensions so that none of the ground cloth is exposed around the edges of the tent. When water hits the top and sides of the tent, it should run down the side and soak into the ground rather than collecting on a waterproof sheet where it can easily flow under and into the tent.

Pockets and gear loft. Most modern tents have pockets sewn into the wall about twelve inches above the floor at the point where the bathtub floor and the tent walls meet. Many camping books consider the number of these pockets to be one of the most important features when evaluating a tent. These books suggest that campers can use pockets to store water bottles, lights, and other gear.

In contrast to this widely held opinion, I argue that pockets are one of the least important features of a tent. If they are available, campers could use them to store empty ditty bags or air-mattress compression cords. But campers should never put full water bottles in pockets, because the weight of the bottle would place considerable stress on the fragile canopy fabric and seam threads, increasing the risk of premature damage. Instead of using pockets, campers should organize their clothing and personal items in specific places along the side of the tent. For example, I place my glasses, headlamp, and sleeping cap in the corner nearest my head; I place my water bottle, medicine, book, iPod, radio, and other electronics on the side near my face; I pack my clothing in a small, soft duffel bag and use it as my pillow; and I place my jackets and pants down beside my legs. Most of the time, I leave my shoes, dirty clothes, soap and personal grooming kit in the car so that we won't have to smell them all night and so that animal scavengers will not be attracted to them.

For many tents, campers can get a gear loft (either as a part of the tent package or as an extra accessory) that attaches to four loops sewn near the top of the tent. Backpackers sleeping in cramped quarters may need these gear lofts for storing their glasses or headlamps, but these lofts are unnecessary for basic tent campers who buy larger tents. Instead of the loft, campers may want to attach a headlamp to one of these loops with a carabineer to have an interior tent light.

Doormat. Most veteran campers also place a doormat just outside each door. These mats provide a clean and dry place to take off shoes and kneel when entering or exiting the tent. Although camping stores sell doormats and some companies such as Big Agnes include them with their tents, most campers purchase ordinary doormats from local department stores. Campers traveling by motorcycle may want to use hand towels since they require less packing space.

Color. Surprisingly, several camping books and articles assert that tent color is an important factor to consider when purchasing a new tent. Some of these sources advise consumers to only purchase green, brown, tan, or gray tents because these colors will blend with natural habitat and be less conspicuous. These authorities argue that brightly colored tents disturb the balance of nature and may offend the sensibilities of fellow campers who want to escape reminders of civilization. A few of these authorities have even argued that brightly colored tents increase the noticeability of the campsite and, consequently, increase the likelihood of being targeted by criminals. In contrast, other books and articles recommend just the opposite. They recommend that consumers purchase bright yellow and red tents because these colors will lift occupants' spirits on dreary rainy days and help hikers find their campsites after several hours on the trail or other daily excursions.

After considering all the arguments and evidence, it seems safe to conclude that a tent's color should be the last factor to consider when evaluating tent models for possible purchase. Anyone who walks around a popular state or federal campground and talks with fellow campers will rarely, if ever, hear one camper complaining about the color of another camper's tent. Factors such as design, size, ventilation, door placement, and price are far more important. Since most tent models are only available in one color, it is possible that these arguments about color are disguised product endorsements. Books that recommend bright red and yellow tents may be indirectly endorsing Big Agnes and Marmot tents. Books that recommend green and brown tents may be indirectly endorsing Eureka Timberline tents. Books that advise consumers to avoid bright colored tents may be indirectly suggesting that consumers avoid Walmart, Kmart, and some Coleman tents.

Tent Recommendations

As previously stated, I believe that individuals and couples who travel in small vehicles and want to ensure maximum mobility should buy simple four-person family camping tents with large rain hoods and no vestibules. Couples with a small child or dog could also camp comfortably in this small four-person tent. Couples with two or more children over age ten may want to consider purchasing two of these tents rather than one larger tent that would be more difficult to set up and take down. Here are some good choices that cost between $200 and $300 unless otherwise noted:

- Eureka Timberline 4—This model is perhaps the most popular tent ever made and should be used as a standard for evaluating newer four-person tents. It is a reasonably priced A-frame tent that is exceptionally long for tall guys, requires little setup space, offers protection from moderate storms, provides ample storage space for two people, and produces the least amount of condensation of any tent on the market. To make it more comfortable and practical, campers may want to add zipper pulls, rain hood pullout cords, and modified loop-and-ball door and window ties.
- REI Family Dome / Camp Dome 4—This tent has been popular for over fifteen years and is a second tent that can be used as a standard for evaluating other tents. It has two doors, is exceptionally easy to set up, and provides ample space for two people and their gear.
- Big Agnes Big House 4—This tent has been named by several camping authorities as one of the best family camping tents available. It has a high ceiling for people who want to sleep on cots or stand in their tent.
- Eureka Copper Canyon 4—This model is a tall cabin tent for campers who want to stand in their tent or sleep on cots.
- Big Agnes Rabbit Ears 4—This tent is a new model but looks like an excellent choice for basic tent camping. The large D-style door is especially attractive.
- PahaQue Green Mountain 4—This is a tall high-end cabin tent with room for cots.
- The North Face Trailhead 4—This is a popular modified dome family camping tent.

- Coleman Sundome 4—This is a popular entry-level summer dome tent that costs less than eighty dollars.
- REI Kingdom 4—This is a new hoop or tunnel tent with near-vertical sidewalls that is becoming popular with veteran tent-camping families. Although its retail price is over $300, it can be obtained for a lower price during special sales.

Basic tent campers who plan to spend several days in windy locations may want to purchase a low-profile, three-season dome tent with a full-coverage rain fly. Here are some examples of these tents:

- REI Half Dome 4—This model is a popular backpacking tent that has won numerous awards over the past ten years. It should be used as the standard for comparing other similar tents.
- Marmot Limelight 4—This is one of several well-made tents with near-vertical walls sold by Marmot. Although Marmot tents are relatively expensive, they are frequently discontinued after a few years and offered at closeout prices. For example, the older Marmot Den 4 that initially sold for $380 was sold for $200 about three years later. It was replaced by the Halo 4.
- Kelty Salida 4—This tent is an economically priced simple dome tent with steeply sloped walls. It is a modified version of the old Gunnison that was popular for several years.

Couples and individuals who travel on motorcycles and bicycles may have to purchase smaller three- or two-person backpacking tents that weigh less than five pounds. Here are some examples:

- Mountain Hardwear Lightwedge 3 DP—This is an older dome tent with one large door on the front that allows easy entry and exit. It was my motorcycle camping tent for six years and weighs five pounds, nine ounces.
- REI Quarter Dome 3—This tent is a newly redesigned version of an old favorite; it weighs three pounds, twelve ounces. It

should be used as the standard for evaluating other tents in this category.

- REI Quarter Dome 2—This is a popular two-person tent that weighs three pounds, one ounce. It has been in production for several years and should be used as the standard for evaluating other two-person tents.
- The North Face Stormbreak 3—This is a new model made by an established company; it weighs four pounds, one ounce.
- MSR Mutha Hubba NX 3—This is a new tent with near-vertical walls that weighs four pounds, seven ounces.
- Big Agnes Copper Spur 2 UL—This is a highly praised hybrid tent that only weighs two pounds, twelve ounces.

Couples with two or more small children may have to consider a six-person family tent but should understand that these tents will reduce mobility because they require more packing space, are more difficult to set up, require larger ground areas that may exceed boundaries of some tent pads, and require more takedown time. These are some possible choices:

- PahaQue Pamo Valley 6—This model is a beautiful and roomy cabin tent for large families.
- REI Kingdom 6—This is a popular family camping tent.
- Kelty Acadia 6—This is an economically priced tent with a full-coverage rain fly.
- Coleman Montana 6—This is an entry-level modified dome tent.

Kitchen Shelters

Virtually all the early pioneer campers erected kitchen shelters as part of their campsites, and today many families camping in established state and federal campgrounds erect kitchen shelters if they plan to stay in their campsites more than one night. Various options available today vary in terms of price, size, shape, packed size, and level of protection.

Shelters with sidewalls provide protection from wind and late-afternoon sun, while shelters with screened walls provide protection from flies, bees, mosquitoes, and other insects. To help readers select the shelter that best fits their needs, let me discuss three basic types.

Screen rooms. Several companies make screen rooms designed to provide protection from rain, sun, wind, and insects. Typically these screen rooms measure ten feet by ten feet or larger and have six- to eight-foot ceilings. Most do not have floors, so they can be set up around permanently fixed picnic tables. Some of the better models will have a twelve-inch sod cloth sewn around the edge so that campers can place a tarp or carpet on the ground overlapping the sod cloth to make a clean, dry floor. When set up, these screen rooms look very inviting, but upon further consideration, they have notable limitations. First, they are expensive and sometimes difficult to set up (even for two people). They all require considerable packing space that may not be available in small cars or on motorcycles, a large ground area to set up, considerable time to set up, and even more time to take down. Some popular examples include the following screen rooms:

- PahaQue Screen Room—this is the Cadillac of screen rooms with roll-up shade and storm walls that can be raised to make extra awnings
- Woodlands Screen House— this is a screen room with a tailored cabin tent look that appears to be relatively easy to set up
- REI Screen House
- Kelty Screen House
- Eureka Screen House
- Coleman Instant Screened Canopy—This model is available at Target and other large department stores

My one experience with a commercially made screen room was not pleasant. Another couple and I bought this screen house one summer while camping in northern Wisconsin during the middle of July. After setting it up, we discovered that three people constantly unzipping and zipping doors got to be aggravating and allowed so many mosquitoes to come in as not having a screen room at all. After a few days, we just left the doors open. Furthermore, most nights we preferred to sit around the campfire rather than in the screen room. When we were ready to break camp, the screen room took as much time to take down and pack as the rest of our camp combined. Granted, we bought an economical model from a discount department store, but this product convinced me that screen rooms are more trouble than they are worth, unless camping several nights in a fly-, mosquito-, or bee-infested area, such as Michigan's Upper Peninsula.

Freestanding canopies. Since most public campgrounds do not have serious insect infestations, many recreational campers opt for freestanding canopies to cover their kitchen and dining areas. These canopies are typically more economically priced than similar screen rooms and require less packing space. Since they are freestanding, they can be set up in any campsite—with or without trees. They can also be set up in parks that forbid tying ropes or cords to vegetation, such as Florida state parks. And on calm days they can be set up as picnic or tailgating canopies on paved parking lots, wooden decks, or sandy beaches. Although a few have completely waterproof roofs, many are primarily designed to provide shade from sun and perhaps protection from light rain. The following models are popular:

- PahaQue Cottonwood—This attractive, nonwaterproof, freestanding dome shelter has a lifetime warranty
- REI InCamp Shelter
- Kelty Sunshade—This is a dome-shaped, freestanding sun canopy.
- E-Z Up Pyramid II
- Coleman Instant Canopy
- Wenzel Smart Shade—This is an accordion-style shelter sold by Walmart, Kohl's, and other chain department stores.
- Texsport Brookhaven Canopy—This freestanding canopy can be purchased at Walmart.

Tarp canopies. Many veteran campers, including me, use ordinary polyethylene (poly) tarps plus four or six poles to make a kitchen canopy. An eight-by-ten-foot poly tarp sells for about ten dollars in most hardware, auto, and department stores. Years ago, campers used canvas tarps, but canvas tarps are heavy and require excessive packing space. Tarp canopies have become popular with many campers because they cost less than commercially made screen houses and canopies and require much less packing space. In rainy areas many campers hang giant tarps measuring twenty by thirty feet or larger from trees to cover their tent and kitchen areas.

I started using tarp shelters in 1968 and have used them on hundreds of camping trips over the past forty-five years, experimenting with various sizes and setup configurations. Gradually, I gravitated to an eight-by-ten-foot polyethylene tarp that can be purchased in any hardware or department store. I like this particular size because it is economical, packs into a small space, can be patched with duct tape, and can be easily replaced whenever it is no longer serviceable. When staying in a campsite for more than one night, I usually add a second eight-by-ten-foot tarp as a sidewall. I support these tarps with three eight-foot Eureka Nested Aluminum Backpacker Poles and one six-foot Eureka Nested Aluminum Backpacker Pole sold by Campmor. These Eureka poles are preferable to other options because they nest inside each other and pack into a very small space. Two or three of these poles can easily be packed on a motorcycle, but they are expensive! The current price of one eight-foot Eureka pole is twenty-seven dollars. REI also makes eight-foot folding tarp-support poles. These poles are a little easier to manage in the campsite, but four of them require more packing space than the Eureka poles. Basic tent campers driving larger vehicles can buy more economically priced stainless steel poles made by other companies.

Campers who do not have a tarp with grommets can make a sun canopy with a full- or queen-size bedsheet. To make the canopy, place small stones in each corner of the sheet, pull the fabric around the stone, tie the bundle with a double-reversed half hitch, and pull the hitch tight. With a few trees and poles, this simple method makes a great canopy that provides shade and protection from dewfall. It is an excellent way for motorcycle campers to shade their tables.

Backpackers and perhaps motorcycle campers may prefer lighter, more-packable tarps made from nylon, polyester, or ultralight silnylon tarps.

Other Shelters

Before concluding this chapter, let me mention three other shelter types that are frequently mentioned in other camping books and occasionally observed in a few public campgrounds. These shelters are designed for backpackers who want ultralight equipment that can be carried comfortably on their backs for several miles. As one might guess, the primary advantages of these shelters are their light weight and small packing space. Their disadvantages are numerous. In particular, these ultralight shelters do not provide room to move about, especially on long rainy days, and may not provide complete protection from rain, bugs, spiders, and other critters. Although these shelters could be tolerated for a night or two, none provide the comfort needed to spend several nights or weeks in the woods. Most basic tent campers will be more comfortable with a tent, but campers riding motorcycles with a backseat companion may want to consider one of these shelters.

Tarp tents. A tarp tent is a thin waterproof sheet that can be erected as a shelter with one or two trekking poles. Some include a mesh inner canopy. Two examples off this type of shelter include the Tarptent StratoSpire 2 and the MSR Twing Shelter.

Hammocks. Several of my camping friends prefer to sleep in hammocks on their camping trips, but hammocks have several limitations. They are difficult to enter and exit, especially with sleeping pads and bags; they do not allow sleepers to change sleeping positions; they are poorly suited for couples; they do not have enough room to store clothing and personal items; they are poorly suited for wet weather and are cold in cool weather; and they cannot be set up in campsites that do not have trees. Although a few companies make more-practical and comfortable hammocks for overnight sleeping, these hammocks still have significant limitations. Two hammocks designed for overnight sleeping include the Hennessy Expedition and the Clark Tropical Ultra. These models have tarp canopies to provide weather protection. Although I personally own four hammocks and often take naps in them during warm days, I would never choose one as my primary camping shelter.

Bivy sacks. Bivy sacks are very small one-person tents that provide a little shoulder and head room but otherwise just cover the sleeping bag. Three examples are the REI Minimalist Bivy, the Black Diamond Bipod, and the Outdoor Research Advanced Bivy. Small campers riding bicycles may want to consider one of these shelters, but they are too small for me.

The Eureka Timberline 4 is a popular A-frame tent that is well suited for basic tent camping.

The Coleman Instant Tent 4 is a popular cabin tent design.

The REI Family Dome 4 is a dome tent that is also well suited for basic tent camping.

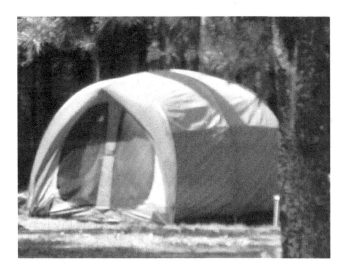

The REI Kingdom 4 is a popular hoop-style tent.

Many camping families set up screen rooms around their tables.

This campsite includes an accordion-style kitchen
canopy as part of the camp setup.

3

BEDDING

After acquiring a comfortable shelter, basic tent campers must turn their attention to the gear needed to sleep comfortably. A hundred years ago, Holding discussed army or horse wool blankets, homemade sleeping bags made from wool blankets sewn together, ground blankets, straw beds, full-length reeded beds, rubber hip cushions, and sometimes hammocks. Along with this gear he suggested that campers dig hip holes into the ground for comfort. Other early camping books recommended the Woods Arctic Eiderdown Sleeping Robe introduced in 1898 and the Johnson Waterproof Sleeping Bag available from Abercrombie & Fitch in 1903.

Today, many inexperienced campers try to save money by packing economical bedding only to suffer through several cold and miserable nights. Pillows slithering away during the night and cold feet are two common problems. After a few camping trips, some inexperienced campers will buy cots, thinking that this will solve their sleeping problems, only to discover that cots require extra packing space, extra setup time, and extra space in a small tent—plus they are cold and uncomfortable. A significant number of these campers will try various combinations of sheets and blankets, egg-crate mattresses, inexpensive sleeping bags sold in department stores, and even small camping trailers. Those who buy small camping trailers will soon realize that they are expensive, require frequent repairs, and greatly reduce mobility. After using them a few years, some owners will trade them for larger and more-expensive RVs or just stop camping altogether. After trying a few different options without success, many inexperienced campers give up camping because they do not want to sleep on the "cold, hard ground" again.

Over the past forty years, I have used many different blanket, mattress, and sleeping bag combinations while looking for the most comfortable sleeping system. I even tried sleeping in a pop-up trailer for three years but decided to go back to tent camping. Eventually, I discovered good-quality sleeping gear sold in backpacking outfitter stores, and I have slept comfortably ever since. In fact, I sleep better in my tent than I do in my bed at home. A basic tent camper needs a mattress, sleeping bag, and warm clothing to sleep comfortably. He or she could add a ground blanket, sheet, and pillowcase (to cover a small duffel bag, day pack, or such to make a pillow) to enhance comfort. These items are described in this chapter.

Mattresses

A good mattress is arguably the single most important piece of bedding for getting a good night's sleep. Without one, campers would have to sleep on the hard, cold ground, and that would be very uncomfortable—even with a fleece blanket and sleeping bag. Frequently, the ground under the tent will have ridges, rocks, and other protruding objects that will stick sleepers in the worst places. In addition to being hard and uncomfortable, the ground is cooler than the air temperature and will chill a person's body by conductive heat loss. Without adequate insulation, sleepers will quickly feel cold and will be unable to sleep well. Just the thought of sleeping on the cold ground is enough to discourage many people who have never been camping before.

A variety of cheap mattresses are available in department stores, but most of them are inadequate for basic tent camping. Economy inflatable air mattresses, such as pool rafts, cost about ten dollars, but these mattresses require considerable effort to inflate, do not insulate users from the cold ground, and are easily punctured. Open-cell foam mats, such as egg-crate foam, can be purchased from department stores for a few dollars but require excessive packing space, provide minimal insulation and comfort, absorb moisture that can chill users, and are difficult to dry. Flocked camping air beds available in many department stores look nice and cost less than forty dollars but require excessive packing space, are difficult to inflate, and are too big to fit into smaller tents.

Insulated inflatable air mattresses. Most experienced outdoor enthusiasts generally agree that an insulated inflatable air mattress is the best choice because it provides maximum comfort yet packs into a small space. These mattresses are superior to more-economical products in terms of convenience, warmth, and comfort. Some are self-inflating, while others have a simple pump system. Regardless of the inflation method, these mattresses can be quickly inflated with little effort. Sometimes campers may have to blow an extra puff of air into the pad to fully inflate it before closing the valve. But within a few minutes after opening, inflatable mattresses are ready to provide a comfortable and warm sleeping surface.

The most recognized brand name in camp mattresses is Therm-a-Rest, first developed in 1972 by two aerospace engineers who wanted to improve upon the generally uncomfortable camping mattresses that were available at the time. These engineers covered an open-cell foam pad with an air- and moisture-tight cover and added a small valve. When the mattress was spread out with the air valve open, the open-cell foam pad expanded and sucked air into the cover. Once the air was inside the cover, the valve could be closed to keep the air inside. After developing and testing several prototypes, these engineers obtained a patent for their mattress and founded Cascade Designs in Seattle, Washington.

Therm-a-Rest mattresses are grouped into three categories based upon their thickness and compressed size. Camp & Comfort pads (blue) are thicker and more comfortable but require more packing space. Eva and I have used the BaseCamp mattress in this group for over six years and hundreds of nights without problem. Trek & Travel pads (green) have a medium thickness and are ideal for campers with economy or sports cars and for some motorcycle riders. Old-style Fast & Light pads (orange or red) were considered to be the best choice for backpacking and motorcycle travel for many years because they packed into small spaces. In 2009, Therm-a-Rest added the NeoAir mattresses to the Fast & Light category. These mattresses compress into a much smaller packing space than any other Therm-a-Rest mattress. Soon after their introduction, they won the Editor's Choice Award from *Backpacker Magazine*. They are ideal for motorcycle travel but expensive.

Therm-A-Rest mattresses are available in four basic sizes. Small pads are only long enough for the upper half of an adult's body. They were designed for summer backpackers who want to travel ultralight and are willing to tolerate mild discomfort. They are also suitable for children. Regular pads are long enough for six-foot-tall people but are only twenty inches wide. They are suitable for slender- to average-build people. Large pads are twenty-five inches wide and seem best suited for average- to large-build people like me. Therm-a-Rest also makes a couple of extra-large pads for even greater comfort and a few women's pads.

The cost of a Therm-a-Rest mattress depends upon its open size, compressed size, thickness, and insulation value. A Trail Scout regular (one inch thick; R-value = 3.4) costs $50, while a Trail Pro large (two inches thick; R-value = 4.0) costs $120. The most compact mattresses suited for backpacking and motorcycle camping include the NeoAir XLite regular (2.5 inches thick; R-value = 3.2), which costs $160, and the NeoAir XTherm regular (2.5 inches thick; R-value = 5.7), which costs $190.

In the past few years, other companies have developed high-quality camping mattresses. Big Agnes makes the Q-Core luxury mattresses plus three other lower-priced mattresses, and Pacific Outdoor makes the ECO Thermo 6 sleeping pad—an environmentally friendly pad made completely from bamboo. Eureka, Exped, Mammut, Montbell, and REI also make high-quality sleeping mattresses. Campers can purchase these pads in camping specialty stores and on the web.

Closed-cell pads. Many backpackers and mountaineers select closed-cell pads made from dense foam sealed with plastic to prevent moisture absorption. These pads are considered to be good options for backpacking because they are lightweight, durable, well insulated, and waterproof. Campers who choose this type of mattress will not have to worry about inflating it every day, accidentally puncturing it, having to repair it, or deflating it before hitting the trail early the next morning. They can count on having a dry, warm mat to sleep on every night. But these closed-cell pads are not as comfortable as air mattresses and require more packing space.

Primary Sleeping Bag Features

Hundreds of sleeping bag models are available and range in price from about $15 to over $800. Selecting the best bag for basic tent camping (or any other camping approach) can seem like an overwhelming task, but it is really very simple. The cost of any particular bag depends primarily upon its comfort rating and weight. Bags with high thermal ratings and high weight are usually priced under a hundred dollars, while bags with low thermal ratings and low weight can be much more expensive. A heavy summer bag rated down to only 40°F would typically cost less than $50 while a lighter three-season bag rated down to 20°F would cost at least $100. And both of these bags would cost less than a lightweight winter bag rated down to 0°F.

Comfort rating. The comfort rating of a sleeping bag is important because each camper needs a bag that will allow him or her to sleep warm and comfortably on the coolest nights during the trips. For many years, sleeping bag manufacturers arbitrarily assigned thermal ratings based upon varying criteria, making it difficult to compare one bag with another. To determine the actual comfort rating, gear experts actually took the bags on cool- or cold-weather camping trips, slept in them several nights, and then reported the lowest temperature they could stay comfortable. They then posted these reports on backpacking websites, such as www.Trailspace.com. Before purchasing a particular bag, consumers were advised to read these reports to estimate the bag's true warmth rating. For several years, experts concluded that most manufacturers overstated their sleeping bag comfort ratings by ten to twenty degrees. A few American manufacturers overstated it by more than twenty degrees. Consequently, camping books typically advised campers to buy sleeping bags that were rated ten to twenty degrees lower than the lowest temperature expected on their camping trips. Campers who expected low temperatures around 30°F were advised to purchase bags rated down to 10°F to 20°F.

Fortunately, consumers no longer have to guess about the accuracy of a sleeping bag's rating. As of January 1, 2005, most sleeping bag manufacturers began using the European Standard (EN 13537) to define the thermal or comfort rating of their bags. According to this standard, the comfort rating of a sleeping bag is defined as the lowest temperature at which a standard woman can expect to sleep comfortably in a relaxed position wearing thermal underwear. It is determined for each sleeping bag model by a standardized laboratory test. Comfort ratings of most bags typically range from about +50°F down to about –25°F. Bags rated down to about 40°F are sometimes called summer bags, bags rated down to about 20°F are called three-season bags, bags rated down to about 0°F are called winter bags, and bags rated down to about –15°F are called severe-cold bags.

In addition to the comfort rating, the EN defines three more thermal ratings. The upper limit indicates how low the temperature must drop before an average man will not sweat in the bag. The lower limit indicates the temperature at which a standard man sleeping in the fetal position will begin to feel cold and be unable to sleep. And the extreme limit indicates the temperature at which the average woman can remain six hours without developing hypothermia.

Manufacturers that first adopted this EN standard included Bergans (Norway), Crux (United Kingdom), Lafuma (France), Mammut (Switzerland), Marmot (Germany), OMM (Poland), and Vaude (United Kingdom). In the spring of 2009, REI was the first American company to adopt the EN. Today, most American companies have adopted this standard, but a few makers of economically priced bags have not. Consumers should look carefully before buying a particular bag.

Although backpackers and mountain climbers who camp in cold weather may buy expensive winter bags rated down to about 0°F or lower, most basic tent campers only need three-season bags rated down to 20°F to 35°F. Three-season bags compress into a relatively small space, can be opened as blankets in mild weather, and yet will keep sleepers warm during cool spring and fall nights.

Weight. The weight of a bag is important for two reasons. Weight is important for backpackers and other wilderness campers because more weight carried in the backpack increases the effort and difficulty of carrying a pack for many miles. Weight is also important because it is directly related to the bag's compressibility. A heavy ten-pound bag will only pack down to the size of a medium-size duffel bag, while an ultralight bag will compress down to the size of a volleyball. Compressibility is especially important for backpackers, motorcycle campers, and a few basic tent campers who travel in small cars with limited packing space.

The weight of a bag depends upon its materials. Modern sleeping bags are constructed as lightweight quilts that have been folded over, partially sewn together, and enclosed with a zipper. They typically have a thin nylon or polyester outer shell and an equally thin but soft inner polyester lining. Between these two layers, bags have some type of thermal insulation material that is secured in place by small sewn-in compartments called baffles. Although all a bag's materials play a role in determining its total weight, the bag's insulating material plays the most important role. Bags insulated with synthetic plastic fibers generally weigh more than bags insulated with duck or goose down feathers.

Other camping books have suggested that down-filled bags are warmer than synthetic-filled bags, but this suggestion is incorrect! In fact, down-filled bags rated down to 25°F are no warmer than synthetic-filled bags rated down to 25°F. The primary differences between these two bags are their weight and cost. Down-filled bags are lighter and more compressible than synthetic-filled bags and cost at least a hundred dollars more. Backpackers prefer down-filled bags because the light weight and compressibility allow them to easy squeeze these bags into small backpacks and carry them many miles with little effort. Motorcycle riders may also want to consider down-filled bags that can be packed into small saddlebags or T-Bags. A few basic tent campers traveling in small vehicles may also have to consider down-filled bags, but most can easily pack more economically priced synthetic-filled bags.

Duck and goose down is graded on a scale ranging from 550 to 850 based upon its fill power, a measure of its fluffiness. Technically, the fill-power number refers to the amount of space filled by one ounce of the feathers. For example, one ounce of large, heavy feathers may only fill about 600 cubic inches, while one ounce of ultrasmall, lightweight down may fill as much as 850 cubic inches. Lower grades of down (550–650) typically come from ducks, are heavier, and cost less than higher grades of down. Higher grades of down (700–850) typically come from geese, are much lighter, and cost more. Sleeping bags insulated with 800 to 850 down require fewer ounces of down and, thus, are very lightweight and compressible—but they can cost up to $700 or $800.

In addition to their expense, down-filled bags have another significant limitation that should be considered before purchasing one. Down-filled bags are extremely sensitive to moisture. Small amounts of moisture from rain, condensation, or body sweat can reduce a bag's thermal efficiency. If a down-filled bag becomes too wet, it will lose its ability to keep its user warm. To protect down insulation from moisture, several sleeping bag makers have recently developed lightweight, comfortable, breathable, waterproof shells and liners, such as Pertex Microlight, but these materials add significantly to the price of the bag. In 2014, Kelty, Sierra Designs, and Big Agnes introduced bags with DriDown, which reportedly is more resistant to moisture—but again, this product increases the bag's price significantly. To prevent accidental soaking, backpackers and motorcycle campers should pack down-filled bags in waterproof bags and exert considerable effort to keep them dry in wet weather. Once they get wet, down-filled bags are virtually useless and require much more time and effort to dry out than comparable synthetic-filled bags.

Synthetic-filled sleeping bags offer a more economical and practical choice for basic tent campers. Good synthetic-filled bags are sometimes made from recycled plastic and polyester and typically cost between $100 and $200. They can provide just as much warmth as down-filled bags but weigh a little more and require more packing space. Furthermore, they will keep users warm when wet and will dry faster when wet.

Over the past twenty years, sleeping bag makers have designed newer synthetic fibers that compress almost as well as down. Some recent highly compressible synthetic insulation materials include Exceloft, Polarguard, Climashield, and Primaloft. These newer materials compress much smaller than older synthetic materials, such as Cloudloft, Insul-Therm, Hollofil 808, Hollofil II, Quallofill, Slumberloft, Thermolite, and Thermashield. Other newer materials, such as Coletherm developed by Coleman and Heatshield Optimal Technology (HOT SL) developed by the North Face, are proprietary fibers that are reasonably priced yet highly compressible.

In addition to their extra weight and packing space, synthetic-filled bags will gradually lose their loft, or thickness, over five to ten years. This loss of loft means that the bag will provide less warmth on colder nights. A three-season bag that first kept its owner warm when the temperature dropped to 25°F, for example, may only keep its user warm down to 35°F after five to ten years. When loft and thus warmth have been lost, the bag can still be used as a summer bag, but people who plan to camp in cooler weather will have to buy another three-season bag.

Secondary Sleeping Bag Features

In addition to thermal rating and weight, sleeping bags offer several features that can enhance overall comfort. Before selecting a bag, consumers should become familiar with all these features.

Shape. Sleeping bags are made in four basic shapes: rectangular, semirectangular, mummy, and double. Rectangular bags were very popular in the 1960s and continue to be popular among a few recreational campers because they, like ordinary beds at home, offer a considerable amount of space for moving around in the night. The limitations of these bags are that they require extra packing space and do not retain body heat efficiently. One example of a good rectangular bag is the Kelty Galactic 30, which measures thirty-three inches wide and seventy-five inches long.

Semirectangular bags have emerged in the past twenty years as an alternative to the less efficient rectangular bags. These semirectangular bags still provide considerable room but pack smaller than rectangular bags and retain body heat more efficiently. A few have hoods but most do not. The following examples are suited for basic tent camping:

- Marmot Mavericks 30—This model is a lighter semirectangular bag.
- Eureka Dual Temperature 20/40—This bag is made with more insulation on one side than the other so that campers can flip it to the side that provides the most comfort for any particular night.
- REI Siesta 25—This bag is thirty-five inches wide at the top and tapered at the bottom to provide a closer fit around the legs and feet.

Over the past twenty years, mummy bags have become the most popular sleeping bag shape, and dozens of models are available for any temperature rating and size. Mummy bags are good bags for basic tent camping because they provide comfort in a wide range of weather conditions. They can be opened in hot weather and used like quilts to cover whatever part of the body may get cool in the night. They can be partially zipped up to enclose the feet in cooler weather, and they can be fully zipped in colder weather. Their hoods can be tightened around campers' heads in extreme cold weather to prevent convective heat loss, but most campers rarely use these hoods. The primary limitation of mummy bags is the confined feeling they create, especially for large people when the bag is too small. The following examples are good bags suited for basic tent camping:

- Marmot Trestles 30—This is a reasonably priced, synthetic-filled bag that should be used as the standard by which other sleeping bags are measured. It comes in a variety of sizes, including extra-wide, and comfort levels. This is my wife's cool-weather sleeping bag.
- Kelty Light Year XP 20—This bag has been available for several years and continues to be a popular choice. I used one for about five years and then gave it to my wife, Eva. She has used it as her summer bag for the past five years.
- Montbell Burrow Bag #1 15—This is reportedly a very warm bag that stretches to provide extra comfort.
- Mountain Hardwear Lamina 30—This bag has been a popular model for several years.
- The North Face Cat's Meow 20—This bag is another good, highly compressible choice.
- Sierra Designs Lazer 30—This bag has a stretchable cover and insulation that can provide extra comfort.

Recently, several companies have offered double sleeping bags for couples who enjoy physical contact during the night. These double sleeping bags are good examples:

- Mountain Hardwear MegaLamina 20
- The North Face Dolomite 20
- Kelty Callisto 35

Size. Sleeping bags are made in several different sizes, and every camping book offers opinions regarding which size is best. Some books recommend that a consumer get inside a sleeping bag before buying it—to see how it fits his or her body. While this advice may have made sense ten years ago, it overlooks the facts that the best sleeping bags may not be available in stores near a person's home and that many people must buy sleeping bags online. Another commonly expressed opinion is that consumers should buy bags that are as small as possible because these bags will have less empty air space that disperses warm air available in the bag and will require less packing space. While this opinion may have some merit for ultralight backpackers who are willing to sacrifice a little comfort to cut every possible ounce, it proves to be bad advice for basic tent campers who want to sleep comfortably all night long and use their bags throughout the year. One more occasionally expressed opinion is that consumers should buy bags that are longer than their body to keep water, batteries, fuel canisters, and clothing warm on cold nights. While this advice may be worth considering by people who enjoy winter camping, most recreational tent campers do not camp in freezing weather. Furthermore, taller campers may not have the option of buying a longer bag.

Regular-size bags are made for campers who are less than six feet tall. These bags typically measure about eighty inches long and about sixty to sixty-two inches in shoulder girth. Long bags are designed for campers who are up to six feet five inches tall. They typically measure about eighty-six inches long and up to sixty-four inches in shoulder girth and will usually cost about ten dollars more than their regular-size counterparts.

Extra-wide bags are designed for big people like me, but only a few companies offer this size. The following models are examples of oversize bags:

- Marmot Trestles 15 Long X-wide—This model has been my cool-weather bag for the past five years.
- The North Face Big B 20—This is an oversize semirectangular bag.
- The North Face Mammoth 20—This bag has been available for several years.
- Montbell Burrow #1 15 Long—This bag stretches to seventy-five inches in shoulder girth.

Other options for big guys are sleeping bag expanders (such as the one made by Mountain Hardwear) that fit most regular or long bags with long zippers or Big Agnes bags, which provide more shoulder girth but are not insulated on the bottom. Instead the bags come with a sleeve to insert a twenty-inch-wide air mattress.

Several companies also make women's bags and children's bags that are smaller than their regular-size bags. Women's bags frequently have extra comforts, such as extra insulation in certain places and fleece-lined foot boxes, that women may appreciate. One example of a women's bag is the Sierra Designs Marlette 35.

Shells and liners. The materials used to make covers and liners that hold thermal insulation in place vary considerably in terms of their comfort, moisture protection, and weight. Simple polyester taffeta shells and liners, used to make economy bags, provide little comfort and a little extra weight. More-expensive all-polyester shells and liners, like those of my Marmot Trestles bag, on the other hand, add considerable comfort and very little weight. In fact, my sleeping bag is more comfortable than my bed at home. Ripstop nylon also makes comfortable shells and liners. Newer ultralight and waterproof materials can add even more comfort to a bag but also can add an extra hundred dollars or more to the price. For example, 10-denier Pertex Quantum is an ultralightweight and waterproof material that adds over a hundred dollars to the price of a bag—plus it tears easily when zippers get snagged.

Zippers and drawstrings. Sleeping bags offer a variety of zippers and drawstrings for closing the bag to retain maximum warmth. Most bags place zippers on the right side or the left side. A few bags have zippers on both sides or in the middle of the chest. Most zippers are full length to allow campers to easily enter and exit the bag and open it to make a quilt, but full-length zippers allow more heat to escape on very cold nights and increase the bag's weight. To prevent cold air from entering through the zipper, more-expensive bags will sew in a draft tube that lies flat on the closed zipper. Other bags have shorter half-length zippers to reduce the heat loss. After considering these options and typical family camping conditions, it seems reasonable to conclude that basic tent campers should purchase bags with long zippers on one side because most of the time these bags will be opened up and used as quilts on warm nights.

One of the most annoying sleeping bag problems is zippers that snag at the most inopportune times. Campers in a hurry to zip or unzip their bags will likely snag the zippers on nearby materials. In particular, zippers can easily get snagged when campers are tired and have turned out the lights to settle in for the night or when they need to get up in a hurry and go to the bathroom. To reduce the risk of zipper snags, some sleeping bag makers sew stiffer material on either side of their zippers. But campers still must be careful when zipping and unzipping these bags. Otherwise they may have to spend several extra minutes trying to free a stuck zipper without tearing the sleeping bag liner or damaging the zipper.

Most mummy bags have hoods and collars that can be tightened with cords or drawstrings. Good-quality sleeping bags have two drawstrings with different shapes located near one shoulder. For example, a round string may be used to close the hood around the head, while a flat shoestring may be used to close the collar around the shoulders and neck. The two strings have different shapes so that the user can easily identify the string he or she needs to adjust in the dark—just by touch.

Some expensive sleeping bags will have fluffy draft collars that create a seal around the neck when the bag is closed. These collars are designed to fit snuggly around the neck without choking the user. They help to keep warm heated air inside the bag and prevent cold air from entering.

Sleeping Bag Recommendations

When buying a sleeping bag, basic tent campers may want to consider the following suggestions.

- Never substitute cotton blankets, comforters, or sleeping bags for good-quality bags. They are useless when wet and require many hours to dry.
- Select a good-quality brand. The Marmot Trestles 15 sleeping bag costs about a hundred dollars and is an excellent choice in terms of packing size and comfort. Other good bag makers

include Mountain Hardwear, REI, Sierra Designs, the North Face, Montbell, Kelty, and Big Agnes. Montbell bags stretch to allow movement, the North Face makes several wide and long bags for big guys, and Big Agnes designs their bags with no insulation on the bottom. All these bags can be purchased from various local and online camping outfitters. In particular, check Backcountry.com, Campmor, Mountain Gear, REI, Sierra Trading Post, and Sundog Outfitter.

- When packing space permits, select synthetic three-season bags rated down to about 20°F that weigh less than four pounds. These bags typically cost between $100 and $200.
- Backpackers and motorcycle riders may have to settle for lighter summer bags or more-expensive down-filled three-season bags that can be squeezed into smaller packing spaces.
- Select bags that allow ample space to move around. Most men less than six feet tall and two hundred pounds should buy regular bags. Tall men should buy long or extra-long bags. Heavy and broad-shouldered men should buy wide bags. Women can buy regular bags or specially designed women's bags. Children and small people can buy short bags or children's bags.

Clothing

Contrary to recommendations expressed by a few self-proclaimed camping experts I have met, basic tent campers should wear as much clothing as comfortable while sleeping at night. Clothing helps to keep the body warm when the temperature drops; protects the sleeping bag interior from body oil and sweat; allows sleepers to easily slide into, around, and out of their sleeping bags; affords decent cover when necessary to walk to the bathroom at night; and provides a warm layer of clothing when the time comes to exit the bag on cool mornings. Combining the right garments with a good three-season bag should keep campers warm even if the temperature drops down to 20°F or lower.

The basic garments worn every night will vary depending upon the predicted low temperature. A camper should always wear a T-shirt and a pair of polyester or nylon shorts or pants. On cooler nights a camper may want to wear a comfortable polyester long-sleeve shirt (which provides a little more warmth than cotton) along with a pair of shorts or athletic pants. On colder nights, a camper may need to add a second polyester long-sleeve shirt, a pair of athletic pants, and a pair of wool socks. On even colder nights, a camper may need a pair of silk, wool, or polyester thermal underwear; fleece sweatpants; an insulated synthetic or fleece jacket; and a wool or polyester knit hat. More details about these garments are provided in chapter 6, "Clothing."

Optional Items

When traveling by car, basic tent campers usually have the space to pack several optional bedding items that provide additional sleeping comfort.

Ground blanket. After setting up the tent, the first item to place on the floor, if possible, is a wool or fleece ground blanket to soften and warm the floor. Wool and fleece will provide an insulated layer that will help to keep tent occupants warm even when water inadvertently gets into the tent. For a four-person tent, a queen-size blanket is ideal, but a full-size blanket will be adequate. Fleece blankets are more economically priced but tend to bunch up and need to be respread every day. Army wool blankets are good choices, but they typically smell very bad when first purchased and must be dry-cleaned and air-dried several times to reduce the irritating moth-proofing odor. The best ground blankets are those made by Woolrich and Pendleton, but these blankets cost $100 to $300.

Sheet. A full-size fitted sheet fits perfectly over two extra-large Therm-a-Rest mattresses and holds them together like an ordinary full-size bed. The sheet is easy to place over the mattresses and easy to remove. Furthermore, it can be easily washed every week with other dirty clothes to keep a clean, fresh-smelling bed no matter how many weeks campers may spend in their tents.

Pillowcases. Although basic tent campers do not have to pack pillows, they should pack a few pillowcases to cover small duffel bags, day packs, or other items to be used as pillows.

Earplugs. Campers who are sensitive to noise may want to pack earplugs for sleeping because many campgrounds are noisier than one's home bedroom. Each campground has its own unique character, but neighboring campers, cicadas, owls, whip-poor-wills, and other creatures frequently sound very loud when you are trying to sleep. In some campgrounds highway traffic and trains can create considerable noise. In Traverse City State Park in Michigan airplanes taking off and landing at a nearby airport create a lot of noise. And of course, thunderstorms occasionally develop during the night.

Unnecessary Items

Other camping books and articles frequently mention a few more bedding items, but these items are unnecessary, require extra packing space, and frequently get in the way when looking for needed items.

Pillows. Most people enjoy having a pillow under their heads at night, but campers must select their pillows with care. Backpackers and ultralight hikers typically do not pack pillows because these items require extra packing space. At night, they typically wrap their hiking shoes or backpacks with extra clothing to make a small pillow. Some luxury tent campers bring large pillows from home or buy small travel-size pillows. But large home pillows require considerable packing space, and travel-size pillows are not firm enough to support many people. Some books suggest using small nylon stuff sacks filled with clothes, but these sacks are hard and can cause numbness or cricks in the neck. After considering all the options, my family has settled upon using small duffel bags and day packs filled with our clothing to make our pillows. To make them even more comfortable, we cover them with nice pillowcases.

Hammocks. A few camping books present hammock camping as a preferable alternative to tent camping, and at least two companies (Clarke and Hennessy) make hammocks with rain flies that are specifically designed to allow users to sleep in them on rainy nights. Furthermore, several campers and backpackers are now using hammocks as their primary sleeping shelters and seem to enjoy them. These people argue that hammocks are lighter and smaller than tents—a feature that appeals to backpackers, bicycle campers, and motorcycle campers who have limited packing space. They also argue that hammocks produce less negative environmental impact than tents since they are not set up on the ground where they could crush fragile vegetation that serves as food and habitat for small creatures.

While I enjoy relaxing in a hammock during the middle of the day, I argue that hammocks should not be used as a primary sleeping shelter for several reasons:

- The lower weight and packing space of a hammock is not an issue for basic tent campers who travel in cars.
- The lessened environmental impact of hammocks is not an issue for basic tent campers, since they typically camp in public campgrounds that provide tent pads made from crushed stone, sand, or dirt.
- Many campsites in coastal beach areas, on the prairies, and in desert areas do not have enough trees to hang hammocks.
- Some environmentalists believe that hammock straps damage trees. Florida state parks, in particular, prohibit hanging hammocks from trees or other vegetation.
- Hammocks are much less comfortable than tents as primary sleeping shelters, especially for couples.
- Hammocks are colder than tents.
- Insulated mattresses and sleeping bags are difficult to manage in hammocks.

- Hammocks are not large enough to accommodate extra clothes bags and personal items.
- Hammocks tied to trees could be dangerous in thunderstorms.

Rather than using hammocks as their primary sleeping shelters, basic tent campers should consider them to be optional camp furniture and use them for lounging during the day and taking occasional naps on warm days. Additional information about hammocks is presented in chapter 5, "Furniture," and chapter 13, "Base-Camp Chores."

Cots. Before concluding this chapter, I want to express a few opinions about cots. During the early 1900s, cots were necessary because tents had no floors. But today, most tents have nice polyester or nylon bathtub floors, and campers can buy very comfortable air mattresses. Furthermore, cots require extra packing space, take longer to set up than air mattresses, may damage tent floors, and take longer to pack up. Having said this, I know from experience that many novice campers are determined to sleep on cots. They think they need a cot to provide a comfortable surface and to elevate them above critters that may be crawling on the floor. Therefore, campers who are determined to sleep on cots should investigate cots that sit low and are less likely to damage tent floors, such as the Therm-a-Rest Luxury Lite.

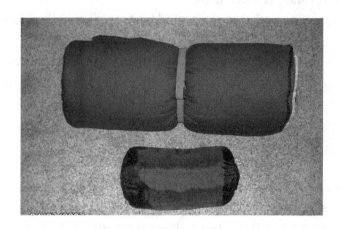

The packing space required for an older Coleman cotton/flannel bag (*top*) is much larger than the space required for a newer Kelty Light Year 25 (*bottom*).

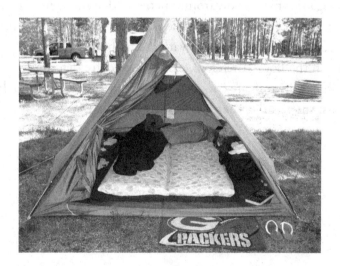

Eva and I use a full-size fitted sheet to cover our two large air mattresses and use regular pillowcases to cover our small clothing-filled duffel bags.

On cool nights, I wear wool socks, long athletic pants, two shirts, and a wool knit cap.

Eva enjoys the warmth of her mummy bag and hood on cold nights.

4

TOOLS

To facilitate mobility and comfort, basic tent campers should assemble a set of tools that will allow them to quickly set up camp, perform routine base camp chores, and take down camp quickly when the time comes to move on to the next destination. Kephart (1917) listed forty-two camp tools, including files, saws, glue, shears, spare buttons, shoe-repair supplies, and gun-cleaning and repair tools. The number of essential and optional tools that modern basic tent campers need is much lower, and most of these tools are small enough to pack in a small car or on a motorcycle. All of them can be packed in a small Cordura nylon tool bag, which is available in most hardware and home improvement stores or from Internet retailers. This chapter covers essential and optional tools, as well as unnecessary tools recommended by other books.

Cord

Many camping books mention rope or cord but provide very little information about it and its uses. They may state that campers should pack some clothesline or parachute cord and show photos of a few knots, but they typically do not explain how much to pack, how to prepare it at home before a trip, how to pack it, how to use it in the campsite, and how to reuse it again on future camping trips. These books and articles seem to suggest that campers just "buy some rope" for a trip and cut off whatever lengths they need for each particular chore. No guidance is provided for reusing it on future camping trips. Presumably, campers can save the random lengths of rope and hope that these lengths will be useful on their next camping trips or just throw them away and buy more cord. Backpacking books typically do not discuss rope at all because rope requires valuable backpack space that could be used to pack food, water, or other necessary gear and because repeatedly tying and untying knots would limit backpackers' mobility.

Basic tent campers should pack 150 to 200 feet of cord to set up their tents, kitchen canopies, tablecloths, clotheslines, garbage bag hangers, and sometimes food storage bags. When they have to set up their tent on pavement, they will need extra cord to extend tent stake-out loops out to the edges of the pavement where they can be staked down into the ground. On other occasions, they may need cord to tie tarps over tables and gear in stormy weather. Procedures for using cord in the campsite are discussed in chapter 14, "Ropes and Knots."

Knives

Other books unanimously agree that a good knife is an essential camping tool, but experts disagree upon the particular type of knife to pack. Some authorities recommend large fixed-blade knives because these knives are stronger for cutting heavy objects such as kindling and opening cans. Other authorities recommend folding knives because they are safer and easier to transport. Yet other authorities recommend multi-tools or Swiss Army knives because they have several extra tools that may be needed to handle common camping problems.

I typically carry five knives on basic-tent-camping trips because different sizes and types are best suited for different camp chores. I carry a medium-size multi-tool in my pants pocket and use it for most camp chores. In addition, I keep a large multi-tool with a heavy-duty blade and large pliers in my tool bag for larger jobs plus a small multi-tool with small pliers for smaller jobs. I also pack a large single-blade folding knife with the kitchen utensils and use it exclusively to cut foods. Finally, Eva carries a large folding knife in her fishing tackle box to clean fish. Other basic tent campers could probably manage with fewer knives. Regardless of the size, knives should be handled with care and should never be used to pry two objects apart. The following multi-tools are good for basic tent camping:

- Victorinox Swiss Army Tinker—This is a perfect pocketknife. It is small and lightweight with smooth, rounded edges that will not tear or wear pants pockets. It also has several tools that can be used to perform many camping and everyday chores, such as opening packages, cutting cord, tightening screws, opening pop bottles, making emergency repairs, dicing fruit or vegetables, cutting meat, and much more.
- Leatherman Juice S2—This small multi-tool has twelve useful tools and smooth edges. It is popular but seems a little heavy to carry every day in your pants pocket.
- Victorinox SwissTool—This large multi-tool is ideal for resolving many camping problems. It has a strong blade, a large pair of pliers, screwdriver bits, and several other useful tools.
- Leatherman Squirt—This small multi-tool comes with pliers and packs into a very small space and is useful when working with small wires and hardware. It can be carried in your tool bag or in a pocket.
- Leatherman E33—This is a heavier folding knife with a strong blade that can be used for preparing food, cleaning fish, or completing other camping chores.

Hatchet

Hatchets (belt axes or camp axes) were indispensible tools for early campers. They were used to fell trees for shelter, bedding, and fuel. After felling trees, axes were used to remove limbs, cut (buck) tree trunks into smaller sections, carve tent poles and stakes, and split logs into small pieces. However, hatchets are rarely discussed in recent camping books. Leave-No-Trace guidelines discourage cutting or damaging live vegetation. Backpackers have learned how to manage without hatchets because they do not want to carry the extra weight. Typically, backpackers drive in tent stakes with rocks and find small pieces of wood for their fires that do not require splitting—or just forgo campfires altogether. Basic tent campers, on the other hand, who travel in small cars (or on motorcycles) and stay in developed campgrounds still need hatchets to drive in tent stakes, split firewood, and shave small wood chips for cooking fires.

When purchasing a hatchet for basic tent camping, consumers should consider four important features:

- Handle length. In general, hatchets with short handles are easier to pack in small spaces but hatchets with long handles are more efficient and safer. For basic tent camping, thirteen to fifteen-inch handles seem to be ideal.
- Handle material. Most accomplished woodsmen prefer hatchets with wood (hickory or ash) handles because these hatchets are frequently made with good-quality, hand-forged heads that will last a lifetime and their handles can be easily replaced when broken. The primary limitation of wooden handles is their shoulders get damaged by inevitable overstrikes and have to be periodically replaced. Basic tent campers who choose to carry wood-handled hatchets should pack a replacement handle and be prepared to replace it in the field. Instructions for replacing handles can be found on the WranglerStar video and other YouTube videos. A second limitation of these hatchets is their eyes can be damaged by common log splitting procedures. Polymer-handled hatchets are gaining popularity among some woodsmen. These tools are economical, lightweight, and relatively durable. Typically, they are guaranteed for a lifetime but if a handle breaks, it cannot be replaced. Steel-handled hatchets are also well-suited for basic tent camping chores but their bits are typically made with brittle steel that is difficult to keep sharp.
- Type of steel. Hand-forged, high-carbon steel hatchet heads are easy to sharpen and hold their sharp edges after several hours of wood processing work. They are ideal for felling trees,

de-limbing felled trees, and bucking logs. But these hatchets typically cost $50 to $150. Dropped-forged hatchets made with harder steel are much more economical, split firewood just as easily as high carbon steel hatchets, and are very durable. They are ideal for typical basic tent camping chores since basic tent campers staying in developed campgrounds will not need to fell trees, de-limb them, or buck logs. The primary limitation of drop-forged hatchets is the difficulty of keeping their edges sharp.

- Weight and shape of the head. The weight of most camp hatchet heads range from 1.25 pounds to 1.5 pounds. Heavier heads increase cutting power with less effort. Wider heads improve splitting efficiency. Hatchets with lighter heads pack into a smaller space. Furthermore, most hatchets are made in one of two basic shapes. Hudson Bay hatchets have relatively large bits compared with relatively small polls while Scout hatchets typically have a more rectangular shape. Although Hudson Bay hatchets may be more aesthetically pleasing and perform most wood crafting chores effectively, their shoulders tend to get damaged faster after splitting firewood compared with scout–style hatchets.

These popular wood-handled models are suited for basic tent camping:

- Wetterling's Backcountry (or Hunter's) Hatchet—These handmade Swedish hatchets are virtually identical with sixteen-inch handles and 1.5 pound heads. The Backcountry was primarily marketed in the USA while the Hunter's Hatchet was primarily marketed in Europe. Their relatively wide heads are especially suited for splitting firewood. Most knowledgeable woodsmen consider these hatchets to be among the finest hatchets available.

- Condor Greenland Pattern Axe—This attractive Hudson Bay-style hatchet has a sixteen-inch handle and a 1.5-pound, hand-forged head. I have used this model on several camping trips and am very pleased with it.

- Gränsfors Bruk Wildlife Hatchet—Many accomplished woodsmen consider this handmade Swedish hatchet to be the best available. It has a fourteen-inch handle and a one-pound, hand-forged head. It is especially designed for felling small trees, limbing, and bucking logs.
- Husqvarna Curved Handle Hatchet—Several experts have praised this economical axe as comparable to the more expensive Swedish hatchets. It has a thirteen-inch handle and weighs two pounds.
- Gränsfors Bruk Hand Hatchet—This model has a ten-inch handle and weighs 1.3 pounds. It would be suited for motorcycle travel, but the short handle reduces its efficiency for driving tent stakes and splitting firewood—and makes it a little more dangerous.

These steel-handled hatchets are also suited for basic tent camping:

- Hart 20 Oz. Hatchet—This all-around camp tool has a very comfortable fourteen-inch rubberized handle and weighs 2.87 pounds. It can be purchased from Home Depot and various online retailers.
- Estwing Fireside Friend—This extra-wide tool has been cited as the best small log-splitting tool available. It has a fourteen-inch handle, weighs four pounds and can be purchased in many hardware stores. Its large poll can be used for driving a few tent stakes but its heavy weight can be tiring after driving in fifteen to twenty stakes.
- Estwing Sportsman's Axe—This attractive tool comes with an equally attractive leather sheath. It has a fourteen-inch handle, weighs 1.3 pounds, and can be purchased from Cabela's, Home Depot, and several other stores. Although it is a popular camp tool, other reviewers have asserted that its long concave (hollow) cheek is poorly designed for splitting firewood.

- Coleman Camp Axe—This is a compact, economically priced camp hatchet that works reasonably well for driving tent stakes and splitting small logs. It has a fourteen-inch handle and weighs 1.8 pounds. Coghlan's, Wenzel, and Stansport make similar tools. Any of these models can be purchased for about ten dollars in most department, sporting goods, and hardware stores. The limitations of all these hatchets are their hard steel bits that are difficult to sharpen and they are sold without a sheath. Although they are not fancy, these hatchets will last a lifetime.
- Kershaw Camp Axe—This small hatchet has a eleven-inch handle and weighs less than a pound. It could be packed in motorcycle luggage but does not split logs as well as other models.

The following polymer-handled models are also suited for basic tent camping:

- Fiskars X7 Hatchet—The head of this hatchet is specifically designed for efficient wood splitting. It has a fourteen-inch handle and weighs 1.4 pounds. Although the handle cannot be replaced if broken, the company claims it is stronger than steel and offers a lifetime warranty.
- Tekton 20 oz. 14-inch Fiberglass Camp Axe— This extra wide tool has a fourteen-inch handle and weighs three pounds. It also comes with a lifetime guarantee.
- Gerber Back Paxe II Axe—This compact tool has a nine-inch handle and weighs just over a pound. It could be used for motorcycle travel but is not a good wood splitter.

When using a hatchet to split firewood, campers must be extremely careful. One small mistake or moment of inattention can cause serious injury. Children should be taught hatchet safety but never be allowed to handle them. Teens should only be allowed to use them under adult supervision. Adults should not try to split logs or perform other chores with hatchets after consuming alcoholic beverages. Other safety procedures for splitting firewood are discussed in chapter 13, "Base-Camp Chores."

Stakes

Tent and canopy stakes are usually discussed in the shelter section of most camping books despite the fact that most tent manufacturers recommend that stakes be packed separately from tents to prevent accidental damage to the tent fabrics. I suggest that they should be considered as essential items in the tool kit. When packed in the tool kit, they are available to set up whatever tent or canopy campers may pack for a particular trip. Depending upon the tent, campers will need six to ten stakes for the tent and eight more stakes to set up a kitchen canopy. To be prepared for any situation, pack twenty stakes.

Several types of tent stakes are sold in department and camping-outfitter stores, but most have significant limitations for basic tent camping in developed campgrounds. For example, the yellow plastic stakes that come with many economy tents are only intended for soft sand or very soft muddy ground. If campers try to drive them into rocky soil or crushed-stone tent pads found in many campgrounds, they will shatter—even if a plastic mallet is used. Similarly, small-diameter steel or aluminum stakes that come with many medium- to high-quality tents are only suited for soft ground. They will bend if campers try to drive them into hard, rocky ground or crushed-stone tent pads. Large V-shaped steel stakes are strong but require considerable packing space and frequently are difficult to remove from the ground. MSR lightweight six-inch needle stakes are ideal for motorcycle trips, but twenty of them are expensive. The best tent stakes for basic tent camping are ten-inch nail-type tent stakes sold in packages of three in most department stores. Motorcycle riders and other campers with limited packing space may want to consider smaller six-inch galvanized nails sold in most home improvement stores. They are relatively inexpensive (about thirty cents each), require very little packing space, and are virtually indestructible.

Pliers

Basic tent campers will need a small pair of channel lock pliers to handle hot frying pans, perform various repairs around the campsite, and, when the time comes to break camp, pull tent and canopy stakes that get stuck in the ground—especially those that have been inadvertently driven into tree roots. As most veteran campers know, many campers are unable to remove these stakes and leave them for the next campsite occupants to deal with. A pair of channel lock pliers will usually remove those stuck stakes when other methods fail.

Other Essential Tools

Duct tape. When tents, sleeping bags, or tarps get ripped, duct tape can frequently be used to make temporary repairs that will serve until the damaged item can be replaced or permanently repaired at home. Duct tape can be used to patch torn tablecloths, tarps, ground cloths, backpacks, and tents. It can be used to splice broken poles, to hold down tablecloths on windy days, to hold bandages in place, to hold soles on shoes, and to solve many other unexpected problems. When possible, basic tent campers should buy small or flattened rolls that requires less packing space.

Gloves. Campers should also pack a pair of leather gloves in their tool kits. These gloves should be worn when handling firewood to provide a better grip and to avoid splinters and spiders. They should also be worn when moving logs, coals, and cooking grates in the campfire to avoid accidental burns. Occasionally, they will come in handy for other camping tasks, such as moving hot pots on a stove. Camp gloves should be made from leather rather than cotton, nylon, or polyester since these fabrics can melt when contacted by hot fires or grills and possibly cause severe burns.

Microfiber towel. The primary uses of a microfiber towel are to dry wet picnic tables, tents, and other camping gear. Tents in particular get wet almost every night and should be dried each morning. Tablecloths should be routinely cleaned each morning to remove dirt and bacteria that may have been left by raccoons or other animals that may have visited the table during the night. Microfiber towels are preferable to cotton towels because they absorb more water, can be washed often, and dry much faster than cotton towels. Sometimes, a towel can be used to sweep dirt in the tent or on a picnic table if a whisk broom is not available. But beware, microfiber towels should not be used as hot pot holders. They are poor heat insulators, so campers can quickly get burned through this material.

Optional Tools

Splitting block. When splitting logs, woodsmen typically recommend placing individual log sections on a tree stump or splitting block to improve the efficiency of each hatchet swing. The splitting block helps to dampen the springiness of the ground and protect the axe's cutting edge from being nicked by small stones in the ground. Unfortunately, most campsites in public campgrounds do not provide splitting blocks. Most campers typically set their logs on the ground to split them. For many years, I struggled with the problem of how to split my firewood logs and frequently improvised splitting blocks from available pieces of firewood. Recently, I decided to make my own portable splitting block with two eighteen-by-twelve-inch pieces of three-quarter-inch plywood glued together. This gave me a nice splitting block that requires minimal packing space in my vehicle.

Small crowbar. Although no other camping book or article has ever mentioned this item as a camping tool, a small twelve-inch crowbar is very useful for performing several campsite chores. It comes in handy for moving hot logs in the fire ring, stirring hot coals, and moving cooking grates. It can also be used to remove stuck stakes, especially when they have been inadvertently driven into tree roots. The twelve-inch size seems to be the best size because it is large enough to perform common chores but small enough to pack in a small tool bag. Realizing the usefulness of a small crowbar was one of the most enlightening discoveries of my camping experience. It is the perfect tool for resolving a problem that baffled me for several years—how to remove those stuck stakes. Now I do not have to leave any more tent stakes in the ground.

A small crowbar also makes a good trenching tool when necessary. Many conservationists become uneasy when discussing trenching, and it should certainly be avoided in pristine wilderness areas. However, trenching may be necessary in public campgrounds where most of the campsites were constructed by pouring crushed stone onto the ground. Trenching can eliminate standing water after heavy rains. If some of the stone settles and causes standing water, it is reasonable to dig trenches around the edge of the campsite and fill in depressions in the center. The procedure for digging trenches with a crowbar is described in chapter 13, "Base-Camp Chores."

Screwdriver. Although campers will rarely need a screwdriver other than the ones on their multi-tools, they may want to purchase a small ratchet screwdriver set with several bit sizes for occasional repairs that cannot be made with a multi-tool. These screwdrivers can be purchased in most hardware stores and cost less than ten dollars. They require very little packing space and occasionally provide the best option when making equipment or campsite repairs.

Carabineers. Inexpensive carabineers have many uses around the campsite and should be packed in a tool bag when possible. They can be used to set up kitchen canopies, hang a garbage bag on a rope tied around a pole or tree, hang a headlamp from the center loop of the tent, and perform several other camping tasks. Carabineers can also be used to attach a camera or water bottle to a backpack or belt.

Spring clips. If space is available, campers should also pack about five one-inch steel spring clips that can be purchased in home improvement stores. These clips can be used as clothespins to hold wet clothes and rags on a clothesline. They can also be used to close food storage bags. Six or seven pack into a small space and will come in handy on most trips.

Small stones. A few small stones or marbles can be used to set up a sheet as a sun canopy or to make a temporary repair to a tarp with a pulled-out grommet. To make an anchor point for a sheet or tarp corner, place the stone near the corner, pull the material around the stone, tie a double-reversed half hitch around the material and stone, and pull the hitch tight. The stone and hitch will provide a secure anchor point that will last until the material rots.

Sewing kit. Many camping books recommend sewing kits as an essential item for making emergency equipment repairs. These books argue that hikers and campers who break a strap on their backpack several miles away from the trail head would have difficulty continuing the trip and getting back to the car unless they had a sewing kit. Some books suggest that dental floss is as good, if not better, than strong thread for making equipment repairs and recommend including it along with a heavy-duty needle in the tool kit.

Basic tent campers staying in developed campgrounds, on the other hand, do not have to worry about repairing backpacks needed to haul their equipment several miles back to a car, but they would probably appreciate having a sewing kit handy if a button needs to be replaced or a seam needs mending. A sewing kit is relatively small and can easily be packed in a small medicine vial in a tool kit. A small dowel with about fifty feet of black bonded nylon upholstery thread plus a few strong upholstery needles can be packed and used to make many repairs. When making repairs with these upholstery needles, campers can use multi-tool pliers from the tool kit to push the needle through thick materials. Campers can also easily purchase a sewing kit from nearby camp or convenience stores in an emergency if they didn't pack one.

Hair ties. Fabric-covered hair ties, sold in the hair-care section of most drug and grocery stores, make excellent tent-pole retainers. Whenever tent poles must be folded and stored, a hair tie holds them well, is easy to remove, and lasts much longer than an ordinary rubber band. Hair ties work much better than rubber bands because they slide along the aluminum and fiberglass shaft surfaces rather than crumpling and tangling. Campers can buy a package of black or brightly colored bands, put them in their tool bag, and then use them to replace the tent-pole rubber bands when repacking.

Tent-pole repair tube. Many tents now come with pole repair tubes. These small tubes are designed to slip over a bent or broken pole and provide support for the bend until the end of a trip. To provide this support, campers must tape the repair tube to the bent pole with duct tape. Although poles rarely need repairing if handled carefully, campers will certainly appreciate having one handy if the need ever arises. To keep it readily accessible, pack it with the tent stakes in the tool bag.

Tent and sleeping-pad repair kits. Other camping books frequently suggest packing tent and sleeping-pad repair kits, but most basic tent campers will never need one, and if they did, the one they bought ten years ago and packed in their tool bag probably will have dried up. Most tears and holes that develop in tent canopies and rain flies are very small and can be ignored until the end of the trip or temporarily repaired with duct tape. Similarly, air mattresses rarely puncture when handled carefully, but if they do, campers can use Seam Grip and Tear-Aid patches to make the repair. If a tarp grommet pulls out, it can be repaired using a small stone, as described previously. If a tarp is severely damaged by wind, campers can easily buy a new one from a nearby store. They only cost a few dollars. Families who have young children who are likely to damage their tents may want to pack Seam Grip and Tear-Aid in their tool kits to be ready for the inevitable. If a tent or mattress is damaged during a trip, campers many want to call the manufacturer after returning home to determine the best way to make the best permanent repair.

Whisk broom. A small whisk broom is useful for sweeping dirt and debris away from the picnic tabletop before covering it with a tablecloth. It is also useful for sweeping dirt and sand that accumulates inside tents after a few days.

Unnecessary Tools

Since other camping books and magazine articles typically recommend several more tools, it seems appropriate to list a few of these tools and explain why they are unnecessary for basic tent camping.

Nails. Although many other camping books and articles list nails as an essential item in camping tool kits, I strongly disagree with this recommendation. Nails (except for nails used as tent stakes for motorcycle campers) are unnecessary for any legitimate camping task. They are unnecessary for setting up tents and tarps with aluminum poles, unnecessary for setting up kitchens, and unnecessary for repairing camping equipment. The primary use for nails is to drive them into trees to hold clotheslines, tarp support lines, and lanterns—but all of these tasks can be easily accomplished with ropes and knots. Furthermore, driving nails into trees causes several problems. Inconsiderate campers drive nails into trees and never pull them out when breaking camp. They just leave the nails for the next campsite occupants to deal with. Hopefully, the next campers will not be injured by an unseen nail protruding from a tree. Furthermore, driving nails into trees is an ecologically unethical practice! Nails can damage trees and leave sharp metal edges that could harm park employees who may have to cut the trees.

Machete. Several older outdoor survival books and articles suggest that machetes are useful tools for cutting small saplings to build shelters and to make tent support poles. The books and articles also argue that machetes can be used to cut live evergreen tree boughs to make comfortable beds. Times have changed considerably since those procedures were practiced. Virtually all state and federal campgrounds now forbid cutting live vegetation for any reason, and Leave No Trace guidelines encourage wilderness hikers and campers to avoid cutting live vegetation. Since machetes cannot be used to make shelters and beds or to split firewood, they have little value in the modern camper's took kit and would not easily fit into a small tool bag.

Shovel. While backpackers may need a small trowel to dig cat holes for their toilets, basic tent campers rarely need them or larger shovels. One possible use for a shovel would be to remove ashes from a campfire ring before starting a fire, but most of the time, fire rings are clean, and when they need cleaning, park staff will clean them if asked to do so. Another possible use for a small shovel would be to dig holes in sand for deadman anchors to rig guy lines for tents and shelters, but deadman anchors are rarely needed. Since shovels require considerable packing space that could be used to pack more useful items, basic tent campers can leave them at home. If holes need to be dug for deadman anchors, campers can use a crowbar.

Saw. Other camping books frequently recommend saws for cutting firewood, but today, basic tent campers staying in developed campgrounds have virtually no reason to pack one. In developed front-country campgrounds, it is unusual to find large dead logs lying on the ground that can be cut into firewood lengths with a small saw. Furthermore, many parks now forbid gathering large logs for firewood because these logs provide food and habitat for small animals and other wildlife. Even if there are no rules forbidding cutting and removing large fallen logs, doing so could have a negative impact upon the park's ecosystem. Instead of trying to cut logs, basic tent campers should buy precut firewood at the camp office or a nearby store.

Large axe. Another tool occasionally seen in established campgrounds is a large axe. Some campers who are planning to spend several days in a campsite and keep a campfire burning most of the time will bring or buy a truckload of firewood that must be split before being used as fuel. These campers sometimes pack large axes to facilitate splitting large loads of wood, but few basic tent campers will ever bring or need such large loads of wood. Most campers can easily use a small hatchet to split a few logs needed for a simple campfire. Furthermore, a small hatchet requires much less packing space, freeing up area that can be used to pack other items, and is safer to use.

Plastic mallet. Many camping books suggest that plastic mallets can be used to drive in plastic tent stakes commonly included with economy tents. These articles suggest that using a plastic mallet will eliminate breakage—but they are wrong. What these books and articles fail to say is that plastic stakes are only suited for soft soil and sandy areas. Trying to drive these stakes into hard crushed-stone tent pads with any tool will break them. On the other hand, driving them gently with a hatchet into soft ground will not break them. Clearly, a plastic mallet is not the solution to the problem. Instead, campers should discard plastic stakes and buy stronger six- or ten-inch nail stakes.

Sharpening stone. Many camping books and magazine articles suggest that campers pack a stone for sharpening their knives and hatchets. Without argument, sharp tools make work much easier than dull tools, but basic tent campers do not need to pack sharpening stones when camping in developed public campgrounds, even for several weeks. While hunters who field dress several animals may have to sharpen their knives once or twice a week, basic tent campers do not use their knives long enough to warrant regular sharpening. Furthermore, most modern knives are made with stainless steel blades rather than older carbon steel blades, and stainless steel blades hold their edges much longer and require less sharpening. Stainless steel blades will hold a good edge for several weeks under normal use. Furthermore, using a sharpening stone effectively requires considerable practice and a special touch. Most people do not know how to use one and would be unable to get a sharp edge.

Stove repair kits. In over forty years of camping, I have never needed to repair a stove in the field. Many years ago, I realized that my old gas stove was no longer working as well as it had when I first bought it. So I used it as best as possible during the camping trip and later replaced the generator assembly after returning home from the trip. Small multifuel backpackers' stoves must be occasionally cleaned at home before leaving on a trip for optimum service. If a stove fails to work properly in camp, basic tent campers can easily cook on a campfire, buy prepackaged foods, or ride to a restaurant. So omit the stove repair kit, and use the limited space to pack more-useful items.

Glue. Basic tent campers rarely, if ever, need glue to stick things together on camping trips. If they do, they can use duct tape or run to a local store to buy a tube of glue. In my experience, people rarely need glue in general, let alone when camping, and when they do need it, they almost always have to buy a new tube because the previously opened tube is dried solid from lengthy storage. I'm sure many campers would have the same problem if they packed glue for camping trips. It would always be hardened by the time they needed it.

Surveyor's tape. Several years ago, I ran across a magazine article suggesting that campers pack a roll of surveyor's tape and use it to reserve choice campsites until the family can complete the registration paperwork and get back to set up. The author of this article argued that the tape would tell subsequent arrivals to the campground that this particular site was claimed.

Although this argument may sound plausible at first, further consideration of typical campsite registration procedures reveals that this logic is flawed. Many campgrounds allow families to reserve specific campsites weeks or months ahead of time, and surveyor's tape will not cancel a valid reservation. Campgrounds that accept walk-up patrons typically use one of two registration procedures. Some allow campers to drive through the campground and identify two or three vacant sites. Then return to the registration station and complete the paperwork. If an earlier arrival has already noticed a particular site and returned to the registration station first, he or she will be allowed to claim the site despite the fact that another camper may have put up tape. Subsequent arrivals will still be riding through the campground while earlier arrivals have the opportunity to return to the registration station and claim one of their selected sites. Other campgrounds tell new arrivals to set up their tent on any unoccupied site and then return to the registration station to complete the paperwork. In either case, surveyor's tape serves no useful function and requires unnecessary packing space and effort. Leave it at home, and use the space to pack more-useful gear.

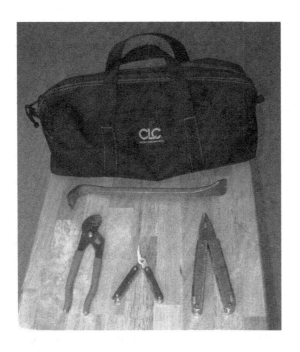

My tool bag contains a small crowbar, a pair of Channel lock pliers, and two Leatherman multi-tools.

Steel-handled hatchets seem to be better suited for basic tent camping than wooden-handled models. *From top to bottom:* an old Wenzel hatchet that I have used for over ten years, a newer Coleman Camp Axe, a Hart 20 Oz. Hatchet, and an Estwing Fireside Friend.

The poll width varies from one model to the other. *From left to right:* Estwing Fireside Friend, Hart 20 Oz. Hatchet, and Coleman Camp Axe.

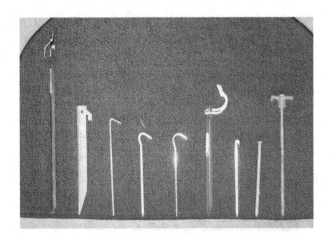

Several tent-stake designs are available for sale, but most have limited usefulness. The two nail-type stakes on the far right can be used in most campsites.

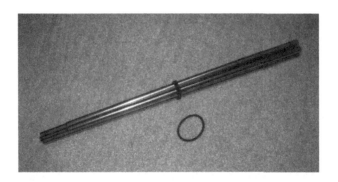

Hair ties make much better tent-pole retainers
than ordinary rubber bands.

5

FURNITURE

For over a hundred years, experienced campers have included camp furniture as an important part of their camping kits. Holding (1908), for example, described tables, beds, chairs (including a tocah reclining chair), stools, and candelabra. Kephart (1917) discussed tables, chairs, stools, folding shelves, wall pockets, cots, and clothes hangers. Today, camping outfitters such as REI and Cabela's offer a wide range of camp furniture from folding chairs and folding tables to kitchen counters and dishwashing stations. In most popular campgrounds, visitors can see a wide variety of folding chairs, folding tables, footstools, and kitchen counters.

Although most state and federal park campsites have picnic tables that provide a place to sit, prepare food, eat meals, play games, and relax, these tables are too low for extended chores such as food preparation and dishwashing. Furthermore, many are too small for dining plus other camp chores. Basic tent campers should consider adding a few more furniture items to enhance their overall comfort—especially when planning to stay several days in a long-term base camp. Since some of these items can occupy a considerable amount of packing space and can be easily damaged by routine use, campers should choose them with care.

A thick plastic tablecloth is the first item to buy. Tablecloths provide a clean surface for preparing foods, eating meals, and playing games. Thick plastic cloths, compared with flimsy cloths, will last several years.

Other furniture items such as chairs and tables should be strong enough to support heavy campers and portable enough to easily move about the campsite. Tables should be strong enough to support the weight of water containers and kitchen equipment. Hammocks add a nice place to relax during the day. Additional details about camp furniture are presented in this chapter.

Tablecloth

Since most state and federal campgrounds typically provide picnic tables with benches in each campsite, additional chairs and tables are not essential for a basic level of comfort. However, a clean plastic tablecloth is essential to cover the table because campground tables can be contaminated by animals walking on them, bird droppings, tree sap, and various foods that may have been spilled by previous campers. After arriving at a campsite, clean dirt and debris off the table, rinse it with water if necessary, allow it to dry, place a clean tablecloth on it, and secure the tablecloth with one or two cords. After camp has been set up, you will then have a clean place to prepare food, eat meals, wash dishes, play games, and relax around the campsite.

Chairs

To enhance comfort, basic tent campers should pack a small folding chair for each person, when packing space permits. Campers can place their chairs near the campfire, next to a table, in the sun, in the shade, or anywhere else they want. Campers can also pack them up and take them to outdoor concerts, the beach, or a fishing spot. Perhaps the best option, especially for big guys like me, is an armless quad chair. These chairs weigh about six pounds, fold into a small space, are very portable, and are extremely strong. Unfortunately, they can be difficult to find. Occasionally, they can be found in local department and sporting goods stores, but most of the time they must be ordered from online retailers. The Alps Mountaineering Adventure Chair is an expensive model but has a four-hundred-pound capacity.

Quad chairs with armrests and high backs may be a little more comfortable, but they require more packing space and break easily. I used these chairs for over thirty years and typically broke one every year or two. I am slightly comforted by the fact that other campers also break these chairs often. In many campgrounds, broken quad chairs can be seen near many garbage receptacles. The heavy-duty chairs rated to hold 350 pounds are not much better. They also break easily. Once it is broken, the chair must be thrown into the garbage. Another limitation of these chairs is they sit lower and require more effort to stand up.

In addition to quad chairs, several other chair designs are suited for basic tent camping. Many campers like director's chairs and deck chairs. Other campers prefer three-legged stools because they offer a good combination of compactness and strength. Motorcycle riders have used Kermit's Kamping Chairs for several years because they can be packed into a smaller space than most folding chairs. Recently, a new generation of compact camping chairs have emerged, including models like the Helinox Chair One.

Campers traveling by motorcycles or small cars may not have the space to pack a folding chair but can use hammocks and the picnic tables furnished in most campsites to relax. When spending several days in a base camp, these campers could buy chairs from local stores after setting up their camp and use them for the length of the camp. When the time comes to move on, they could ship the chairs back home or give them to a campsite neighbor.

Table

Although most campgrounds furnish a picnic table with every campsite, these tables are not always large enough or high enough for various camp chores. For example, families with children need much more space to prepare food and eat meals. Furthermore, picnic tables are typically too low for comfortable standing necessary for many food preparation tasks. Sporting goods stores and outdoor outfitters sell a variety of folding tables that could be used for camping chores, but these tables are usually too low for food preparation and too flimsy to hold much weight.

A popular camp-table design is a small, lightweight rolltop table that packs into a small tube sack with a shoulder strap. These tables are a good height for eating meals and playing games but are too low and flimsy for comfortable food preparation, cooking, and dishwashing. Most rolltop tables are made from aluminum with plastic slides and clips, but a few are made from wood or other materials. Most of them are about thirty inches square. The following models are popular:

- REI Camp Roll Table—This is a very solid table that could be used as a standard by which other tables are measured.
- Stylish Camping Aluminum Roll-Top Table—This model is similar to the REI table.
- Coleman Compact Outdoor Table—This table is similar to the REI table but less expensive.
- Camp Time Roll-A-Table—This is a highly praised table made with plastic-encased wooden slats. Many reviewers give this table high ratings because its plastic top allows for easy cleanup and because its legs are attached without braces, allowing users to pull up to the table with their knees and legs under the table. However, this table is much shakier than other models.

Another popular camp-table design is a resin- or aluminum-topped table with folding legs, similar to a card table. These tables typically measure about forty-eight inches long by twenty-four inches wide. They are sturdier than rolltop tables but require more packing space and are too low for comfortable kitchen work. Campers with limited packing space could tie this table on their car's luggage rack if they have one. The following models are examples of this type of table:

- Samsonite Folding Table
- Coleman Pack-Away Folding Table
- Lifetime Height Adjustable Folding Table
- Stansport Plastic Folding Camping Table

Perhaps the strongest and most practical type of table is a homemade wooden tabletop supported by two adjustable-height folding sawhorses. The tabletop could be made with five one-by-six-inch boards cut five feet long. To support these top boards, attach three one-by-four-inch boards of the same length to the bottom as support braces. To give the tabletop a finished look and to prevent possible injury, round the corners and cut the ends of the bottom support boards at a slight angle. A pair of sawhorses, like Stanley Adjustable Sawhorses, could be purchased from a local home improvement store for about sixty dollars. The adjustable height allows campers to raise the table to a comfortable counter height for food preparation and lower it to a dining-table height.

When traveling in a small vehicle, this tabletop can be tied on the luggage rack with short ropes and trucker's hitches. Once attached to a luggage rack, the sawhorses could be tied on top. Always check this load anytime you stop.

Milk Crates

Over the past fifty years, I have experimented with a variety of kitchen-gear packing containers, including homemade wooden crates, plastic tubs, and storage boxes. After considerable trial and error, I have concluded that milk crates make the best storage containers for camp kitchens and nonperishable foods because they are large enough to carry food and kitchenware, compact enough to be packed together in a small space, and square enough to be used as shelving after setting up camp. Milk crates have several other practical features as well:

- Handle cutouts on each side make them easy to carry to and from the campsite.
- Their light weight allows a person to carry two or three at one time.
- Flat vertical sides allow campers to pack them side by side on garage shelves or in car trucks without losing valuable packing space.

- The twelve-by-twelve-inch, square dimension is perfect for packing pots and pans, including a ten-inch frying pan with its handle removed, and full-size dinner plates.
- Square shape and bottom lugs allow three or four to be stacked without worrying about them falling over.
- Ten-inch depth is perfect for packing several pans, plates, and tumblers.
- Rigid construction allows them to be used as footstools and step stools when necessary.

One major problem with genuine milk crates is that they are difficult to obtain. Although they can be observed around town and are commonly used for storing record albums and serving as rear trunks on delivery bikes and motor scooters, dairies refuse to sell them, and some states have passed laws that make it illegal to sell them in flea markets. The best place to get them is an online wholesale packaging company called Uline (1-800-295-5510) that sells strong imitation milk crates. The minimum order of three crates costs thirty dollars. Although these imitation crates are not quite as strong as genuine milk crates, they are certainly stronger than the cheap milk crates sold in discount department stores and seem to be strong enough to last for dozens of rugged camping trips over several years.

Hammocks

When possible, campers should pack a hammock or two for casual day lounging and napping. Many people especially enjoy taking naps after lunch and casually reading books or listening to music until they drift off to sleep. In addition to napping, campers can use them as hanging chairs when sitting around the campsite and talking with their companions. Several styles and brands of hammocks suited for daytime siestas are available. Small fishnet hammocks, which can be purchased in many department stores, camping supply stores, and military surplus stores for about ten dollars, pack into a small space and are functional—but they are not particularly comfortable. Hammocks made from parachute nylon, such as those sold by Eagles Nest Outfitters (ENO), are much more comfortable. The ENO DoubleNest hammock costs a little more and does not seem to offer any advantages over the SingleNest. Although it is promoted as a hammock for two people, it would be very uncomfortable if two large adults tried to get in it together. Other well-known hammock makers include Clark, Crazy Creek, Hennessy, Lawson, Speer, and Trek Light Gear.

Hammocks can also be used to take naps in highway rest areas on travel days. Older campers taking various medicines for blood pressure and high cholesterol may get sleepy while driving in the middle of the day. Rest areas typically provide bathrooms, vending machines, and picnic tables but do not provide a good place to nap. Since many rest areas have large shade trees around their tables, campers could set up a hammock and take a very relaxing nap. Procedures for hanging hammocks will be described in chapter 14, "Ropes and Knots."

Other Optional Items

Bath mats. For a little extra comfort in the campsite, campers may want to pack one small rubber-backed, fuzzy bath mat for each person. After setting up their campsite, campers can place each mat on a picnic table bench. The mat provides a comfortable, dry, and warm place for them to sit—especially when camping on cool, early-spring or late-fall weekends and when the campsite has concrete benches.

Extension cord. Many state parks and a few other public parks offer campsites with electrical outlets that can be used to charge cell phones and other electronic devices and to power laptops, portable DVD machines, portable TVs, fans, and more. In other words, having readily available electrical outlets can add considerably to a family's overall comfort during a tent-camping vacation. However, these outlets are not always conveniently located near the central areas of the campsite. To make the electrical outlets more accessible, basic tent campers should pack a fifteen-foot outdoor extension cord along with their camp furniture so that they can bring the electrical outlets to their picnic table or tent.

Unnecessary Items

Retail stores sell other camp furniture items, and camping books frequently recommend some of these furniture items, but I think they are unnecessary and inhibit mobility by getting in the way when searching for another needed item. Some unnecessary items are discussed below.

Tablecloth clips. Most camping outfitters sell tablecloth clips, and several camping books suggest that campers use them to hold their tablecloth in place on windy days. Typically a set of clips consists of six to eight metal spring clips designed to be placed strategically around the table edge to hold the tablecloth in place. Many campers buy and pack these clips but rarely use them because they are too small to fit many camp tables. Typically, these clips just get in the way when looking for other needed items, and they are easily lost. Instead, campers should use one or two lengths of cord to secure their tablecloth to the table and heavy objects such as water jugs, coolers, and canned goods to weigh down the corners. If necessary, duct tape can be used to hold down edges.

Kitchen station. Many camping outfitters offer a variety of folding cabinet units for food preparation, cooking, and other kitchen chores. For example, Cabela's sells a Deluxe Camper's Kitchen, and Gander Mountain offers a variety of kitchen stations that range in price from $100 to $200. Other well-known kitchen stations include the Kelty Basecamp Kitchen and the Bass Pro Shops Basic Camp Kitchen. In its *2014 Gear Guide, Backpacker Magazine* listed the Grub Hub Mesa 1 kitchen station as a top choice for base camping.

While these kitchen stations may be nice for luxury tent campers, they are expensive and impractical for most basic-tent-camping families who travel in small vehicles. A simple homemade countertop as described earlier in this chapter or a folding table would be a more economical and practical option.

Shelving and utensil organizer. Older camping books recommend packing some type of shelving to store clean cookware, dishes, and utensils when not in use. Kephart (1917), for example, displayed in his early book a homemade folding shelving unit that collapsed into a small space for travel. Other camping books suggest campers place boards on top of storage boxes to make shelves. Today, several companies offer a variety of folding cupboards. Some examples include Oztrail Folding Cupboard, Portable Cupboard's Camping Pop-Up Cupboard, Creek Company Hanging Camp Cupboard, the and Camp-let Quick Erect Cupboard. These folding cupboards can be purchased from Cabela's and other camping outfitter stores. Although they are especially popular among luxury tent campers, they are not practical for basic tent camping. Instead of buying expensive shelving, basic tent campers can use milk crates to make functional shelves and counter space. Milk crates can also be turned on their sides and used to store pots, pans, plates, utensils, cups, and extra gas cylinders.

Portable sink. A few modern camping books and magazine articles suggest that campers pack a portable sink for washing dishes, clothes, and other things. At first, this advice may seem reasonable, but upon further consideration, a portable sink will quickly become excess baggage. It will be rarely used and will get in the way when looking for other items. Instead campers can wash clothing on rocks or concrete benches. For washing dishes, any pot or bowl can hold soapy water. A small bucket could be used to catch soapy gray water after rinsing dishes, wash clothes, and take baths when showers are unavailable.

Armless quad chairs make good camp chairs because they pack into a small space and are strong enough to support large people.

This 5' x 2.25" homemade table with two sawhorses makes a perfect kitchen counter. Milk crates provide good storage.

A folding table comes in handy when a picnic table is unavailable.

These small bath mats help to make the table benches
more comfortable. Notice that the table cloth is
secured with a cord rather than metal clips.

6

CLOTHING

Older camping books and articles typically devoted considerable space to describing clothing suited for camping. Holding (1908), for example, devoted two chapters to camp clothing, one for men's clothing and one for women's. In the men's chapter he discussed Norfolk jackets with pleats and large pockets, thin waistcoats, flannel underwear, knickerbockers, well-soaped stockings to prevent blisters, brown boots, tweed caps, oilskin or Mackintosh waterproof trousers, and spare clothes. In the women's chapter, he included unlined, semifitted coats with inside pockets; narrow, soft, and pliable corsets; Angola knickerbockers; wool undergarments and hose; toques or tweed hats; sensible brown boots with low heels; single-breasted, rubber-lined waterproof coats; and waterproof skirts.

Today, basic tent campers who want to be prepared for possible weather conditions must assemble large sets of garments that are suited for hot, rainy, and cool weather. Furthermore, they need clothes for various recreational activities. The needed clothing includes shoes, socks, underwear, shirts, pants, dresses, jackets, hats, and many other items. Before each trip, campers must select the garments that are best suited for the particular activities planned during the trip and the probable weather.

To facilitate maximum mobility, basic tent campers should find garments that can be stuffed into tiny crevices without wrinkling, dried quickly when wet, and layered to provide considerable warmth on cooler days. For the most part, these garments should be made from polyester, nylon, wool, and silk. Having this set of garments allows campers to select the best clothing for the weather, pack quickly each morning, throw duffel bags into vehicles or tents without worrying about wrinkling or damaging other equipment, dry clothing even in cloudy weather, and stay warm in cooler weather.

Apparel Companies

Over the years, several companies have established reputations for making high-quality outdoor apparel suited for basic tent camping. Basic tent campers should become familiar with these brands, visit retail stores, try on these garments, and use them as standards for evaluating the appearance, workmanship, and price of garments made by other companies.

Woolrich. Woolrich began in 1830 as a wool mill located in Little Plum Run, Pennsylvania. The company first sold woolen yarn and fabrics to local farm families and loggers and later made blankets for Union soldiers during the American Civil War. After the war, the company made wool uniforms for military personnel and outdoor clothing. By 1989, it had grown into a multimillion-dollar company and began making down insulated jackets. Over the past thirty years, the Woolrich brand name has become associated with black-and-red-plaid wool shirts and jackets. In 1999, its jackets were featured in the movie *The Horse Whisperer*. Today, its garments are sold by several retailers, including L.L.Bean, Cabela's, Lands' End, and Amazon.com.

L.L.Bean. After a long, cold, and wet Maine hunting trip in 1911, Leon Leonwood (L. L.) Bean asked a shoemaker to sew warm leather upper panels around a pair of rubber work boots, and this idea evolved into a new line of footwear and apparel for outdoor enthusiasts. Today, L.L.Bean shirts, pants, and rain gear are highly prized by many veteran backpackers. They are available only from the L.L.Bean website.

Champion. Champion initially was founded in Rochester, New York, by the Feinbloom brothers in 1919. By 1950, the company had established a reputation for making quality garments and began supplying uniforms for the NBA and other professional athletic teams. Over the past fifty years, it has supplied uniforms for dozens of university athletic teams and several foreign professional sports teams. Today, the company is a subsidiary of Haneswear, and its garments are sold in Target stores and other retail outlets. These economically priced performance shirts, shorts, athletic pants, thermal underwear, and light jackets make excellent camping garments. They are lightweight, warm, moisture wicking, and fast drying.

Columbia. The Columbia Hat Company was established in 1938 near Portland, Oregon, by Paul and Marie Lamfrom after they fled from Nazi Germany. Twenty-two years later, the Lamfroms' daughter, Gert Boyle, assumed control of the product line, and in 1960 she changed the company's name to Columbia Sportswear Company. Over the next several years, the company introduced Gore-Tex parkas (1975), the Quad Interchange System Parka (1982), the Bugaboo Parka (1986), Omni-Dry outerwear (1987), Titanium jackets (1994), and Omni-Shade sun-protection garments (2008). Columbia was the official supplier to NBC Sports during the 1994 and 2002 Winter Olympic Games and the 2005 X Games. In the past ten years, the company has acquired Mountain Hardwear, Montrail, and Pacific Trail product lines. Today, Columbia garments are sold in many large sporting goods stores, and these garments are recognized as quality outdoor apparel for a reasonable price.

Recreational Equipment Inc. (REI). REI is an outdoor recreational equipment cooperative that was founded in Seattle, Washington, in 1938 by Lloyd and Mary Anderson. The Andersons began making ice axes and buying climbing gear to sell to fellow mountain-climbing enthusiasts. After a few years, the company began buying camping and mountaineering equipment at wholesale prices and selling this equipment to co-op members for less-than-retail prices. In 1972, the co-op received considerable attention when it introduced its own High-Light tent with huge screened side windows for unequalled ventilation. Today, REI makes and sells a complete range of high-quality outdoor apparel suited for basic recreational tent camping. REI's garments have a reputation for being warm, lightweight, very well made, and reasonably priced.

Patagonia. In 1957, Yvon Chouinard (a French Canadian mountain climber and outdoor adventurer living in southern California) bought a small blacksmith forge and began making equipment and hardware for mountain climbers. Initially, his company was called Chouinard Equipment. In the 1960s, he began selling colorful clothing suited for climbing. In 1972, he changed the name of the company to Patagonia and soon introduced a complete line of sportswear. The company was the first to introduce the concept of layering clothing for warmth. It introduced Synchilla in the early 1980s and Capilene thermal underwear with at least 50 percent recycled polyester in 1984. Capilene 1 is the lightest weight designed for warm or mild weather, Capilene 2 and 3 are midweights designed for cool weather, and Capilene 4 is the heaviest weight designed for the coldest weather. Early in its history, Patagonia began using environmentally clean materials and lobbied for other companies to do the same. In 2008, Patagonia received the Eco Brand of the Year award.

Sierra Designs. In 1965, George Marks and Bob Swanson resigned their jobs at a Berkley, California, ski shop and started Sierra Designs, making jackets and clothing for snow skiers. Almost immediately, they began making outerwear for the North Face and introduced their Cagoule Parka made from Reevair, a breathable material before the advent of Gore-Tex. A year later, the company introduced its 60/40 Parka, and this garment was an instant hit with outdoor enthusiasts. Eventually, the 60/40 Parka became a classic with a cult-like following. Over the years, Sierra Designs developed down insulated jackets, synthetic-fiber insulated jackets, and wind/rain gear. Recently, the company merged with JanSport, Kelty, and Slumberjack.

The North Face. The North Face was established in 1965 by Douglas Tompkins and Kenneth Klopp in San Francisco, California. The company was initially established as a retail store selling high-quality gear for mountain-climbing enthusiasts but soon began making its own garments. According to the company's website, its name was selected because mountaineers consider the north face of a mountain to be the most difficult side to climb. Within a few years, the company was also making backpacks, jackets, sleeping bags, and tents. Throughout its history, the North Face has sponsored over forty mountain-climbing and polar expeditions, and videos of these expeditions can be found on YouTube. Since its inception, the North Face has introduced several popular jackets, including the Sierra Parka (1969), the Stowaway Jacket and Pants (1982), the Mountain Gore-Tex Jacket (1985), and the Mountain Light Jacket (1988). During the 1980s, wilderness chic came into style, and the North Face logo became so popular that some people began selling counterfeit the North Face jackets and thieves began stealing the North Face jackets from individuals for resale. Today, the Denali fleece jacket is very popular among young adults.

Mountain Hardwear. Mountain Hardwear was founded in 1993 by a group of people who had worked for Sierra Designs for several years. In their first year of operation, the group introduced the Ergo Hood jacket that allowed one-hand hood adjustments and allowed wearers to turn their heads without having their vision obstructed by the sides of the hood. In 1996, the company's Ethereal Parka won the Editor's Choice Award from *Backpacker Magazine*. Over the next ten years, the company made jackets with Conduit waterproof membranes and Gore's WindStopper fabrics. During this time several of the company's jacket styles won awards from the outdoor-apparel industry. In 2006, the company again won *Backpacker Magazine's* Editor's Choice Award for its Torch Jacket. Today, Mountain Hardwear makes all its apparel from green, eco-friendly materials and recycled polyester. The Monkey Man 200 is a very popular fleece jacket.

In addition to the above-named companies, several more companies have emerged as producers of high-quality garments suited for basic tent camping. Campmor, for example, offers a full line of economically priced shirts, pants, underwear, and thermal layers suited for camping and other outdoor activities. SmartWool makes T-shirts, socks, and hats from merino wool. Terramar makes economy priced underwear from special blends of silk, wool, and polyester. PrAna makes beautiful and comfortable pants and dresses for women. And numerous companies, such as Merrell, Keen, Vasque, Salomon, Timberland, and Asolo, make a variety of shoes and boots suited for basic tent camping.

Fabrics

Several fabrics are used to make outdoor clothing, and each type of fabric has unique properties that determine its suitability for basic tent camping in various conditions. To ensure dry, warm, and comfortable trips in various weather conditions and to help preserve our fragile environment, basic tent campers should become familiar with a few basic facts about common fabrics so that they can select the best set of garments for any time of year.

Cotton shirts and T-shirts, made from plants grown in hot, dry climates such as the southern United States and India, are well suited for hot summer camping trips in the southern United States because they are relatively inexpensive and help to cool the body in hot weather. Cotton fibers readily absorb and hold moisture for a long time. This moisture helps to produce a cooling effect for the wearer, especially if a gently breeze is blowing. Light-colored, loose-fitting sleeveless cotton T-shirts are especially good choices for hot summer camping trips because they can be packed into a relatively small space—but campers should always have a jacket available to maintain warmth after rain or temperature drops. Cotton shorts and dresses may also be good choices for hot summer weather. On the other hand, cotton socks should be avoided in all weather because they make the feet feel wet and can produce blisters. Cotton underwear should also be avoided because it will feel uncomfortable after sweating and increase the risk of rashes.

Cotton jeans and flannel shirts should be avoided because they are heavy, require considerable packing space, chill the body when wet, and require long drying times that reduce mobility.

Polyester, made from petroleum and occasionally recycled plastic drink bottles, is used to make a broad range of underwear, shirts, shorts, and fleece that are well suited for basic tent camping. Polyester garments compress well, are fast drying and long lasting, hold body heat, and resist wrinkles. Polyester is also good at wicking moisture away from the body, like REI's Moisture Transport System (MTS), which REI uses in its underwear and thermal underwear. Several companies make polyester clothing that is suited for spring, summer, and fall camping trips. A few companies also make garments that are well suited for colder weather.

Polartec makes fleece from polyester in three thicknesses: 100 is relatively lightweight, 200 is a midweight, and 300 is the heaviest and warmest weight. The primary limitation of fleece is that it does not block the wind. Therefore, in cool, windy weather, outdoor enthusiasts will typically wear wind-resistant jackets (such as hard-shell rain jackets) over their fleece garments to keep the wind from chilling their bodies. Polartec also uses a lightweight polyester fabric called Power Dry to make thermal underwear. In addition, several companies make T-shirts from 50 percent cotton and 50 percent polyester that are reportedly more comfortable than polyester but hold body heat better than cotton.

Polypropylene, made from natural gas, is extremely warm, lightweight, compressible, and fast drying. In fact, makers claim that it is the warmest of all fabrics, with the highest moisture-wicking properties. Polypropylene is used to make many different garments, but the specific garments of interest to basic tent campers are sock liners and thermal underwear. In the past, polypropylene had a tendency to develop an unpleasant odor after brief use, and sometimes retained the odor even after washing. A new manufacturing process using silver threads reportedly reduces its odor-retention properties. Furthermore, polypro is unusually heat sensitive and must be hand-washed or machine-washed in cool water on a gentle cycle.

Nylon is a strong thermoplastic thread made from coal. It is highly abrasion resistant and dries quickly. It is used to make pants, shorts, and water-resistant or waterproof jackets and pants. Nylon threads can made in several thicknesses, designated by denier (D) values. The denier value refers to the weight, in grams, of nine thousand meters of fiber. In practical language, garments with lower denier numbers are made from smaller-diameter yarn and, consequently, are thinner and more compressible. For example, Patagonia's Rain Shadow lightweight rain jacket, made from 50 D ripstop nylon, packs into a very small space. Jackets with higher denier numbers are thicker and more durable but require more packing space. Cordura is a heavier type of nylon designed to be especially tough and abrasion resistant. It is the tough stuff used to make backpacks, boots, tool bags, and military equipment. It is also used by Aerostich to make their Darien waterproof motorcycle riding jackets and pants. The primary limitation of nylon garments, like polyester garments, is their sensitivity to heat. Consequently, campers must be careful around campfires, stoves, and hot pots.

Spandex is a synthetic fiber comprised of at least 85 percent polyurethane and is reportedly stronger and more elastic than rubber. This fabric also has high moisture-wicking properties and is used to make a wide variety of snug-fitting athletic and outdoor clothing (such as swimsuits, shirts, tank tops, compression shorts, underwear, socks, and jeans). Lycra, made by DuPont, is the best-known brand of spandex. Lightweight campers who want tight-fitting clothing for hiking, swimming, and other recreational activities may want to consider a few garments made with spandex. Although spandex dries faster than cotton, it will not dry as fast as polyester or nylon.

Silk is made from the threads in cocoons spun by silkworm larvae. Silk garments are very comfortable, lightweight, warm, and compressible. Furthermore, these garments have high moisture-wicking properties and do not retain odors. Silk can be used to make thermal underwear and other garments. Thermasilk, sold by Terramar, combines silk with Quick-Dri fibers to make very comfortable underwear and long underwear for men and women. Silk thermal underwear, compared with polyester, polypropylene, or wool underwear, is cool and still smells okay after several days of wear. One limitation of silk is that it is a fragile material that may tear after a few weeks of wear and washing.

Wool, typically from sheep, has been a major insulating material for many years and has been used to make jackets, clothing, blankets, and many other items. Wool fibers are crimped, creating small air pockets that trap warm air from the body, thus insulating the body from the cooler external temperatures. In addition to serving as a good insulator, wool is very breathable and can keep the wearer warm even when wet. Despite the warmth wool garments provide, these garments have been unpopular in the past because older wool irritated the bare skin of many people. Today wool and wool blends are much more comfortable to the touch. In particular, merino wool is the softest wool available and claims to have superior heat-retention and moisture-wicking properties. It is used to make socks, underwear, thermal layers, and T-shirts. Wool socks have become the popular choice for backpackers and should be strongly considered by basic tent campers as well. Wool undershorts, T-shirts, and thermal underwear are also popular with backpackers but may be too expensive for most basic tent campers. Remarkably, some backpackers claim that merino wool T-shirts are cooler than cotton shirts in hot desert weather. Wool long-sleeve shirts or jackets combined with a rain jacket can provide considerable warmth in cool weather. SmartWool and Woolrich are two well-known companies that make a wide range of woolen garments suited for basic tent camping.

Rayon (or viscose) is a soft, silky, eco-friendly fabric that is made from renewable bamboo or pine-tree pulp but is poorly suited for outdoor living. Although it is compressible, smooth, and comfortable, it requires extra-long drying time, retains body moisture after mild exertion in cool weather, and can feel extremely hot in direct sunlight.

During the past ten years, several new fabrics have been developed to make garments suited for camping and outdoor activities. In general, these fabrics are made from plentiful and renewable plant resources. Cocona, for example, is made from coconut shells and used to make moisture-wicking, fast-drying, odor-resistant shirts and other garments. GoLite uses Cocona to make the Carara Convertible Skirt. Coffeenna, made from coffee grounds, is another new fabric for outdoor clothing.

This material is reportedly very breathable and odor resistant with high moisture-wicking properties. Kühl uses Coffeenna to make the Café Hoody and T-shirts. Bamboo has been used to make rayon for several years and now is used to make other ultrasoft and comfortable fabrics with high moisture-wicking properties. Bamboo shirts and skirts reportedly are very comfortable but also a little pricy.

Footwear

Each camper will need at least two pairs of shoes: a pair of shoes (or boots) for daily activities plus a pair of sandals for showers and casual camp wear. Each camper will also need up to six pair of socks depending upon the length of the trip.

Shoes or boots. Experienced hikers prefer heavy shoes or boots over lightweight sneakers because heavier shoes provide more stability on uneven surfaces and more ankle support. These heavy shoes or boots are also desirable for basic tent camping because many campsites and footpaths have uneven surfaces such as rocks, roots, and landscape timbers that could cause falls and injuries. Furthermore, sturdier boots provide protection from sharp rocks, heavy objects such as axes and firewood, and other hazards that may be encountered in an outdoor camping environment.

A pair of work or hunting boots sold in local shoe and department stores would be an economical option for recreational camping. These boots typically cost between fifty and a hundred dollars a pair. Most brands are relatively comfortable for camping, walking, and short-distance hiking. Campers should look for a pair that is relatively lightweight with a nonslip (Vibram) sole. Wolverine boots, for example, are economical and comfortable. Motorcyclists like these boots because their Vibram soles give extra traction and confidence on wet surfaces. Other well-known work boot brands include Chippewa, Dunham, Durango, LaCrosse, Red Wing, Thorogood, and Timberline. Before embarking upon a trip, campers may want to apply a waterproof treatment such as Nikwax or Camp Dry to make them a little more water resistant.

Hiking shoes and boots are also suitable for basic tent camping. These shoes and boots are sold in outdoor outfitter stores and are made for intermediate- to long-distance hiking. They usually cost a little more than work boots but typically are more comfortable. They are designed to be worn for many hours and for several days in a row. Prices of good hiking footwear typically range from $80 to $400 a pair. These shoes are frequently classified into four categories: trail-running shoes, light hiking shoes, midcut hiking boots, and mountaineering boots.

Trail-running shoes can be used for basic camp wear in hot weather but do not support the foot on uneven surfaces as well as heavier shoes and boots. They typically weigh just over a pound, are cut low, and have lots of mesh that will dry quickly when wet. Their mesh makes them breathable, comfortable in hot weather, and well suited for water activities. They usually have a little stiffer midsole than sneakers or tennis shoes, which provide minimal protection from roots, rocks, and other hazards found in many campgrounds. However, they may not provide adequate foot protection for long-distance hikers carrying medium-size packs.

Light hiking shoes provide a little more support and protection and seem to be the best camping shoe for warm weather. They are cut low, provide ample ventilation for hot summer activities, and have a stiffer compressed EVA midsole designed to protect the feet from rocks, roots, timbers, holes, and unpredictable surfaces that might be found on the trail. Typically, these boots weigh about two pounds and cost about ninety dollars. Some models are waterproof but waterproof boots should be avoided in summer weather because they feel extremely hot.

Midcut (or three-quarter) hiking boots typically cost about $110 and are ideally suited for cool-weather camping trips. They just cover the ankles, weigh about three pounds, have a stiffer midsole than light hiking shoes, and are designed to provide foot and ankle support needed to hike five to ten miles a day while carrying twenty-five to forty pounds in a weekend backpack. Some of these boots are made with lots of mesh, while other models are made from leather. Some have Gore-Tex or eVent waterproof liners that make great choices for wet and cool-weather camping trips.

Heavy-duty mountaineering boots are designed for long-distance hiking and backpacking over rough terrain but are not particularly well suited for basic camping trips because they are expensive and heavy and provide much more support than basic tent campers need. They are cut well above the ankle, have very stiff metal or hard nylon shanks, weigh four pounds or more, and may cost up to $300. Many are made with top-grain leather and have waterproof liners. Before wearing these boots on a hiking trip, owners should break them in over several weeks to prevent blisters and other foot problems.

Shower shoes. In addition to general-purpose shoes or boots, campers will need a pair of lightweight shoes or sandals for bathing and casual camp wear. These shoes should be waterproof or fast drying so that campers can wear them in the shower or the river and expect them to dry in a few minutes. Several options are available. Economical plastic-thong flip-flops pack into a small space and dry quickly, but they can be uncomfortable for extended wear. Fabric thongs between the toes may be a little more comfortable, but the fabric does not dry quickly, especially on cloudy days, and they are still uncomfortable for many people. Slides, such as those made by Nike, Adidas, and Crocs make relatively good shower shoes but do not pack into as small a space as other options. Nylon or spandex water shoes pack into a small space and can be used for river activities but may not dry quickly.

Socks. Most backpacking books advise hikers to wear clean wool or polyester socks every day—and this advice applies equally well for basic tent camping. Wool and polyester socks, compared with cotton, provide more warmth and padding for all recreational activities. They also pack into a small space, dry quickly, have good moisture-wicking properties, insulate feet from both hot and cold temperatures, and help to keep feet dry and comfortable. Typically, they cost about fifteen dollars. Even if campers are caught in rain showers and their wool socks get wet and wick water into their shoes, their feet will still feel warm and comfortable. Cotton socks feel miserable when wet. Some good choices are made by SmartWool, Thorlo, Columbia, Fox River, REI, Wigwam, and Wrightsock.

Base Layers

Underwear. Campers traveling in cars typically have the space to pack up to six pairs of polyester, nylon, or wool underwear because these garments require very little packing space. Campers traveling by motorcycle will usually pack fewer pairs and wash them every day or two. Polyester, wool, or nylon underwear can be washed and dried anytime and provides warmth and comfort even when wet. Motorcycle riders will especially enjoy these materials because they, compared with cotton, reduce the chances of developing "monkey butt" after long rides. ExOfficio boxers made with nylon and spandex are especially comfortable but are expensive. Other good brands include REI, Terramar, Patagonia, Champion, and Under Armour. SmartWool merino wool boxer briefs are much more expensive but may be worth their expense in cold weather. Each of these companies also makes good-quality briefs for women at comparable prices.

Short-sleeve T-shirts and tank tops. Campers traveling by car could pack up to six short-sleeve T-shirts or tank tops depending upon the length of the trip. In hot weather, campers may want to pack cotton T-shirts or tank tops, but in cooler weather, campers should pack polyester or wool shirts. These shirts will pack into a small space, provide more warmth than cotton shirts, wick moisture away from the body, and dry quickly after washing. Furthermore, they can be easily layered with other garments to provide considerable warmth in cold weather.

Women may want to pack tank tops with built-in shelf bras. These garments should be comfortable and attractive enough to be worn for casual wear and water activities and should be made from compressible, fast-drying, moisture-wicking fabrics (not cotton), such as those used to make athletic tops, and without excessive padding or wires that make them less compressible and less comfortable.

Several companies make good polyester T-shirts suited for outdoor activities, and these shirts typically cost between fifteen and twenty-five dollars. Some good brands include REI, Champion, Terramar, Nike, Adidas, New Balance, Russell, ExOfficio, Outdoor Research, and, Zumba Fitness. Some hikers have praised wool T-shirts for hot-weather conditions, but they are much more expensive than other T-shirts.

Close-fitting long-sleeve T-shirt. Each camper should also pack at least one close-fitting polyester or wool long-sleeve T-shirt, even in hot weather. This shirt can be used as a thermal layer (long underwear), outerwear, and sleepwear, especially if the temperature drops lower than expected. In cooler weather, campers could pack up to four of these shirts. Good-quality long-sleeve T-shirts are made by the same companies that make short-sleeve T-shirts described above.

Long thermal-underwear pants. In hot summer weather, campers may not need a pair of long-underwear pants. But in the early spring, late fall, and winter, campers will need at least one pair of long-underwear bottoms made from polyester, polypropylene, silk, or wool. In very cold weather, campers should wear one pair and pack a second pair. These bottoms can be worn under pants during the daytime and under athletic pants at night. Long underwear made from silk seem particularly good for basic tent camping because they are reasonably priced, compressible, comfortable, moisture wicking, and fast drying and can be worn several days in a row and still smell relatively clean. Long underwear made from polypropylene is very popular among hikers, campers, and backpackers but may develop an unpleasant smell that is difficult to wash out.

Outerwear

Shorts, pants, and dresses. Basic tent campers traveling in cars usually have the space to pack up to five shorts, pants, or dresses. These garments should be made from nylon, polyester, or spandex because these fabrics can be crammed into small spaces without wrinkling and dry quickly after washing or water activities. Before each trip, campers should select a combination that seems best suited for planned activities and predicted weather. Men typically select a combination of shorts and pants while women may want to pack a dress or two in addition to shorts and pants. In hot weather, one of these garments should be a swimming suit.

The most versatile garment for basic tent campers would be a pair of nylon or polyester convertible pants with zip-off legs. In cool weather these pants can be worn as long pants, and in hot weather, the lower legs can be removed and the pants worn as shorts. Two pair of these pants can be packed into a small space and effectively provide four different garment options. In fact, convertible pants have become the standard "uniform" for backpackers (especially men). Big men may want to consider REI 3X pants, which are very comfortable. Other companies that make good-quality convertible pants include Campmor, Mountain Hardwear, and the North Face.

Female campers may want to pack a pair of capri pants or a dress for casual wear and special occasions. Several companies make beautiful pants and dresses designed for recreational camping and other outdoor activities. These dresses are typically made from polyester and spandex, can be packed into a small space, will not wrinkle, and will dry quickly when wet. Some companies that sell dresses designed for outdoor activities include prAna, Patagonia, and Toad&Co (formerly Horny Toad). Regardless of the particular type of garments preferred, five is the maximum number needed for any trip. Campers must choose wisely and plan to wash about once a week.

Athletic pants. In addition to the pants and shorts discussed above, campers should also pack a pair of polyester athletic pants—regardless of the weather. These pants can be worn as casual camp wear and sleepwear. Unlined Champion polyester athletic pants sold in Target stores are a great choice. They are economical, warm, and comfortable for most weather. Sometimes they are ideal for recreational activities or daily activities when everything else is dirty or wet. These pants combined with a good pair of wool socks, thermal underwear, polyester shirts, and a fleece jacket hold in enough body heat that campers may not need their sleeping bags on many cooler nights. In cold weather, campers may want to consider a pair of fleece pants with elastic cuffs. In hot summer weather, campers could substitute a pair of cotton scrub pants but should never pack cotton sweatpants, because sweatpants require excessive packing space, chill the body when damp, and take forever to dry.

Loose-fitting long-sleeve shirts. Campers should pack at least one loose-fitting, polyester, nylon, or wool long-sleeve shirt—even for hot weather trips—in case the temperature drops a little more than expected or a cool summer shower passes through the area. In very hot weather, campers may want to select light-colored cotton and linen shirts that provide the maximum amount of cooling. Several companies, including Champion and REI, make economically priced long-sleeve T-shirts and mock turtleneck shirts. Another good choice is a quick-drying nylon travel or fishing shirt such as the ones sold by Campmor and Columbia. In cooler weather, campers may want to pack fleece or wool shirts. Woolrich makes a line of wool shirts for hunters and outdoor enthusiasts that may require a little more packing space but will also provide considerable warmth on cool nights. SmartWool makes very comfortable wool long-sleeve T-shirts. The companies listed in the section on short-sleeve T-shirts also make good long-sleeve polyester shirts.

Vests and Jackets

Travel vests. Basic tent campers need a place to carry personal items that might be needed at any time during a camping trip—such as sunglasses, pens, notepads, cell phones, wallets, and cameras. Women typically carry these items in their purses, but most men would not consider this option. One possible option is a small fanny or waist pack, but these packs seem to be going out of style. A newer trend is to wear a travel vest with lots of pockets. Several companies now make travel vests. For example, Duluth Trading Company makes lightweight travel vests that are generously cut for big guys and have several pockets. Other good travel vests are offered by L.L.Bean, Filson, Orvis, ExOfficio, Cabela's, and Columbia.

Insulated sweaters or jackets. On cool-weather camping trips each person will need an insulated jacket. This jacket can be worn as an outer layer in cool weather and layered with a long-sleeve shirt and waterproof jacket in cold weather. These garments combined with a short-sleeve T-shirt create four layers that should keep most people warm even when the temperature drops down to freezing.

For many years, wool sweaters were commonly worn to provide insulation from cold weather. These sweaters retained body heat well and did not absorb moisture. But they were uncomfortable for many people and too bulky for packing. Then fleece emerged as an alternative insulating material that provides almost as much heat retention as wool plus feels more comfortable and does not require dry cleaning. Polartec was the first company to make fleece, and it continues to make three different weights of fleece—lightweight, midweight, and heavyweight. Many other companies, such as the North Face, Patagonia, and REI, use Polartec fleece to make their insulated shirts and jackets.

More recently, warmer materials, such as synthetic polyester fibers (Polarguard) and goose down feathers, have been used to make quilted insulated sweaters and jackets. These newer materials are compressible and provide a tremendous amount of warmth for their weight. Nau, for example, makes a down shirt that reportedly compresses to the size of a grapefruit. Other makers of down and synthetic vests and jackets include Arc'teryx, Marmot, Mountain Hardwear, Outdoor Research, Patagonia, and the North Face.

Waterproof coats or ponchos. Each camper should pack a raincoat or poncho for every trip. Although it may not be needed on many trips, it is good to have handy when showers and storms develop. Raincoats come in a wide range of options. The cheapest option is a polyurethane-coated poncho or raincoat sold in local grocery and department stores, but this type of coat has two distinct limitations. First, it will not compress as small as better-quality rain gear and, thus, requires more packing space.

Second, it will not breathe as well as better-quality gear. People wearing these coats on warm days or during vigorous activity, such as hiking or splitting wood, will sweat, and this sweat will be trapped inside their coats, making them just as wet as if they had no coats at all. Their clothes will become quickly soaked with sweat rather than rain. How counterproductive is that? They might as well not wear raincoats at all.

Good-quality rain gear, on the other hand, is waterproof, breathable, and compressible. Perhaps the most popular type of raincoat is a lightweight hard-shell jacket that also serves as a wind blocker. These jackets are typically made from nylon or polyester fabric that has been laminated with Gore-Tex or some other thin, waterproof, breathable membrane. The membrane has pores that are large enough to allow warm water vapor (steam) to evaporate but small enough to prevent cooler liquid water droplets from penetrating.

Gore-Tex, introduced around 1969, was the first waterproof fabric and is still widely used to make breathable rain gear. Some companies that use Gore-Tex to make their hard shells include Arc'Teryx, Asolo, Marmot, Merrell, Montrail, Mountain Hardwear, Outdoor Research, the North Face, and Vasque. Over the past ten years, other companies have developed their own proprietary waterproof, breathable membranes for hard shells. The best known of these newer membranes are eVent, PreCip (Marmot), TEK (L.L.Bean), Conduit (Mountain Hardwear), Elements (REI), H2No (Patagonia), HyVent (the North Face), MemBrain (Marmot), Omni-Tech (Columbia), and Pertex Shield (Outdoor Research). All these newer materials seem to perform about the same as Gore-Tex in terms of water protection and breathability. In addition to these waterproof membranes, most companies coat the nylon exterior of their garments with a durable water repellent (DWR) wax to give an extra measure of moisture protection.

In recent years, a new type of rainwear, soft-shell jackets, has emerged on the market. These garments stretch and are much softer to the touch than the older hard shells. Like the hard shells, they are waterproof, but they breathe much better and feel more like fleece. Some popular makers of soft-shell rain jackets include Mountain Hardwear, the North Face, and Patagonia. Many backpackers and other outdoor enthusiasts have begun to use these soft-shell rain jackets, but lightweight tent campers may not find them to be as practical as the hard shells, especially when they need to pack them into a small space, as these shells do not compress as small as the hard shells.

In colder weather, campers should select an insulated waterproof coat or jacket to provide warmth as well as protection from rain. Most garment makers, including Columbia and Woolrich offer several jacket options for cold-weather camping.

Accessories

Hats. Most camping books recommend that campers wear full-brimmed hats during the day to protect their eyes, faces, and necks from cancer-causing ultraviolet rays. In addition to protecting the skin from ultraviolet radiation, hats shade the eyes from the sun, keep the rain out of the face, and help to retain body heat in cool weather. Since camping trips and activities can be hard on hats, campers may want to buy crushable hats and pack two or more to be comfortable in various situations.

On hot summer days, a full-brimmed, light-colored, ventilated, straw or cotton hat such as the Henschel Breezer Aussie or Dorfman Pacific Mesh Safari keep the head as cool as any hat available. They protect bald heads from sunburn, help to keep wearers cool, shade the eyes from the sun, block light rain, and can withstand a certain amount of mild abuse. On colder days, wool felt hats such as the Stetson Spencer provides warmth, skin protection, and eye protection. Many outdoorsmen wear Tilley hats for rain and mild weather. For casual wear around the camp, short-brimmed baseball, military, or cadet caps allows wearers to lie in their hammocks without having to remove their hats. For sleeping in cool weather, campers may want to pack wool or polyester knit caps, such as a SmartWool stocking cap for warmth and comfort.

Gloves. In addition to the leather camp gloves packed in the tool bag, campers may need a second pair of gloves in cooler weather.

Knit glove liners compress into a small space and may be sufficient in mild weather. Nylon work gloves also compress into a small space and should be adequate for cooler weather. On colder days, campers may need more-insulated gloves that provide less finger dexterity. When riding motorcycles, campers may have to wear a pair of Gore-Tex-lined, insulated nylon gloves suited for snow skiing.

Gaiters. Anyone who plans to camp in wet or snowy weather or ride motorcycles may want to add a pair of gaiters to his or her rain gear. Gaiters are especially helpful for motorcycle riders because they protect the boots, socks, and lower pant legs from water that is slung up from the front wheel when riding on wet roads. This protection is especially important because wet socks will quickly wick large quantities of water down inside the boots. Backcountry hikers also like gaiters because they keep pants dry when hiking through wet grass or undergrowth. When wearing gaiters, campers should wear them inside their rain pants so that rainwater will run down the pant leg and off the gaiters. In addition to protection from rain and wet grass, gaiters provide additional warmth for lower legs in cold weather. Several brands and sizes are available. Some models barely cover the ankles, while others are longer and cover more of the lower leg. A good choice for lightweight camping is midcalf-length gaiters such as the ones made by Mountain Hardwear or Outdoor Research.

Rain pants. In addition to a rain jacket, some campers, especially those riding motorcycles or hiking through high grass, may want to add a pair of rain pants. Many of the companies listed above for jackets also make rain pants. Marmot PreCip pants are economical, lightweight, compressible, and waterproof. In colder weather, campers may want to wear a heavier pair of insulated, waterproof ski pants.

Dirty-clothes bags. Campers should also pack a small mesh bag to hold their dirty clothes. Mesh bags allow wet clothes to dry, but mesh laundry bags filled with dirty clothes can get smelly, so leave them in the car with your shoes and personal grooming kit rather than bringing them into the tent.

Liquid detergent. For every trip, campers should pack a small bottle of liquid detergent for washing clothes. Any brand is fine, but Woolite can be used to wash delicate fabrics and is environmentally safe. Pack a small bottle with the dish detergent in the kitchen-gear box.

Most of the summer, we wear fast-drying
nylon or polyester shirts and shorts.

Eva especially likes this Patagonia fleece jacket on cool days.

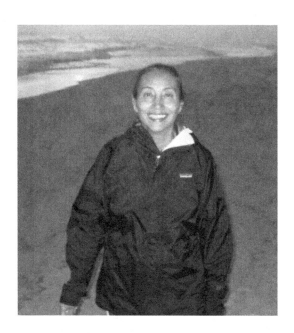

Eva wears this Patagonia hard-shell jacket as a windbreaker or raincoat. In cold weather, she wears it on top of her fleece jacket and a couple of polyester shirts to provide considerable warmth.

This Woolrich hat and jacket are very comfortable for cool-weather camping.

7

PERSONAL ITEMS

In addition to a watch and cell phone, basic tent campers will need several personal items to ensure comfort and enjoyment for each trip. The specific items needed will vary from person to person but will include a few common items such as headlamp, bath supplies, and grooming kit. To be able to pack all these items in a small space, campers should look for travel-size items, compact items, and nesting items. Although the list of personal items is rather long, most of these items can be purchased in small containers and packed into a small space. In fact, all the essentials can even be packed for a motorcycle trip.

Highway Maps

While cell phones and GPS receivers can be great navigational tools, it is a good idea to have a good map for every state to double check these electronic devises and to provide assistance when satellite signals are weak. Travelers can usually get these maps free of charge by sending e-mail requests to state departments of transportation or by picking them up in state welcome centers or rest areas. When free highway maps are unavailable, travelers can buy good-quality maps in gas stations and convenience stores. Some people may want to get two maps for each state—one to plan trips at home and a laminated folding map for quick reference while traveling. The passenger can serve as the navigator and use the map to identify upcoming highway numbers on the chosen route. Laminated maps are good for car and motorcycle reference because they hold up to the constant folding and unfolding that occurs during each trip and inevitable moisture.

Pocketknife

Each camper will need a knife for many camping chores such as cutting fruit and meat, removing ropes left by previous campers, opening packages, and cleaning fish. Sometimes campers use knives to cut kindling and open cans. When the time comes to use a knife, campers should have it handy to avoid wasting time looking for it. Each camping book recommends a different type of knife. Some books recommend sturdy fixed-blade sheath knives, while other books recommend folding multi-tools. After using dozens of knives over my lifetime, I have concluded that multi-tools are the best all-around choice for basic tent camping. In particular, I like the Victorinox Swiss Army Tinker, which is small and light enough to carry in my pants pocket. It has a sturdy blade and has several other useful tools that can be used to open bottles, pull splinters, punch holes in leather, drive screws, and trim tough toenails. Other popular multi-tools are offered by Leatherman and Gerber.

Headlamps

To be able to move safely in the dark, find small items in the tent, and perform various routine chores, basic tent campers need a reliable light source. Over the past several years, large flashlights and gas lanterns have become obsolete. They require excessive packing space and have several other limitations, such as requiring fuel that is costly, messy, sometimes unavailable, and potentially deadly. Furthermore, lanterns are so bright that they can annoy neighboring campers who prefer to relax in the dark. Flashlights are impractical because they must be held in one hand, forcing campers to juggle the flashlight while performing various camping chores in the dark. Battery-powered lanterns are a better choice, but they are large and unwieldy.

Without a doubt, headlamps offer the best type of light for basic tent camping. Headlamps have been used by miners for decades and were adopted by backpackers as the ideal light source several years ago. They pack into a very small space, focus considerable light anywhere users look, and allow wearers to use both hands when performing camping chores. To be prepared for the unexpected, each camper should pack one headlight and each camping party should pack one or two extra headlamps in case one gets damaged. Together these items require less packing space than an average flashlight and are much more practical.

Economical headlamps can be purchased in department stores for about ten dollars, but these lights are heavier, provide less light, and require more battery changes than better-quality LED models sold by camping outfitters. Better headlamps are made by Petzl, Princeton Tec, Black Diamond, and Mammut. In particular, the Petzl Tikka 2 is an excellent choice for basic tent camping. It weighs about three ounces, sells for about thirty dollars, uses three AAA batteries, and provides light for about one hundred hours. Other headlamps have rechargeable batteries and brighter lights, but they are more expensive.

Extra Batteries

To ensure that headlamps, radios, cameras, and other devices are ready when needed, campers should pack several extra batteries in a food storage bag. Headlamps typically need three AAA batteries, and radios and cameras typically require one or two AA batteries.

Three basic types of batteries can be used by campers: alkaline, lithium, and rechargeable. Alkaline and lithium batteries (technically called primary batteries) must be disposed of after they discharge and contain some chemicals that can be harmful to the environment. Alkaline batteries are more economically priced but provide fewer hours of power. Lithium batteries provide more hours of power but cost more. Rechargeable batteries (technically called secondary batteries) provide many more hours of power than primary batteries but contain more toxic chemicals that pose an even greater environmental hazard than primary batteries. Ideally, all batteries should be recycled, but many campgrounds and communities have been slow to establish battery recycle programs.

Day Packs

Basic tent campers do not need large, expensive backpacks like the ones typically carried by backpackers and wilderness travelers but will find small day packs very handy. They can use these day packs to pack warm clothes for day hikes and supplies for beach trips. When camping on the Florida Gulf Coast or Michigan western shoreline, campers could use the packs to carry water, towels, sunscreen, snacks, and books out to the beach. When camping in the mountains, campers could carry rain gear, water, and a few snacks when hiking trails. When camping in hike-in or boat-in sites, small day packs can be used to carry small personal items from the car to the campsite. At night, day packs can be turned inside out, stuffed with clothing, covered with pillowcases, and used as pillows.

Day packs range in load capacity from about 500 cubic inches to 1,800 cubic inches. Some just hang on the shoulders, while others have hip belts and chest straps as well. Many day packs come with features and adjustments that make them reasonably comfortable for longer hikes, even with lots of gear packed inside. Some have several small compartments, while others have only one main compartment. Some are packed through one main top opening (top loaders), while others are packed by opening one of several horseshoe-shaped zippers (panel loaders). Simple Cordura backpacks can be purchased in department stores for about ten dollars, but they do not make comfortable pillows. Nylon packs cost a little more but are lighter and more comfortable— and make comfortable pillows at night. Nice lightweight nylon day packs can be purchased in camping or backpacking specialty stores or on websites such as Campmor, REI, and Mountain Gear. These lighter packs typically cost between fifty and a hundred dollars.

Bath Supplies

Before each trip, campers should pack eight specific items together as bath kits. After arriving at the destination and setting up the tent, each camper can easily grab his or her bath kit without having to rummage around through the luggage in the dark. In most public campgrounds, campers will carry these kits to a nearby shower building, but in the few campgrounds without shower facilities, campers will use these items in their campsites to bathe.

- shower shoes
- plastic or nylon shower bag to carry all other items
- towel
- washcloth
- soap
- clean pair of shorts or athletic pants to wear after the bath
- clean T-shirt or tank top to wear after the bath
- headlamp to provide light in the dark

A woman's kit may include the above-named items plus small travel-size bottles of shampoo, conditioner, and other items.

Shower shoes are essential because many campground shower stalls are not as clean as one might hope. In fact, a sizable number of showers in public campgrounds have mold and mildew growing on the walls and floors. Some campground showers have standing water, and a few may have foot fungi (athlete's foot or some other contagious condition) left by previous users. Shower shoes will help to protect campers from these and other possible problems. Shower shoes can also be worn for casual camp wear and walking to the bathroom in the middle of the night. Some people prefer plastic flip flops, while others prefer slides. Certainly shower shoes should be waterproof or fast drying.

The best type of bath towel to pack for basic-tent-camping trips is a small twelve-by-twenty-inch microfiber kitchen or shop towel that can be purchased from any department store. Although large cotton beach towels may be nice for home use, these towels require excessive packing space and long drying time that could reduce mobility. A small microfiber hand towel, on the other hand, requires much less packing space, provides ample absorption, and dries quickly. It can also be washed in the bathroom sink after each use and dried on a clothesline within a few hours. Small backpacking towels sold at camping outfitters can also be used, but ordinary microfiber towels sold in department stores are more economical and seem to smell better.

The best type of soap for camping again depends upon personal preference. Bar soap lasts longer than liquid soap and is convenient to use in the shower, but it can get messy if not dried immediately after use. Liquid soap packaged in plastic bottles does not require drying but does not last as long as bar soap. Backpackers and other wilderness campers who must dump their soapy bathwater on the ground typically prefer biodegradable liquid soap such as Campsuds, Sea to Summit Wilderness Wash, or Coleman Camp Soap.

Grooming Kits

Each camper will need several travel-size items for personal grooming that can be packed together in a small bag. Although some multi-tools include tweezers, these tweezers may not be strong enough for some grooming chores such as pulling hair. Basic items for a camper's grooming kit include:

- toothbrush
- toothpaste
- floss
- razor
- hairbrush
- deodorant
- nail clippers
- tweezers
- cotton swabs
- hand soap in a small plastic bottle

A woman's kit may also include small containers of day cream and night cream, any desired makeup, and nail polish.

To reduce size, basic tent campers may want to cut the handle off of a regular toothbrush or buy a folding travel toothbrush (available in most pharmacies and department stores) to make it easier to pack in the grooming kit. A small bottle of hand soap will be needed because many public campgrounds do not furnish hand soap near their sinks. In these bathrooms, campers must carry their own personal hand soap each time they visit the bathroom.

Other Essential Items

Sunglasses. Most basic tent campers and other people enjoying outdoor activities need a pair of sunglasses for protection from harmful UV radiation.

Digital camera. Although cell phones can take a few basic photos, they cannot capture the detail and clarity that is possible with good digital cameras. And although others may consider cameras to be optional equipment, I consider them to be essential because I want to have a complete photographic record of every camping trip I have taken. Modern cameras are small enough to carry in a breast pocket and strong enough to make great images despite distance and light limitations, I use them to photograph campsites, unique buildings, attractions, animals, and many other things encountered on my trips. After returning home, images can be organized and saved on small flash drives, printed for photo albums, or enlarged for framing.

Medicine. Many people, especially older campers, must take medicine every day for high blood pressure, high cholesterol, diabetes, and other chronic medical conditions. Before each trip, these campers must pack enough medicine for the entire trip plus a few extra days because buying prescription medicine away from home can be difficult.

Cell phone charger. Cell phones have become a necessity for camping as well as for everyday life. Campers will frequently use them to call campgrounds to get necessary information, tourist attractions to get schedules, restaurants to make reservations, family members to stay in touch, and occasionally emergency responders to report problems. To ensure that phones will be ready when needed, campers should always pack a charger and charge their phones often. When traveling by car, they may want to pack two chargers—one that plugs into the car cigarette lighter and a second one that plugs into a 110-volt power outlet. In addition to the convenience of being able to charge their phones at any time, it is comforting to have a backup in case one is damaged.

Handkerchiefs or folded paper towels. Many books recommend that campers carry handkerchiefs all the time. The handkerchief can be used to wipe away sweat, wipe up spills, and blow the nose. It can also be used as a dressing for severe lacerations when a sterile gauze dressing is unavailable. Alternatively, a good paper towel can serve all the functions mentioned above plus can be used as toilet paper in a pinch and flushed down a toilet. Viva paper towels, in particular, are soft enough to wipe one's nose several times a day but strong enough to clean up a lot of spilled liquid before falling apart.

Butane lighters. Each camping family will need two or three butane cigarette lighters to light camp stoves and campfires and to sear nylon rope ends. These lighters can be purchased for a few cents in most convenience and grocery stores.

Spare keys. Every camper should carry extra keys to his or her vehicle because the unfamiliar routine of vacation travel occasionally leads to car keys being inadvertently locked inside cars. Travelers who do not have an extra set of keys will have to find a locksmith and pay fifty to a hundred dollars. Campers who have emergency roadside assistance insurance such as that provided by the American Auto Association (AAA) may not have to pay the cost of the locksmith but could still lose an hour or two waiting for the serviceman to arrive. The best safeguard against losing valuable travel time and money is to carry extra keys.

Optional Items

GPS receiver. GPS navigation receivers have become extremely popular over the past fifteen years—especially among truck drivers, backpackers, and geocachers. They are also useful for basic tent campers traveling to unfamiliar destinations by car or motorcycle. Campers who do not own a GPS receiver should strongly consider purchasing one as soon as possible. As campers drive, a GPS shows major streets, intersections, and geographic features that lie ahead on the route. It announces which lane to position the vehicle in before turns and provides step-by-step directions to gas stations, restaurants, private campgrounds, and other businesses along the route. And it gives information about speed, travel time, the number of miles to the destination, and approximate time of arrival. Travelers who know the GPS coordinates of their destination can enter these coordinates and get valuable navigational information that allows them to find their destination even when highway directional signs are confusing or obscured by darkness. Excellent receivers are offered by Garmin, Magellan, and TomTom. These receivers can be purchased in many department stores and other retail stores. Waterproof GPS receivers for motorcycles can be purchased from Rider Wearhouse for $270 to $1,000. Campers with smart phones could download the Google Maps app for no cost and enjoy most of the benefits afforded by GPS receivers.

Notepads and pencils. Some people like to carry notepads and pencils to jot down important names, phone numbers, and ideas they want to remember at a future time. Having a notepad and pencil handy makes it easy to record this information quickly without rummaging around through other items. A small notepad and pencil can be easily carried in a travel-vest breast pocket.

Electronics. Most Americans have become dependent upon various electronic devices and frequently pack them for business and vacation travel. Some of these electronic devices, such as cell phones, help travelers stay in touch with their families and business contacts, while other devices are used for entertainment and relaxation. Laptops, notebooks, tablets, e-readers, game players, portable media players, weather radios, AM/FM radios, and DVD players have all become very popular. Many of these items are available in a compact size that is suited for basic tent camping. For example, Sangean makes a great pocket AM/FM/weather-alert radio. Campers who want to watch movies could pack a small portable DVD player or tablet. In the past, portable analog TVs were great for watching the news and important sports events, but the switch to digital broadcasting in 2009 has made it much more difficult to find TV signals in remote camping areas. Most digital TV antennas can only receive stations located within twenty-five miles but the Mohu Leaf antenna packs small and reportedly is able to receive stations located as much as fifty miles away.

Books and games. Many people enjoy reading books on their vacations, and books require relatively little packing space. Reading books can be an entertaining way to relax around the campsite and pass time while waiting for the rain to stop. Furthermore, reading books helps some people fall asleep at night. Other families prefer to play games such as dominoes or rummy in the evening. Simple games require very little packing space.

Hobby supplies. Campers with unique interests may have a wonderful opportunity to pursue these interests on trips to distant destinations. For example, some camping destinations offer great fishing and bird-watching opportunities. Regardless of their particular interests, campers can usually find good compact equipment for their hobbies that can be packed into limited packing space. Fishermen can find collapsible rods and compact tackle boxes. Bird-watchers can find compact field guides, such as the *Peterson Field Guide to Eastern Birds*, and compact binoculars.

Folding wagon. Families that enjoy camping in walk-in campsites may want to consider purchasing a folding wagon to haul their gear from their vehicle to the campsite. Several companies make folding wagons, but the Mac Sports wagons seems to be very popular. These wagons can be collapsed into a relatively small space when traveling and then opened to a convenient size after arriving at the campsite. They can also be used to haul supplies to distant picnic or beach areas. Although the makers specifically state that these wagons are not made for children, Eva's and my two-year-old grandson loves riding and sleeping in ours.

Rooftop cargo carrier. Families with children should consider purchasing a rooftop cargo carrier. Along with the space available in the car trunk, rooftop cargo carriers provide ample space to pack all the equipment needed for safe and comfortable family camping trips. In fact, these carriers also provide a place to haul a canoe or kayak. Cargo carriers are made for almost any car or SUV model and cost between $100 and $600, depending upon the brand and features. Consumers typically purchase the specific parts needed to adapt the carrier to their particular vehicle and then purchase the carrier itself. Vehicles without rooftop luggage racks will usually need four towers, two side rails, two load bars, locks, and fairings, plus the cargo carrier. Cargo carriers range in quality from higher-priced lockable cargo boxes to average-priced cargo baskets down to lower-priced cargo bags. Well-known makers of cargo carriers, such as Thule and Yakima, offer online software that allows consumers to enter the make and model of their vehicle and determine the specific parts needed to build the cargo carrier. For more assistance, campers can go to camping outfitters such as REI where sales staff can provide needed assistance. Other companies that offer cargo carriers include Whispbar and SportRack.

Bicycles, canoe, golf clubs, and tennis racquets. Many campers enjoy a variety of sporting activities that require large, bulky equipment that would be difficult to obtain in a distant location. To have this equipment available, they must pack it in or on their vehicle before leaving home. To haul this equipment, campers may have to buy a rooftop cargo carrier, hitch-mounted racks, or small trailer. Evidence of the popularity of these recreational items can be seen in any popular campground. On nice summer weekends, most camping destinations are filled with children and adults riding bicycles around the paved park roads plus dozens of canoes and kayaks on cars and lakeshores waiting to be launched. Many public parks offer bicycle trails, water access, golf courses, and tennis courts.

Solar charger. Although I have not purchased a solar charger and do not plan to purchase one in the near future, many hikers are now buying these chargers to charge their rechargeable headlamp batteries, cell phones, personal locator beacons, tablets, and other electronic devices in the wilderness. Basic tent campers who plan to camp in campgrounds with limited electrical access, such as those in Great Smoky Mountains National Park, may want to investigate these chargers. Several models sell for less than $50, but better-quality chargers typically cost up to $250.

Unnecessary Items

Before concluding this chapter, I want to mention a few unnecessary items that are frequently recommended in other camping books. These items are unnecessary for different reasons. Some are rarely, if ever, needed in developed public campgrounds; others perform no task that could not be performed by another item, or they can be easily purchased in local stores whenever they may be needed. Since these items cost extra money, require extra packing space, and typically get in the way when looking for needed items, basic tent campers can leave them at home.

Compass. Many camping books and articles list a compass as the first item on their list of essentials. According to their arguments, campers will need a compass along with a topographical map to avoid becoming lost in the forest. To support their argument, these books cite statistical studies showing that hypothermia resulting from being lost overnight in a forest or in a cave is one of the top reasons for search-and-rescue missions. My response to this argument is that most basic tent campers stay in developed front-country campgrounds where they pull their cars into paved parking spots near their campsites. Those who enjoy hiking will usually hike short, well-marked trails. Very few basic tent campers hike miles into the wilderness areas where they could get lost. Therefore, a compass seems to be an unnecessary item for most basic tent campers.

Waterproof matches. Many camping books also suggest that campers pack waterproof matches as one of the essential items, stating that campers need a way to start fires in rainy and damp conditions. Certainly, all campers need a reliable method for starting fires, but butane lighters are far more practical than waterproof matches. These lighters can be purchased in almost any local store, pack into a small space, and do not require separate waterproof cases. Campers should pack two or three of these lighters so that backups will be available when one runs out of fuel.

Candles. Although many camping books recommend emergency candles, these candles are impractical and possibly dangerous. Basic tent campers should never consider packing one. Candles cannot be used in or around a tent because a small flame can quickly damage tent fabrics, cause carbon monoxide poisoning, and injure campers whose polyester clothing accidentally contacts the flame. In addition, candles can easily be blown out by the wind and provide too little light to read books or perform various camping chores. Instead of packing candles, campers should pack an extra headlamp or two plus a few extra batteries.

Lantern. For over fifty years, family campers considered gas lanterns to be an essential item for providing light around the campsite after dark. But lanterns have become unnecessary over the past twenty years. Compared with headlamps, lanterns have numerous limitations as a light source. For example, lanterns plus their fuel require considerable packing space, and fuel spills can be messy. Lanterns do not provide focused light in specific places where it is needed. Gas or propane lanterns cannot be used in tents because they present fire and carbon monoxide risks. Finally lanterns are so bright that they may be objectionable to neighbors who want to relax quietly in the dark or enjoy their campfires. For these reasons, basic tent campers should give up their lanterns and adopt personal headlamps instead. Headlamps are brighter, safer, more practical, and more economical and require much less packing space.

Hair dryer. Although many people like to dry their hair after swimming or bathing, they really do not need to pack a hair dryer for camping trips. Hair dryers require packing space that could be used for other items and frequently get in the way when looking for other needed items. Furthermore, leaving hair damp after swimming or bathing will actually help cool the body on hot summer days, and hair will naturally dry in an hour or two. Towels can be used to remove most moisture, and many campground bathrooms have hot-air hand dryers that can be used to dry hair if necessary. In cooler weather, campers can wear polyester or wool knit caps to prevent the head from getting too chilled.

Portable toilet. A few camping books suggest that campers pack a portable toilet, but portable toilets are rarely needed because most developed campgrounds have nice bathhouses with either flush toilets or vault toilets. The only time campers might need a portable toilet is if they were camping in a dispersed campsite in a national forest or in a small campground with only a smelly pit toilet. Even in those situations, portable toilets would be difficult to pack because they are relatively heavy and require considerable packing space that frequently is unavailable in small vehicles.

Portable heater. Before discussing this topic, I must confess that I have used portable heaters in the past and now thank God that I am still alive. Although portable gas, kerosene, and propane heaters are sold in many stores and seem to offer warmth for cold fall and spring nights, they are extremely dangerous! Novice campers should never even think about using one of these heaters. They can cause fires in the confined quarters of a tent that will quickly consume the tent, bedding, and clothing. To see a vivid example of this phenomenon, watch the movie *Wild Hogs*. Furthermore, gas heaters can produce poisonous carbon monoxide gas. Since campers typically do not have fire guards that stay awake all night, they could easily go to sleep with a heater and never wake up the next morning. Furthermore, heaters are expensive, require valuable packing space, and can be messy. Electric space heaters may be a little safer, but they still can cause fires and possible electric shock. The best way to prepare for cold weather is to pack a good sleeping bag rated for colder weather and a warm set of garments that can be layered for maximum comfort. After learning how to dress for cold weather and acquiring a good sleeping bag, campers will be able to sleep comfortably even on cold mornings when the temperature drops down into the twenties. For additional information about the dangers of portable heaters, see chapter 16, "Safety."

Umbrellas. Some backpacking books recommend that backpackers pack small umbrellas to provide temporary covers for cooking meals and exiting doors of small tents. These ultralight campers need umbrellas because they do not have kitchen shelters to cover their cooking/eating areas in rainy weather. But basic tent campers who have larger tents, rain gear, and kitchen shelters over their picnic tables will not need umbrellas. Furthermore, umbrellas require packing space that could be used to pack more-useful items. Although a small collapsible umbrella may be nice to have on a few rainy days, it is an unnecessary luxury that may never be needed.

Fire starter. Many camping books recommend that campers pack some type of fire starter to start their campfires. Some of these books, in fact, describe how campers can make their own fire starter out of paraffin, shredded newspaper, fat pine, cotton balls, petroleum jelly, and other materials. While these discussions are interesting, they do not make a strong case for spending time and money for homemade or commercially made fire starters. Instead, basic tent campers can easily use crumpled newspaper and twigs in dry weather and a few Match Light charcoal briquettes in damp weather. This charcoal can be purchased in almost any grocery or convenience store. In rainy weather, campers may want to forget the campfire and use a camp stove to cook their meals.

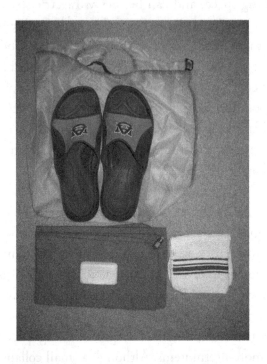

My bath supplies include a shower bag, towel, washcloth, soap, and shower shoes.

My grooming kit includes several travel-size items.

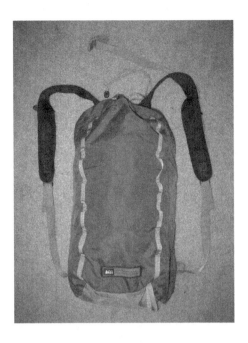

The REI Flash 18 can be used to carry personal items during daily excursions and to make a pillow at night.

I enjoy listening to music and news on my iPod Shuffle and my Sangean pocket radio. The radio receives weather channels that allow me to monitor local forecasts.

8

PROTECTION AND
FIRST AID

Since the early 1900s, tent-camping authorities have recognized the need to pack mosquito repellent and first aid supplies. For example, Holding (1908) discussed bandages, plasters, and finger stalls plus treatments for cuts, indigestion, headache, colds, lumbago, and sunburn in his chapter titled "Medical and Surgical." Kephart (1917) addressed this topic in two places. In the "Personal Kits" chapter, he argued that first aid kits should be small enough to carry on the person at all times since many injuries occur away from camp. Then he described a "soldier's kit" that contains a triangular bandage, one or two compresses of sublimated gauze, two aseptic safety pins, and instructions for dressing gunshot wounds. He recommended that campers go to druggist stores and obtain these items plus an assortment of supplies such as aspirin, potassium permanganate, calomel, and Epsom salts to make their first aid kit. In a subsequent chapter titled "Pests in the Woods," he described a variety of concoctions that could be used to prevent mosquitoes, ticks, chiggers, fleas, flies, and scorpion bites or stings.

Modern camping books seem to focus more upon wilderness survival rather than common camping injuries and recommend a large number of first aid and medical supplies that basic tent campers will probably never need. *Camping and Wilderness Survival* by Paul Tawrell (2006), for example, contains over one thousand pages suggesting that camping means survival in the woods. He describes hundreds of potential injuries ranging from lightning strikes and hypothermia to bear attacks. The book lists thirty-two items for a first aid kit and describes how to treat any type of injury imaginable. Over the past ten years, *Backpacker Magazine* has published several articles describing backcountry life-or-death experiences and suggesting specific medical supplies that could help prevent or treat these unusual injuries.

While these books and articles may be interesting to read, they are misleading and provide little guidance for ordinary families who want to know which particular first aid supplies should be packed for vacation trips to developed state and federal campgrounds. These books and articles are misleading because they overdramatize injuries that are very unlikely to occur and suggest that campers buy supplies that may never be needed. In contrast to these other books, this chapter describes the protection and first aid items that ordinary families will likely need for a basic-tent-camping trip.

In addition to packing prevention and first aid supplies, campers should also become familiar with basic principles of first aid and CPR so that they will be able to respond appropriately should an emergency ever develop. These classes are offered for little cost by the American Red Cross and other agencies.

Sunscreen

For several years, medical experts have advised people engaging in outdoor recreational activities to apply sunscreen several times during the day. Sunscreen helps to avoid painful sunburn and exposure to potentially harmful ultraviolet radiation. Most people should apply at least 30 SPF sunscreen, but people with fair complexion should apply 50 SPF or higher. Several companies, including Coppertone, Banana Boat, and Hawaiian Tropic, sell compact tubes of sunscreen that can be easily packed in a car, on a motorcycle, or on a bicycle. Experts recommend that sunscreen should be applied whenever a person will be outside for more than fifteen minutes—even on cloudy days. Campers should apply sunscreen at the beginning of the day and continue to reapply several times during the day.

Insect Repellent

Each camping destination has its unique collection of insects. Destinations near rivers, lakes, and standing ponds frequently have lots of mosquitoes. Destinations in Michigan's Upper Peninsula, northern Minnesota, and North Dakota have swarms of mosquitoes plus biting black flies. Destinations in the south have red bugs, or chiggers, in the grass. And destinations all over the country have ticks and other pesky insects. Campers who are unprepared for these insects can quickly become miserable.

To be ready for insects, campers should always pack some type of insect repellent. Several effective products are available on the market, and each product has its strengths and limitations. For many years, products with DEET, such as Off! Deep Woods spray and Repel lotion were considered to be the most effective. Studies published by *Consumer Reports* and other consumer groups concluded that products with DEET provided the longest effective protection against the mosquitoes that cause West Nile Virus. Repel lotion is particularly effective and convenient. Unfortunately, many scientists assert that DEET is an environmental and personal health hazard. In particular, it may cause cancer and present additional harm for young children. It also will dissolve plastic tablecloths and other plastic items in seconds after contact.

Several companies have developed alternative products with more environmentally friendly ingredients, but for several years, these products provided less protection than products with DEET. Examples of early products include Avon Skin So Soft lotion, lemon eucalyptus oil, citronella, and other plant products. Most recently, picaridin-based products, such as made by Sawyer, have emerged as excellent repellents. In fact, Sawyer's picaridin repellent reportedly repels mosquitoes almost as well as DEET and also repels flies and ticks better than DEET-based products. Natrapel is another picaridin-based product that reportedly provides long-lasting protection with no harm to gear and with less-harmful environmental effects. Permethrin is another insect repellent and is made to be sprayed on clothing. It reportedly has no harmful effects on clothing, camping gear, or the environment.

Hand Sanitizer

Many Americans commonly contract respiratory and intestinal infections caused by pathogens that are transferred from contaminated hands to the mouth and smooth tissue around the nose, mouth, and eyes. The best way to prevent these infections is to always wash hands after going to the bathroom, before preparing food, and before eating. Campers are particularly susceptible to these illnesses because many campground bathrooms do not have soap and many campsites do not have clean water spigots. Therefore, campers should pack a small container of hand sanitizer and use it often. Purell is a well-known brand, but several other brands are available for nominal expense.

First Aid Supplies

Campers should always pack a small first aid kit in their vehicles in case of injury. Common camping problems include minor burns from the campfire, minor cuts, insect bites, intestinal upset, sunburns, sprains, and headaches. The first aid kit should include items to treat these common problems and should be accessible at all times, even when traveling with all camping gear packed in the back of the vehicle. When hiking a few miles away from camp, campers should carry a first aid kit in a day pack. A first aid kit should include these items:

- rubber gloves (two pairs) for when aid must be given to a stranger
- aloe gel for burns
- Itch Eraser for insect bites
- Neosporin antiseptic cream for cuts
- medium-size Band-Aids for cuts and blisters
- Benadryl for insect stings and allergic reactions
- ibuprofen for pain and muscle soreness
- aspirin for chest pain

- antacids for upset stomach
- Zanfel poison ivy wash
- large sterile gauze pads (four) for severe lacerations
- elastic bandage for wrapping sprains, for applying pressure, and for holding large gauze pads in place

If other intestinal or medical problems develop on a particular camping trip, campers can easily drive to the nearest pharmacy to purchase necessary medicine or medical supplies.

Campers should also know how to respond to serious medical issues that could occur while camping. For serious lacerations, allergic reactions, snakebites, and most other problems, call 911, stabilize the injury, and help to evacuate the injured person to the nearest medical facility as quickly as possible. For falls involving possible head, neck, or spinal injuries, keep the injured person still, clear the airway, cover him or her with blankets to maintain body temperature, and call 911.

Complete first aid kits are available in department stores and camping outfitters. These kits include all the basic items plus a few extra items, such as scissors, and are able to handle a wide range of minor medical problems. Examples of such kits include the Adventure Medical First Aid 0.5, Campmor Camp Medical Kit, Adventure Medical Day Tripper, and Adventure Medical Ultralight Pro. Instead of purchasing prepackaged medical kits, campers can choose to assemble their own first aid kits.

Hats

Most camping and hiking authorities recommend that each camper wear a full-brimmed hat to provide protection from potentially harmful ultraviolet radiation. Since campers typically spend many hours outside, they should wear hats to protect their faces and necks from sun damage that could lead to melanoma and other skin cancers and to protect their eyes from damage that could lead to premature cataracts. Hats with brims also provide shade for the eyes, cover from rain, and warmth in cool weather. Additional information about hats is provided in chapter 6, "Clothing."

Optional Items

Lip balm. Constant exposure to sun and wind will lead to chapped lips. A small tube of lip balm will make them feel much better.

Head nets. A few camping destinations, such as Michigan's Upper Peninsula and Minnesota's Boundary Waters Canoe Area Wilderness, sometimes have swarms of mosquitoes and biting flies that can make outdoor camping life unbearable. An inexpensive way to reduce these insect problems is to purchase a head net that fits over a wide-brimmed hat. These head nets can be purchased in most department stores, sporting goods stores, and camping outfitters for five to fifteen dollars. Well-known makers include Coleman, Coghlan's, and Sea to Summit.

Bug-repellent clothing. If mosquitoes and biting flies are expected to be especially bad, campers may want to pack one or two bug-repellent shirts and pants in their duffel bags. Several companies, including Columbia, ExOfficio, No Fly Zone, Outdoor Research, and Zorrel make insect-repellent garments. Or campers can spray their clothing with Sawyer Permethrin Premium Insect Repellent.

Sun-protective clothing. In the desert and other open areas, campers may want to pack shirts and pants that are designed to protect the skin from potentially harmful ultraviolet radiation from the sun. L.L.Bean sells a range of sunblock garments, as does REI, Campmor, and most camping outfitters. Columbia makes a line of Omni-Shade garments that are sold in many stores. Although these garments offer sun protection, many people camping in the eastern United States, including the Florida Gulf Coast, just use sunscreen and wear light-colored, lightweight cotton garments and hats and experience few problems.

Unnecessary Items

Snakebite kit. Although snakebite kits are sold in most camping outfitter stores and apparently sell well, these kits are unnecessary for at least four reasons. First, the overall risk of dying from a venomous snakebite in the United States is almost zero. Large snakes are solitary creatures and typically move away from human activity and noise. Most campers will never see a venomous snake in a developed state or federal campground unless people have left human or animal food out that attracts mice. Second, if a snake does venture into a campground, it will avoid people and hide under logs and other objects unless physically threatened. Most people who have been bitten by venomous snakes either stepped on them in the dark or tried to catch or handle them. Third, if a person is bitten by a venomous snake, the recommended procedure is to apply ice to slow circulation and evacuate him or her to a medical facility as soon as possible. Since cars and telephone service are readily available in developed campgrounds, the victim can be evacuated immediately without wasting time trying to use a snakebite kit. Once in the medical facility, the victim will be monitored to determine whether antivenin is necessary or not. And finally, an untrained person trying to use a snakebite kit can do more harm than good. Applying tourniquets and cutting the skin will cause injury that will require additional medical treatment beyond the treatment required for the bite.

Pepper spray. Some books recommend that backpackers pack cans of pepper spray in case they happen to encounter aggressive bears or people. In such situations, the backpackers might be many miles and many hours away from assistance and thus must be prepared for the worst-case scenario. However, basic tent campers who camp in developed campgrounds and exercise proper care in food-handling procedures should never have to worry about bear attacks.

Although bears have caused problems in developed campgrounds in the past, rangers in most parks are now able to keep bears away from campers most of the time. In bear habitats, such as Great Smoky Mountains National Park and the Cherokee National Forest, campers will see posted signs regarding personal safety. When registering for a campsite, campers will be advised by park rangers regarding standard precautions to take. Rangers will usually tell campers to store all food and fruity-smelling personal items in the car or a metal locker located in the campground. Sometimes rangers will advise campers to hang their food and other fragrant items from a high cable. Rarely will they advise campers in developed campgrounds to purchase pepper spray.

Emergency blanket. Many books recommend emergency blankets to survive extra-cold nights. Although these blankets require little packing space, they are intended for wilderness hikers who may get lost and have to survive a cold night in the woods with no shelter or bedding. Most basic tent campers will never use one and should instead buy good-quality clothing and sleeping gear that will keep them warm at night. If it gets too cold, campers can get into their car and turn on the heater. If necessary, they can even drive to a motel.

Pistol. A few early camping articles plus several recent motorcycle-camping publications recommend that campers pack a pistol for protection on camping trips. I would like to respectfully disagree with this recommendation. For most of my camping lifetime, firearms were illegal in national and state parks and, fortunately, were never needed to protect myself or family. Although recent laws now allow people to carry firearms in state and federal park areas, firearms are still prohibited in many campground areas and are unnecessary. Granted, some small, remote campgrounds have occasional problems with drunkenness and disorderly behavior, but campers should avoid these campgrounds as much as possible. Instead, basic tent campers can stay in large, supervised campgrounds where unregistered people are unable to enter, camp hosts are on duty, and park rangers patrol the campground at night. On the rare occasion in which a potentially violent person is encountered, campers should avoid contact with the person, leave the area, and call park rangers or 911. Rather than packing a pistol, campers should refrain from alcohol consumption, avoid rough places, and treat other people with respect.

Eva and I always carry insect repellent, sunscreen, aloe burn gel, poison ivy soap, and our first aid kit in our vehicle so that these items are available when we may need them.

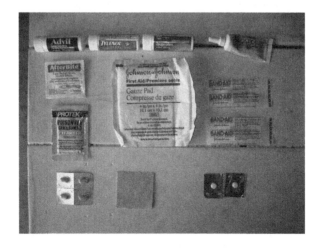

Here are a few items in our first aid kit.

9

KITCHEN

To travel economically, basic tent campers should assemble a set of nesting kitchen items that can be used to prepare and serve a wide variety of simple, good-tasting meals in the campsite. In general, kitchen items should be lightweight and compact, and smaller items should nest inside larger items during travel.

Early camping books and magazine articles clearly emphasized that eating well played an important role in determining the overall comfort on a camping trip. In fact, these early resources devoted considerable space to describing kitchen gear and staples that were small enough to pack for camping trips yet versatile enough to prepare a good variety of simple but great-tasting meals. Holding (1908), for example, discussed his kitchenware in two chapters. He described stoves in one chapter and various plates, cups, utensils, containers, and baskets in another chapter. Kephart (1917) listed over forty kitchen items—including a coffeepot, dipper, skimmer, white enamel cups, and white metal dessert spoons—needed to prepare and serve meals in the woods.

Contemporary camping outfitters sell a wide variety of cups, cook sets, utensils, and stoves that can be packed for camping trips. Indeed, they sell far more items than most people can even imagine. People who are unfamiliar with these items may have difficulty deciding which specific items to select. Consequently, this chapter will provide an overview of modern camp kitchen gear and recommend specific items.

The particular kitchen items that a family should pack for a camping trip depends primarily upon the amount of packing space they have available. Couples traveling by motorcycle, for example, with little packing space can pack a few small items and plan to eat a few meals in restaurants, purchase prepared foods in grocery stores, and cook a few more items on campsite grills. Couples traveling in small cars can pack small kitchen sets and prepare a wider variety of simple, great-tasting meals in their campsites. Families traveling in large SUVs can pack complete kitchen sets and plan to cook almost every meal in their campsites. Regardless of the amount of kitchen gear packed, all campers should learn to prepare a variety of simple, economical, good-tasting meals that will satisfy their hunger and add considerable comfort to their camping experience.

Essential Items

Regardless of the particular meal and travel plans for any given trip, basic tent campers should always pack eleven basic kitchen items. These items, listed below, are essential for cooking and eating various types of meals on any camping trip.

- water bottle for each person
- cup for each person
- spoon for each person
- tongs
- butane lighters (three)
- GI can opener
- paper towels (at least ten sheets)
- dishrag
- dish detergent
- plastic garbage bags (three)
- water jugs (one to four)

With this set of essential items and a pocketknife, campers can buy several foods in restaurants or grocery stores and bring them back to their campsite to eat. They can also cook bratwursts, hamburgers, steak, and other meats on the camp grill and can cook several fruits and vegetables, such as apples, potatoes, and onions, in aluminum foil on the grill or in the campfire coals. If they want to warm soup or other canned goods, they can buy disposable aluminum loaf pans in any grocery store and heat the food on the campfire.

Despite the number of essential items, they all can be packed into a small space with a little planning. The lighters, can opener, dishrag, garbage bags, and dish detergent can all be packed inside a cup. The spoons and tongs can be packed in any small space, and the empty water jug can be attached to the outside of the luggage with a carabineer, cargo net, or short length of cord. If two people are traveling together on a motorcycle, the water bottle for the second person can be nested inside his or her cup. Additional suggestions for these essential items and other recommended items are presented below.

Personal water bottles. Most camping books and magazines articles recognize the importance of having personal water containers and make various recommendations regarding the best ones. A few books recommended military-style or western-style canteens, but most recent books and magazine articles recommend high-quality plastic or metal bottles. Most camping outfitters sell a variety of plastic, aluminum, and steel water bottles. Plastic bottles, especially hard plastic bottles such as those made from Lexan, are very durable, convenient, and widely used. Other options include BPA-free plastic bottles, such as Nalgene Choice and Camelbak; aluminum water bottles, such as those made by SIGG; and stainless steel bottles, such as those made by Klean Kanteen, New Wave Enviro, and L.L.Bean.

After trying several types and sizes of personal water containers, I have concluded that basic tent campers should choose a container that holds about sixteen ounces. It should be large enough to carry sufficient water for a daily excursion but small enough to bring into the tent at the end of the day. Klean Kanteen stainless steel bottles are excellent choices because they are easy to hold in one hand and have wide mouths for ice cubes. Recycled Gatorade or Powerade drink bottles also make great personal water bottles. They are economical, durable, and shaped to fit into backpack side pockets and automobile beverage holders. But before using plastic water bottles, campers should become familiar with BPA and its possible health risks. See chapter 17, "Ethics," for more information.

Cups. Each camper needs a good insulated cup or mug for hot chocolate, coffee, tea, juice, milk, hot soups, oatmeal, and other foods. Campers who have their own cups and coffee or tea bags just have to find a little hot water in the morning to get a nice warm beverage to start the day. Camping outfitters sell a wide range of cups and mugs, and every camping book expresses a different opinion about the best ones. Each design has certain strengths and limitations. The most practical cups have at least five qualities:

- insulated to keep hot beverages hot and cold beverages cold
- large enough to hold at least twelve fluid ounces
- durable enough to withstand light abuse and very hot liquids
- comfortable to hold without burning one's hand
- designed to nest well with other gear to conserve packing space

Acrylic and plastic cups look very nice but can crack with hot beverages. Stainless steel Sierra cups are popular among backpackers because these cups can be used to dig cat holes and have wire handles that can be clipped to backpacks with carabineers—but they are usually small and uninsulated. Campers can easily burn their fingers and lips while using these cups. Furthermore, Sierra cups with wide rims and narrow bases do not nest well with other kitchen items. Orikaso cups and squishy cups pack into small spaces but are small and uncomfortable to hold. Plastic- and metal-lined tumblers without handles are reasonably good choices, but they are rather large and require extra packing space. In general, cups with folding handles, such as the Snow Peak titanium insulated cup, are ideal for basic tent camping—but this Snow Peak cup costs about forty dollars. Other good options are offered by MSR and REI.

Spoons. Each person will need a soup spoon to stir and eat his or her food. When used with pocketknives, campers should be able to eat almost any food imaginable. Metal spoons sold for home use could be used, but they are heavy and could damage nonstick cookware. Camping outfitters sell a variety of compact backpacking utensils made from lightweight Lexan, stainless steel, or titanium. Backpackers and wilderness campers seem to like Snow Peak titanium or GSI Lexan sporks/foons because they function as both spoon and fork, are lightweight, and require minimal packing space. Basic tent campers with more packing space should consider heavy-duty Lexan utensils such as GSI Outdoors Tekk Spoons because they are durable, relatively lightweight, and can be used to stir foods in nonstick cookware.

Tongs. This particular utensil can be used to cook a variety of foods. It can be used to flip pancakes and hamburgers and fry bacon. It can also be used to move aluminum foil food packs on the grill or in campfire coals. And it can be used to remove corn and potatoes from boiling water. Small metal tongs sold for home use are economical and suited for most camping chores, but nylon tongs sold in camping outfitters can be packed into a smaller space and used with nonstick cookware without damaging the finish. People riding motorcycles should seriously consider folding tongs sold at camping outfitters.

Butane lighters. Contrary to what other camping books may suggest, basic tent campers should pack small butane cigarette lighters rather than waterproof matches or other fire-starting items. Butane lighters require less effort and have a lower risk of failure, even in damp weather. These lighters are handy for starting campfires, lighting stoves, and burning the ends of nylon cord. Campers should pack at least three of these lighters so that they will have backups when one runs out of fuel. Although smokers routinely carry one or two of these lighters already, nonsmokers may have to make a special effort to acquire and pack this item.

Paper towels. Paper towels have a large number of uses around the campsite. They can be used to clean hands and wipe up spills. They can also be used as napkins, dish towels, tissue paper, and emergency toilet paper. Viva brand paper towels are an excellent choice. They are strong yet soft enough to be used comfortably as tissues and toilet paper when necessary. People traveling in cars can just pack a roll with their kitchen gear or toss a roll into the trunk. Campers traveling by motorcycle can tear about ten sheets off the roll, fold them, and pack them in a quart-size food-storage bag.

Dish detergent. On most trips, campers will need a small amount of dish detergent for washing dishes and hands in the campsite. Dish detergent sold in grocery stores comes in large bottles that require excessive packing space and have much more soap than needed for any camping trip. To make the detergent more packable, campers should fill a travel-size plastic bottle with a few ounces of detergent before leaving home and pack this small container with the rest of the kitchen items.

Garbage bags. Campers will routinely need plastic garbage bags to collect their trash every day. In the past, some campground registration offices gave garbage bags to campsite registrants, but this extra touch has generally fallen to budget cuts. Plastic grocery bags make great campsite garbage bags. They are free, pack into a small space, are a good size for campsite trash, can be easily hung with a rope and carabineer attached to a tree or tarp support pole, and have handles that can be easily tied together to contain the contents. Three of these bags can be stuffed into a tiny packing space and may come in handy on the first day or two of a new camp. After settling in, campers will usually go to buy more supplies from a local store, where they can acquire more plastic bags for the remainder of the trip.

Water jugs. Large water containers are essential for basic tent camping. Campers will frequently want water in the campsite to drink, cook, wash hands, wash dishes, brush teeth, and shave. Having bottles or jugs of fresh water at the table makes all these chores much easier and keeps campers from having to make multiple trips to the bathhouse or water spigot. Having relatively large containers allows campers to bring ample amounts of water each trip and make fewer trips back to the water spigot.

After using many different water containers, I have concluded that recycled three-liter Ocean Spray Cranberry Juice jugs make the best water containers for basic tent camping. These jugs are perfect because one jug can hold a relatively large amount of water but is small and lightweight enough to allow one person to easily carry the water several yards back to a campsite. In fact, one person can easily bring two jugs back—one in each hand. These jugs are durable enough for many camping trips, are designed for one-handed pouring, and can withstand light abuse. When one cracks, campers can easily buy a replacement in any grocery store.

The number of containers to pack for a particular trip depends upon the amount of packing space. Having more water jugs reduces the number of trips to the well or spigot. Families traveling in large vehicles may want to pack three or four containers in a milk crate. Couples traveling in small cars may only have room to pack two containers. And people traveling by motorcycle may only be able to tie one empty container to the outside of their luggage. If Ocean Spray jugs are unavailable, campers could use ordinary one-gallon milk or water jugs, but these containers are not as durable as the Ocean Spray jugs.

Stove

Small, portable stoves suited for camping and travel have been available since the 1850s. One of the first models, called the Rob Roy, burned alcohol as its fuel. Another early model, called the Primus stove, burned pressurized kerosene. It quickly became a favorite of campers, and in the early 1900s, T. H. Holding praised it as an excellent camp stove. The Primus continues to be a popular stove design today. Around 1945, the Coleman Company entered the portable stove market. Today, Primus, Coleman, and a few other companies make a variety of portable stoves suited for basic tent camping. These stoves can be purchased from most sporting goods stores and outdoor outfitters. Some stoves use propane as their fuel, while others use wood, butane, white gas (Coleman fuel), solid fuel pellets, Sterno fuel, unleaded automobile gas, or other fuels.

Having a small stove plus a small pot and frying pan allows campers to prepare many different foods at the picnic table under a kitchen canopy. Campers can quickly boil water for hot chocolate, tea, or coffee. They can also heat a variety of canned and frozen foods, such as chili, soup, and beef stew. Or they can easily cook a variety of rice- and pasta-based meals, such as macaroni, spaghetti, and fettuccini Alfredo. Being able to cook meals under a kitchen canopy is especially nice when it is raining.

Two-burner camp stove. When campers have sufficient packing space, they should strongly consider adding a two-burner camp stove. These stoves are designed to burn either propane or white gas. Propane models seem to be a better choice because propane cylinders, compared with white gas containers, are easier to store and use. Pouring white gas from a one-gallon can into a small gas tank with a small funnel can be difficult, and repeatedly pumping air into the tank can be a hassle. Several companies, including Coleman, Primus, Century (L.L.Bean), Camp Chef, and Stansport (Target), make propane stoves and offer a variety of options, such as self-ignition and grill tops. Coleman stoves and propane cylinders seem to be the most popular option.

Backpacking canister stove. Backpacking canister stoves burn a propane-fuel mixture that comes in small prefilled canisters. To use the stove, campers simply screw a fuel canister onto the stove, open the valve, and light it. When the fuel runs out, campers can easily unscrew the empty canister and screw on a new canister. These stoves are very simple and typically cost forty to a hundred dollars. They are popular among backpackers and are ideal for both motorcycle and small-car camping trips.

A popular model is the MSR PocketRocket. It is a small and durable stove that folds into a package smaller than a twelve-ounce drink can and works like a small blowtorch. It can boil a pot of water in about five minutes. Its small four-ounce fuel canister costs about four dollars and can cook ten to fifteen meals. In many ways it is a great camping stove, but it has four limitations. Its flame is easily affected by light wind, it does not simmer foods as well as some other stoves, it may not work well in cool weather and high altitudes, and its replacement fuel canisters may be difficult to find in remote camping areas. Other popular canister stoves include the Coleman Exponent F1 Ultralight; Snow Peak LiteMax; Primus Express Spider; Primus Power Stove Set, which includes a boil pot and windscreen; MSR Reactor Stove System, and Jetboil GCS.

Backpacking gas stove. This third type of camping stove is a single-burner stove designed to burn white gas (Coleman fuel). These stoves have small refillable bottles. Whenever the gas runs out, campers must unscrew the refillable gas bottle and pour white gas into it with a small funnel. To make this refill process easier, campers should first pour the gas from the one-gallon can into a small measuring container and then pour the gas from the measuring container through the funnel into the bottle. Once the bottle has been filled, users must pump air into the bottle and sometimes prime the stove. These gas stoves range in price from $80 to $160. Some of the more-expensive models can also burn kerosene, unleaded gasoline, and other fuels. The advantages of this type of stove are it works well in cold weather and high altitudes, its flame can be adjusted low enough to simmer foods, and its fuel is easy to find even in remote, rural areas. The limitations are the gas container, transfer container, and funnel require extra packing space; it is more expensive than a canister stove; it requires more time and effort to refill the fuel container; and it requires regular cleaning and maintenance. Some popular examples of these stoves include the MSR WhisperLite, Coleman Exponent Fyrestorm Ti (which can also burn canister fuel), and the MSR SimmerLite.

Ultralight backpacking stove. Camping outfitters also sell a variety of unusual stoves designed for ultralight hikers and backpackers with limited packing space. Some examples of these ultralight stoves include aluminum alcohol stoves such as the Mini Trangia stove, which weighs about twelve ounces; solid-fuel Esbit stoves; Sterno stoves; and small woodstoves that burn small amounts of twigs and leaves readily found near most campsites. Backpacking magazines also explain how readers can make small alcohol-burning stoves from cat-food cans. Although these ultralight stoves may be smaller and lighter than other stoves, they produce less heat and require longer boiling times. Consequently, most backpackers forgo these unusual stove designs and pack more-reliable propane or white gas stoves. Basic tent campers, including those traveling by motorcycle, would be well advised to do the same.

Pots and Pans

Pots and pans suitable for basic tent camping are typically made from one of four materials, and each material has notable strengths and limitations. Stainless steel pots are lightweight and cheaper than pots made from other materials, but they do not distribute heat efficiently. While they are great for boiling water for dehydrated backpacking meals, they can easily scorch food that needs to be simmered for several minutes. Titanium pots are popular among backpackers because they are extremely lightweight and boil water rapidly, but they are expensive, do not distribute heat as well as aluminum, and can easily scorch food. They are well suited for ultralight backpackers who are seeking lighter weight and fast boiling times for dehydrated foods but are poorly suited for basic tent campers who may want to prepare meals requiring long simmer times. Many gourmet cooks prefer cast iron pots and pans because they require less heat and distribute that heat more evenly over the entire cooking surface. Classic tent campers, canoe campers, equestrian campers, and luxury tent campers spending several days in a base camp frequently bring cast iron Dutch ovens and pans to prepare a variety of stews, roasts, breads, and desserts. The primary limitations of cast iron cookware are weight and rust proneness. Backpackers would never carry a cast iron pot because of its weight, and basic tent campers who only spend a few days in each campsite will probably want to leave these heavy items at home. As Holding observed over a hundred years ago, aluminum pots seem to be the best choice for basic tent camping. They are lightweight, distribute heat efficiently, and allow campers to simmer food for long times. Their primary limitations are they are easily dented and scratched and can warp from rapid temperature changes.

Pots. Over the past forty years, I have used army mess kits, cheap department store pots with handles removed, and backpacking pots. When riding my motorcycle on camping trips, I looked for the ideal camping pot that could be packed on a motorcycle yet could easily cook meals for two people. Most large pots and pans sold in department stores required too much packing space, and smaller army mess kits and backpacking pots were too small to cook meals for two people. Plus backpacking pots sold in camping outfitters are designed to heat water rapidly but not to simmer foods for several minutes.

After trying several different backpacking pots and being disappointed with each one, I noticed a one-and-a-half-quart aluminum pot sitting on a friend's stove one day and realized that this size would be perfect for motorcycle camping. It is relatively small to pack but large enough to cook food portions for two people. A few days later, I went to a local department store, bought a similar pot with a nonstick surface, removed the handle, and used this pot for several years. I was generally satisfied with this pot because it was small enough to pack on my motorcycle but allowed me to cook several different meals on a campfire or backpacking stove. Although I subsequently purchased more-compact camp cook sets, I still believe that economical one-and-a-half- and two-quart aluminum pots sold in department stores are ideally suited for basic tent camping when driving larger vehicles. To facilitate nesting, handles should be removed, and hot pots must be handled with pot holders or pliers.

Frying pan. After several disappointing attempts to fry bacon, eggs, and other foods with backpacking frying pans, I have concluded that these pans are better suited as serving trays than frying pans. To increase the diversity of foods that can be cooked in the campsite, campers need a good frying pan—one that is thick enough to disperse heat, large enough to cook portions for two, and small enough to pack in a small space. Coleman makes a ten-inch steel camp frying pan with a folding handle that works very well, but small aluminum nonstick frying pans sold in department stores are also very good. Their only limitation is their handles must be removed to facilitate packing. These department store frying pans are large enough to brown a half pound of ground beef for spaghetti or to cook several pieces of bacon but small enough to nest with pots and pack into a milk crate. In particular, T-fal frying pans are excellent. A set of two costs about twenty-five dollars. The larger ten-inch pan is ideal for two-burner camp stoves, and the smaller eight-inch pan works well with a backpacking stove.

Complete cook set. Several companies now offer complete cookware sets that include pots, frying pan, lids, plates, and sometimes cups that all nest together. The GSI Bugaboo Base Camper set, for example, includes a two-liter pot, a one-and-a-half-liter pot, two plastic strainer lids, a metal lid/pan, and a handle. It is ideal for campers who prefer to add their own plates and bowls. Eva and I have used this set for ten years. Bugaboo also makes a larger Camper Set that includes the above mentioned pots and frying pan plus four small plates and four cups/bowls. In addition, the company makes a smaller Backpacker Set that could be used by campers that travel by motorcycle or small car. Other companies offering complete cook sets include REI and MSR. For motorcycle camping, the GSI Dualist and the MSR Quick Solo System are two more choices.

Utensils

To cook and eat a variety of simple, good-tasting meals on a campfire, grill, or gas stove, basic tent campers need a few basic utensils in addition to their pocketknives and tongs. To keep these utensils organized, campers should pack them in empty coffee cans or canvas water bottle holders such as those available from Duluth Pack.

Nylon mixing spoon. A nylon mixing spoon can be used to stir food in nonstick cookware and disposable aluminum pans or pots. It also can be used to serve food when fully heated. Mixing spoons are preferable to serving spoons because mixing spoons are flat and pack into a smaller space. Nylon spoons, in contrast to metal spoons, are durable, lightweight, and will not damage nonstick surfaces on pots and pans.

Kitchen knife. In addition to their personal pocketknives, campers may want to consider another knife reserved exclusively for kitchen chores. A sharp knife will be needed to cut fresh fruits, vegetables, and meats. Many different types of knives could be used, but a folding knife with one large, lockable blade seems to be the best choice. This type of knife can be packed into a small space and is safe to handle when closed.

Spatulas. When packing space permits, campers should pack two spatulas. A small nylon spatula is needed for flipping eggs, pancakes, toast, and grilled cheese sandwiches in nonstick pans, and a larger metal spatula is needed for flipping burgers on a grill or cast iron griddle. Most basic tent campers can find a variety of small spatulas in local grocery and department stores. Motorcycle riders can find very compact spatulas at camping outfitters.

Utensil sets. At camping outfitters, shoppers will find a variety of utensil sets designed for backpacking and basic tent camping. One nice set is the Guyot Designs MicroBites Utensil Set consisting of a small nylon spoon and spatula that snap together and can be used for a variety of food-preparation tasks.

Eating utensils. In addition to spoons, many people may want to have forks and knives for eating certain foods. Campers could use metal table forks sold in department stores, but these utensils are heavy and could damage cookware. Lexan forks weigh much less and are very durable.

Dishes

Bowls. If packing space is available, campers can add two or more bowls to assist with food preparation and meal presentation. Both plastic and metal bowls are suitable for basic tent camping—but glass and ceramic bowls are not because they can break and cause personal injury. Eva and I pack four plastic bowls that we bought in a discount department store. Camping outfitters offer a wide variety of bowls suited for basic tent camping. Some of these bowls include Sea to Summit X-Bowls made from food-grade silicone with walls that collapse for travel, GSI baked enamel bowls, Seattle Sports Nylon Pocket Bowls, and Flatworld Orikaso bowls that fold flat. Snow Peak makes lightweight titanium bowls, and GSI offers stainless steel bowls. Two other options are disposable paper bowls and aluminum pie pans.

Plates. Adding plates to a kitchen set will further enhance eating pleasure. Campers have several options regarding their plates. Campers with ample packing space could purchase large plastic dinner plates sold in department and grocery stores, or they could buy high-quality plastic, stainless steel, or titanium bowls at camping outfitters. REI, for example sells Chefware plates made from Lexan. MSR makes nice stainless steel plates that nest well with small pots and pans. They would be suitable for both motorcycle and small-car trips. Motorcycle riders with little packing space could purchase a couple of plastic salad plates, which pack into a small space and hold small portions of food. Alternatively, campers with limited packing space could wait until they set up camp and then go to a local store to buy paper plates.

Coolers

Backpacking books typically do not discuss coolers because backpackers are unable to carry these heavy and bulky items in their backpacks. Instead of carrying perishable foods, backpackers typically eat dehydrated foods that require no refrigeration. Basic tent campers staying in developed state and federal campgrounds, on the other hand, will have ample space to pack a cooler in their car and convenient places to buy ice near most campgrounds. Having a cooler allows basic tent campers to pack several perishable foods such as butter, salad dressing, and cheese and prepare a much wider range of good-tasting meals.

A variety of cooler sizes, shapes, and styles are available in most grocery and department stores. To ensure that the cooler will keep foods cold for a reasonable length of time and will not leak, buy a brand name such as Coleman, Igloo, Thermos, or Rubbermaid rather than a generic brand. Medium-size forty- to sixty-quart coolers seem to be ideally suited for basic-tent-camping trips. They hold enough perishable food to last several days but are small enough to be carried by one person and packed into most cars. Typically, they require one large fifteen-pound bag of ice on the first day and, depending upon the outside temperature and amount of time opened, one or two small seven-pound bags each subsequent summer day. Examples of good coolers in this category include the Igloo 48-Quart Breeze, Rubbermaid 48-quart Chest, and Coleman 50-Quart Chest.

Large coolers over sixty quarts are poorly suited for basic tent camping since they are too large to pack in most cars and too heavy to carry more than a few yards. Small coolers less than twenty-five quarts are too small to be the primary cooler for most car-camping trips but could be added as a drink cooler for travel and daily excursions. The soft-sided REI Go Box Cooler is ideal for motorcycle trips because it is large enough to hold butter and a few eggs but small enough to pack in a saddlebag or T-Bag.

Although soft-sided coolers are easier to pack and carry, they have one notable limitation: they leak and sweat, and this moisture can soak other clothing and camping gear. Furthermore, they require more ice fill-ups to keep contents cold. Yeti coolers are relatively new to the market. They are well insulated and made for camping and other outdoor activities. In addition, they reportedly keep food cold for up to four days without having to repack the ice and are bear proof. Their main limitation is their price. The forty-five-quart cooler costs about $350, and the fifty-quart cooler costs about $380. They seem to be especially popular with boaters and canoeists but have not been widely used by basic tent campers who can easily buy ice every day for about two dollars a bag.

Optional Items

Griddle. Many cooks prefer to use griddles rather than frying pans to cook foods like pancakes and grilled cheese sandwiches. Consequently, some campers may be tempted to pack ten-inch square griddles in their kitchen equipment. A Lodge single-burner cast iron griddle is especially nice because it requires minimum heat and cooks evenly. A good-quality aluminum griddle is much lighter and cooks almost as well. But griddles are usually poor choices for basic tent camping. Cast iron griddles will begin to rust after one or two days in damp conditions. Frying pans are much more versatile, and griddles are another unnecessary piece of equipment that must be packed and always seems to get in the way when looking for other items.

Dutch ovens. Dutch ovens are typically made from cast iron and weigh about ten to fifteen pounds. Backpackers would never pack these because they would add unnecessary bulk and weight to their loads. But many luxury tent and canoe campers include Dutch ovens in their kitchen equipment. They use these ovens to bake pot roasts, lasagna, breads, and desserts. Lodge Dutch ovens seem to be the particular brand of choice. After considering the strengths and limitations of Dutch ovens, it is easy to see that motorcycle campers cannot pack them and that basic tent campers traveling in small cars can easily live without them. They will be used for few meals, rust easily, are heavy, and require extra packing space that could be used more effectively.

Dish towels. Two types of fabrics are used to make dish towels. Cotton is relatively inexpensive and can be used to hold hot pans. Polyester microfiber towels absorb more water and dry faster but won't protect from burns if used to pick up hot pots. Campers who want to use their towels as potholders certainly must buy cotton towels despite the fact that they require longer drying time.

Aluminum foil. Campers who do not have space to pack pots and pans in their vehicle but want to cook a few meals in their campsite can cook a variety of foods with aluminum foil. The basic items needed for foil cooking are sheets of twelve-inch, heavy-duty aluminum foil; a pair of tongs; spoons; butter; salt; and pepper. These items require very little packing space but allow campers to cook several delicious meals over hot charcoal or a campfire. Campers can cut and fold a few sheets of foil before leaving home or can purchase a small fifty-foot roll of foil in a local grocery store after setting up camp. For more details about aluminum foil cooking see chapter 15, "Meals."

Disposable aluminum pans. Campers who are unable to pack pots in their vehicle can purchase disposable loaf pans in most grocery stores and use them to heat water and canned foods on a campfire. These pans are inexpensive and come in a variety of sizes. They can be used to heat water for hot chocolate, dehydrated meals, or washing dishes. Pie pans can be used as plates or bowls to hold individual food servings. The major limitation of these pans is that they are lightweight and flimsy. Lifting them requires two hands and full attention to avoid spilling the contents.

Cutting board. Although campers can survive without a cutting board, having one makes it easy to cut meat, vegetables, and fruit without cutting the tablecloth. A recent article in *Backpacker Magazine* suggested using the flexible plastic cover from a three-ring binder as a cutting board. The plastic cover can be trimmed to any size to fit a particular packing plan. Campers who cook many meals in their campsites should consider this small luxury for their kitchen kit.

Bucket. If space permits, campers should consider packing a two-gallon bucket for collecting gray dishwater, washing clothes, and taking baths when showers are unavailable. We use a simple paint bucket sold in most hardware and home improvement stores. When traveling, we fill our bucket with onions, potatoes, apples, oranges, bananas, and other fresh vegetables and fruit. Other campers prefer folding buckets, such as the Sea to Summit 10-Liter Bucket, because they require less packing space.

Cooking grate. Although most public campgrounds have fire rings with cooking grates or grills, a few do not. In fact, most Michigan state parks have nice steel-clad concrete fire rings with no cooking grates. To grill burgers, brats, or steak in these campgrounds (or cook other foods), campers must bring their own cooking grate. Several camping outfitters sell rectangular and round grates. Campmor, for example, sells a rectangular Rome Pioneer cooking grate. In campgrounds with no fire rings or grills, campers can use stones or large logs to support the grate or buy a large lasagna pan in a grocery store to grill hamburgers or brats.

Cooking tripod. Since some campgrounds do not have cooking grates and other campgrounds do not have adjustable grates, many avid outdoorsmen who enjoy cooking in the woods bring their own tripods to hang cooking grates over campfires. The grate is suspended by a chain that can be raised or lowered to adjust the amount of heat for any specific food. Several examples of these tripods can be found on the Internet. Lodge is a well-known brand. Instructions for making a collapsible tripod, using materials like aluminum electrical conduit and eyebolts, can also be found on the Internet. Although these tripods may be useful in long-term base camps, they require considerable packing space, limit mobility by requiring additional time to set up and disassemble, have many parts that can easily get lost, and are unnecessary in most campgrounds. Also, the chains frequently interfere with moving pots on and off the grate.

Folding campfire stove. After using a tripod for several years, I concluded that there must be a better way. Eventually, I conceptualized and built a small folding campfire stove. It has a solid-steel-plate back that is fourteen inches wide by eight inches high and two folding sides that are six inches high. When set up, it accommodates an eleven-by-sixteen-inch cooking grate or cookie sheet. The front is open so that coals from a larger fire can be easily moved under the cooking grate as needed. When folded, it is flat and packs into a very small space. Although it was designed for wood fires, it can be easily adapted to accommodate charcoal. See photos at the end of this chapter.

Portable grill. Although a small cooking grate is all that is needed and although many cars are too small to accommodate full-size grills, families traveling in medium-size vehicles and planning to spend several days in a base camp may want to consider packing small, portable grills. In particular, people who plan to camp in primitive areas such as dispersed campsites in national forests and state parks without cooking grills may want to pack small grills. One compact choice is the Fire Sense Notebook Charcoal Grill. This is a relatively sturdy grill that can easily handle meals for two to four people, such as hamburgers, steaks, pork chops, chicken breasts, bratwursts, corn, and shish kebobs. Although it allows campers to cook a variety of foods in any campsite, it requires extra packing space and requires frequent cleaning, consequently impairing mobility.

Unnecessary Items

Before concluding this chapter, let me comment on a few frequently recommended but unnecessary kitchen items.

Electric coffeemakers. A large number of people apparently feel that they need several cups of strong coffee in the morning before they can start the day. Although I am not one of these people, I have been around them for much of my life and sympathize with their apparent early-morning discomfort. When considering a camping trip, these people seem to think that an electric coffeemaker is the first and most important essential item to pack. But coffeemakers and accessories can occupy considerable packing space and greatly reduce the ability to pack up quickly in the morning. Therefore, coffee drinkers should consider other options for satisfying their morning coffee and caffeine needs.

The best, but perhaps less tasty, option is to pack small coffee bags (that can be steeped in hot water like tea bags) plus a few small packets of creamer and sugar along with a coffee mug. Each morning campers only have to boil some water or beg some hot water from a neighbor. A second option is to boil a small amount of freshly ground coffee in a pot of water and pour or dip the brewed coffee carefully so as to avoid transferring the grounds into a cup. A third option is to pack a large thermos and walk or drive to the campground office or store each morning and fill the thermos. Campers who select this option should ask park rangers or personnel in the registration station where they can find coffee the next morning. If coffee is not available in the office or store, campers can find fresh-brewed coffee in most convenience stores or restaurants. A fourth option is to drink instant coffee, but I know most coffee aficionados wouldn't consider this to be a real option. The last option is to buy a small old-fashioned percolator that can be used on a campfire or camp stove to percolate fresh coffee.

Pasta strainer. Several camping books recommend pasta strainers with the underlying suggestion that campers will cook pasta several times during a camping trip. In reality, most basic tent campers will only cook pasta one or two times a week and can use pot lids or plates to drain the water. If necessary, campers can use tongs to remove the pasta from the water. Campers who have any of the Bugaboo cook sets will not need an extra strainer, because the set includes plastic strainer lids with holes to drain water.

Large water container. Most camping outfitters sell three- to five-gallon water containers, and several recent camping books and magazine articles suggest that campers add these containers to their camping kits. The rationale for this recommendation is that bringing large amounts of water back to the campsite each trip saves several trips to the water spigot over a week's vacation. In reality, however, this rationale is flawed. Large containers filled with water are extremely heavy. One gallon of water weighs over eight pounds and five gallons weighs almost forty-two pounds. A filled five-gallon container is so heavy that children and smaller women could not possibly carry it back to a campsite more than twenty or thirty yards away. In fact, larger and stronger men would have considerable difficulty carrying it very far. Smaller three-gallon containers are a little easier to manage but still require considerable effort. After getting these large containers back to the campsite, they are very awkward for pouring water into pots or glasses. Although a few people may be strong enough to pick a full container up with one hand and pour water into a cup or glass held in the other hand, most people could not. Furthermore, these large containers require considerable packing space and do not facilitate nesting. After considering the limitations of these larger containers, it seems more practical to obtain a few small one-gallon containers rather than struggle with one of these larger containers.

Portable oven. A few backpacking books have described portable ovens such as the *E-Z Camping Reflector oven* for baking breads, desserts, and even pizza. This oven, designed to be used next to a large campfire, folds down to a small flat package for travel. Other books have suggested the *Backpacker's Pantry Outback Oven*, which is designed to be used with some backpacking stoves. After considering the limitations of these ovens, it seems reasonable to leave them at home because they require excessive packing space and are not needed. When basic tent campers want baked foods, they can easily drive to a store or restaurant to buy them.

Bear canisters. Many recent camping books, magazine articles, and websites recommend that campers pack their food in bear-proof bags, barrels, or other containers. The reasoning used to justify these containers is that campers in bear habitats must keep their food and garbage secured for their own personal safety and for the long-term benefit of the animals living in the vicinity. Without a doubt, campers should secure their food and garbage whenever they leave their campsite and when they retire for the night. However, most campers staying in developed state and federal campgrounds do not need to purchase or pack large bear canisters. When registering for campsites, campers should inquire as to the best way to protect their food from animal scavengers. In some campgrounds, rangers recommend that campers secure food items in the trunks of their cars. In other campgrounds, campers can store small coolers and other food items in metal lockers scattered around the campground. Yet other campgrounds offer different food-storage options and recommendations.

Water-purification equipment. One of the most important kitchen items for backpacking is water-purification equipment and supplies. Backpackers cannot carry enough clean drinking water for a multiday trip in their backpacks. As a result, they must collect water every day from nearby streams and lakes. But water in the backcountry may be contaminated. Therefore, backpackers must pack water-purification equipment for every camping trip.

Basic tent campers staying in most developed state and federal campgrounds, on the other hand, do not need this equipment. Most public campgrounds provide clean (potable) drinking-water spigots in the campground, and some campgrounds provide them in each site. All campers need is a few containers to bring it back to their table. Anyone with serious health problems or anyone who does not trust the purity of the local water can easily drive to a nearby store and buy pure drinking water in one-gallon jugs or smaller personal-size bottles.

Kitchen sink. One or two camping books have suggested that campers bring a sink for washing dishes. Several companies offer small, collapsible, waterproof sinks and containers designed for washing dishes. But an extra sink is unnecessary because any pot or bowl can be filled with soapy water to wash dishes. Instead of packing a sink, basic tent campers should pack a small bucket to catch soapy gray water for proper disposal.

Coleman camp stoves provide reliable service for many years. I used this propane model for over ten years.

This MSR PocketRocket is a compact, economical, and dependable stove that can be easily packed for motorcycle or small-car trips.

I built this wood stove so that we could cook in campsites that did not have cooking grates. It folds flat for travel.

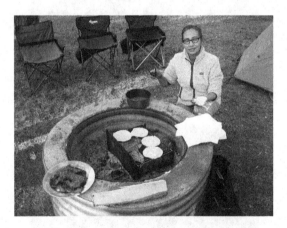

We can cook complete meals with this homemade wood stove. This night we cooked carne asada and pinto beans, served with tortillas.

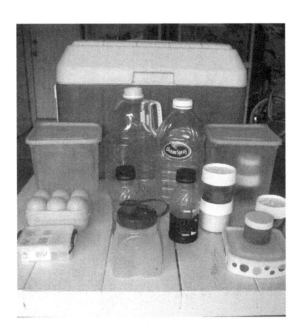

We use a variety of plastic containers to pack perishable foods for our camping trips. We pack these food containers in a fifty-quart cooler that can be easily packed in the back of most vehicles.

10

PLANNING

To camp in the most-popular campgrounds and enjoy the most-interesting tourist attractions, basic tent campers must plan trips and make reservations several months before their trip. For example, to stay in Peninsula State Park in Wisconsin during the month of July, campers must make reservations eleven months in advance. To stay in Ludington State Park in Michigan, they must make them six months in advance. In other words, campers must begin planning their summer camping vacations in August and September of the previous year. If they delay making their reservations a few days, most of the prime campsites will have already been claimed. In late September 2013, for example, only 5 campsites out of 471 in Peninsula State Park were still available for the second week of July 2014. In February 2014, no campsites were available in Ludington Sate Park for the third weekend in July.

Calendar

The first step in planning a camping trip is to secure a calendar for the upcoming year. Most office supply stores stock calendars for the next year by July of the preceding year. Pocket planners seem to be ideal for planning camping trips. They are small enough to keep on a desk or carry in a pocket if necessary yet large enough to make detailed vacation notes. After securing the calendar, campers should begin looking at possible vacation dates for the following summer. Each family will have to anticipate their unique employment and social obligations for the following year and then block out a week or two for their vacation. For many families, July is the best month for a vacation, and the week around the fourth is the best week. Consequently, many campgrounds fill quickly several months ahead for this time of the year. After raising children and retiring, most families have more flexibility for planning their camping trips and will be able to plan trips at less popular times. In September and October, most campgrounds have nice sites available for last-minute walk-up arrivals, but a few, such as Unicoi State Park, Georgia, still require advance reservations.

Once plans have been made and campsites have been selected, campers must visit the campground's Internet reservation page (or call the reservation phone number) and reserve a specific site for the selected dates. Then they should jot important details, such as date of arrival, length of stay, site number, and reservation number, on the calendar. After making the reservations, campers should plan travel routes, overnight camp reservations, and other details and then note these plans in the calendar to avoid confusion and possible conflicts. As the date of the trip approaches, make copies of the page to have an itinerary that can be easily carried in your pocket and another one or two to give to family members in case of an emergency.

This planner can also be used to plan other activities and appointments during the year. For example, avid basic tent campers like Eva and me usually take several shorter three- to five-day camping trips from March through November. During March, April, May, and November, we typically plan trips to warmer destinations, such as southern Alabama, southern Georgia and the Florida Gulf Coast. During June, August, and September, we plan trips to cooler destinations, such as southern Illinois, southern Indiana, and Great Smoky Mountains National Park. During October, we always plan a long weekend trip to Helen, Georgia, for Oktoberfest. As we plan each trip and make our reservations, we jot important details in the calendar.

Best Campgrounds

Many years ago, travelers could camp almost anywhere along rural roads but those days are over. Recent camping books advise readers to find "good campgrounds" and "good campsites" but typically do not explain how to identify these good campgrounds and campsites. Some books suggest that the best camping destinations are small, remote, and private campgrounds. Fishermen assert that the best camping destinations are located near good fishing holes. Horse riders define them as those with the most bridle trails and good saddle barns. Many RV guide books suggest that the best campgrounds are those with long paved parking pads, pull-through sites, water and electrical hookups at each site, and dump stations.

To date, I've found no book listing factors that define the best basic-tent-camping destinations. So I want to offer my own definition of good campgrounds and campsites. The best campgrounds are those that provide safe, family-centered environments; comfortable campground amenities; and lots of recreational opportunities. As a general rule, these are large, popular campgrounds located near major tourist attractions. They are campgrounds where adults and children can walk and play safely in the roads and everyone can sleep peacefully during the night.

To assess the safety and amenities of a particular campground, campers should visit MapQuest.com or similar website to view satellite images of the park and surrounding area, visit the park's home page to read descriptions and view photos, and read other reviews and descriptions posted on the web. As a general rule, state and federal parks with more than seventy-five campsites, posted rules, entrance control stations, and reservation procedures are safe and tranquil camping destinations. Specific features and amenities to consider are summarized below.

Safety Features

- entrance-control stations and gates that prevent vagrants and criminals from entering the property—especially after dark

- registration process that determines the identities of all people entering the property
- posted emergency procedures with phone numbers
- strong cell phone reception
- at least one host camper for every fifty campsites
- park rangers or law-enforcement personnel who drive through the campground frequently
- enforced speed limits of 5 mph and quiet hours between 10:00 p.m. and 7:00 a.m.
- enforced restrictions on alcohol possession and disorderly behavior
- enforced rules requiring dog owners to restrain their pets with six-foot leashes and pick up poop in public areas and possibly prohibitions of certain dog breeds
- at least ten other families camped in the campground

Campground Amenities

- large, level, unobstructed campsites with grass or crushed-stone surface (ideally elevated tent pads) and at least 1,600 square feet of unpaved ground space
- sturdy tables (ideally movable), fire rings, and cooking grates
- buffer zones with trees and undergrowth between campsites that provide shade, privacy, and noise dampening
- numerous mature trees that provide morning and afternoon shade as well as places to hang clotheslines and hammocks
- potable water spigots and gray water disposal stations located within 250 feet of every campsite
- clean and spacious bathrooms with at least one flush toilet, shower, and sink for each gender for every thirty campsites
- clean and well-groomed grounds that help to control animal and insect problems
- electrical outlets for charging cell phones and other electrical devices

- camp store or convenience store located within one mile of the campground
- Laundromat located within five miles

Recreational Opportunities

- swimming area
- visitor center with educational programs and exhibits
- interpretive programs on history/ecology of the park and camping-skills demonstrations
- hard-surface biking or walking trails
- boat ramps, fishing/marine supplies, fish-cleaning stations, and boat rentals
- additional recreational areas such as playgrounds, hiking/bridle trails, tennis courts, volleyball courts, basketball courts, and horseshoe pits
- children's activities such as hayrides, face painting, craft classes, and games
- family entertainment such as movies, concerts, hymn sings, campfire programs, and live theatre
- opportunities to see unique scenery, plants, birds, and animals
- Wi-Fi zone and TV room for watching news, weather, and movies
- popular tourist attractions located nearby

Popular campgrounds will have most of the above-listed amenities, while small, remote campgrounds will have fewer of these amenities. For example, both Peninsula State Park in Wisconsin and Ludington State Park in Michigan are very popular tent-camping destinations that feature entrance-control procedures, enforced rules, frequent patrols, children's activities, beaches, hard-surface trails, camp stores, and regularly scheduled family programs.

Best Campsites

After selecting their travel dates and a good campground, campers must select a good campsite. Most public properties publish maps showing the overall campground layout and photos of campground facilities on the Internet. Campgrounds that accept reservations may also post descriptions of individual campsites and sometimes photos. Campers should examine these maps, descriptions, and photos and look for the following features:

- large, level, unobstructed site with at least 1,600 square feet of unpaved ground surface
- crushed-stone, dirt, or grass surface
- elevated tent pad or slightly sloped surface that will drain rainwater
- sturdy table that can be easily moved
- sturdy fire ring with cooking grate located near the front edge of the campsite
- tree stump or large tree round for splitting firewood
- ten-foot buffer zones along the sides
- mature trees that provide midday and afternoon shade and places to hang hammocks (Morning shade is desirable as well but is not as important.)
- relatively close bathroom and water spigot
- close-by recreational areas such as the beach, volleyball courts, and pavilion
- close proximity to camp hosts
- location at least two hundred feet away from lakeshores or riverbanks to allow wildlife access to the water and avoid snakes and possible flooding after rainfall.
- location relatively far from garbage dumps
- scenic view

Public Campgrounds

Public campgrounds vary considerably in terms of their safety, amenities, and price. As a general rule, large public campgrounds with over fifty campsites are safe places for families and their children and have many amenities that can enhance overall vacation enjoyment, but they cost more per night than smaller campgrounds. Most large campgrounds have entrance-control stations and/or gates, volunteer campground hosts, park rangers who patrol the campground at night, nature centers, beaches, boat ramps, visitor centers, various recreational opportunities, and many other amenities. Some excellent campgrounds offering many of these amenities are listed on my website, www.BasicTentCamping. com. These large, popular campgrounds frequently require advance reservations, and their cost ranges from about twenty dollars to as much as sixty dollars per night.

Smaller, more-remote campgrounds typically offer large, spacious campsites with large buffer zones that provide privacy from neighboring campers, but they have fewer safety features and amenities. The smallest campgrounds with less than twenty-five campsites may only have one water spigot, a pit or vault toilet, a picnic table in each campsite, and no showers. These small campgrounds frequently do not require or accept reservations and, consequently, are popular with people who wait until the last minute to plan their camping trips. Although these campgrounds are usually safe for adult camping, they frequently are used for all-night drinking parties—especially on summer weekends. Campers who choose to stay in these campgrounds may have to endure a lot of loud music, talking, and swearing. Presumably, these campgrounds are patrolled by county deputy sheriffs. These officers will respond to disturbance calls, but the response time can be painfully slow. Specific types of public campgrounds and their typical amenities are briefly summarized below.

State Department of Natural Resources (DNR) campgrounds.
Most states have a department of natural resources that manages several dozen state parks and recreation areas with campgrounds.

These DNR properties typically have over fifty campsites with good overnight security, flush toilets, hot showers, ample water sources, electricity, hiking/biking trails, swimming pools or beaches, children's programs, and many other amenities. A significant number of them offer visitor centers, naturalist programs, playgrounds, picnic areas, convenience stores, snack bars, Laundromats, bicycle rentals, canoe/boat/kayak rentals, historic buildings, geological features, and other popular amenities. Furthermore, many DNR properties are located near popular tourist areas where campers can find many festivals, museums, concerts, plays, and tourist attractions. As a general rule, these DNR campgrounds are more expensive than other camping destinations. Their prices, including park admission fees and camping fees, range from about twenty dollars per night to sixty dollars per night. Rustic tent sites cost less, while sites with 50-amp electrical service and sewage cost more. For safety and comfort reasons, families with small children should strongly consider large state parks as overnight and main-destination camps when traveling.

These DNR properties are easy to identify on official state department of transportation (DOT) highway maps. The approximate location of each property is denoted on the map with a small symbol, and all properties are usually listed in the margin with basic details. These properties are also easy to find on the web, but some websites are incomplete and poorly organized. To find the most-popular DNR-managed campgrounds in a particular state, campers should search the web for "best state parks or campgrounds [state]." To identify the most-scenic state parks with exceptional cultural and historic significance, campers may want to consult National Geographic's *Guide to State Parks of the United States.* To find the most-secluded state park campgrounds, campers may want to consult *The Best in Tent Camping* for that particular state, if one is available. To identify the best state parks in Wisconsin, Michigan, Illinois, and Indiana, readers should obtain a copy of my book *The Family Camping Guide to Wisconsin, Michigan, Illinois & Indiana.*

A few DNRs also manage forests and wildlife areas with rustic campgrounds. Typically these state forests and wildlife areas are smaller campgrounds located in more-remote areas with fewer tourist attractions and amenities. The primary recreational activities in these forests and wildlife areas are fishing, shooting, hunting, and sometimes trapping. Although many may have campground hosts on duty, a significant number do not have showers and flush toilets. The Wisconsin DNR, for example, manages the Northern Highland–American Legion State Forest in the far north-central part of the state with four developed campgrounds and fourteen rustic campgrounds plus dozens of rustic hike-in and canoe-in campsites. The Michigan DNR lists 133 state forests in the Lower and Upper Peninsulas with a total of 2,658 rustic sites. The price of a campsite in these rustic campgrounds typically ranges from ten to twenty dollars per night.

National Park Service (NPS) campgrounds. The National Park Service is an agency within the US Department of the Interior that manages 59 national parks and 342 other properties, such as national seashores, national lakeshores, and national recreation areas. Many of these properties have campgrounds, but the amenities of these campgrounds vary considerably from one property to the other. Most national park campgrounds have good security, flush toilets, convenience stores, and naturalist programs but limited, if any, shower facilities, electrical outlets, and swimming pools. They also tend to be located in more-remote wilderness areas away from major highways and popular tourist attractions. On the other hand, many national seashores, lakeshores, and recreation areas have more amenities, including nice showers and electrical outlets, and tend to be located near popular tourist areas. The price of a campsite in these properties typically ranges from twenty to thirty dollars per night, but seniors over sixty-two can get these sites for half price. For retired couples, these NPS properties are excellent choices for extended base camps.

Identifying NPS campgrounds on state highway maps can be a little difficult. Although DOT highway maps may use green shading to identify the NPS property boundaries, they frequently do not identify individual campgrounds within the property. For example, the Tennessee DOT highway map shows the Big South Fork National

River and Recreation Area on the border of Tennessee and Kentucky but does not show individual campgrounds or provide information regarding their amenities. To get this information, families could search the web for campgrounds in that particular property, or they could get a copy of the *National Park Service Camping Guide.* This book explains that the Big South Fork National River and Recreation Area has three campgrounds: Brandy Creek (149 sites), Blue Heron (45 sites), and Alum Ford (6 primitive sites). This book also provides other important details such as driving directions, address, amenities, and activities.

National forest campgrounds. The US Forest Service (USFS) is an agency within the US Department of Agriculture (USDA) that manages 155 national forests and 20 national grasslands plus several national recreation areas. To find these national forest properties, campers can refer to state DOT highway maps or visit the *U.S. National Forest Campground Guide* (www.forestcamping.com/) which contains basic details about most national forest campgrounds. On highway maps, these properties are usually shown with green shading, but they typically cover a large area, and individual campgrounds may not be identified.

Located within each national forest are several developed campgrounds. These campgrounds vary considerably in terms of their amenities and price. A few very remote rustic campgrounds are free. Smaller rustic campgrounds with ten to forty spacious campsites and vault toilets cost about ten to twenty dollars per night. A few USFS campgrounds have fifty to two hundred developed campsites with electrical and water service, flush toilets, and even hot showers. These developed campgrounds typically cost over twenty dollars per night, and some of them are leased to private profit-driven concerns that may charge more. Older campers with a senior pass can still camp for half price.

Smaller national forest campgrounds typically have self-registration stations for walk-up campers and do not accept advance reservations. Furthermore, many of these small national forest campgrounds do not have full-time overnight security. Therefore, campers should call the local USFS district office and ask questions about safety and security before deciding to spend the night in these campgrounds.

US Army Corps of Engineers (COE) campgrounds. The US Army Corps of Engineers is a federal agency that manages many exceptionally nice public campgrounds. These COE properties are usually located on large rivers and reservoirs that offer a variety of water recreational activities. These campgrounds typically have entrance-control stations; beautifully maintained grounds; large, level campsites; and some of the nicest shower-and-bath facilities of any public campground. Their prices range from twenty to thirty dollars a day, but seniors with a pass can camp in them for half price.

Unfortunately, these campgrounds are difficult to find if one does not know how to identify them. They are rarely marked on state DOT highway maps and only have a few small, easily overlooked signs along major highways. Although most RV owners know about these campgrounds and often select them as their favorite destinations, few basic tent campers know of their existence. For example, I drove up and down I-57 through Illinois over thirty-five years and saw signs to Rend Lake but never realized until a few years ago that these campgrounds were some of the nicest public camping destinations in the state.

To find COE campgrounds, campers can search for them on the Internet or obtain the book *Camping with the Corps of Engineers*. It describes all the COE parks and campgrounds by state. Illinois, for example, has four COE properties with a total of twenty-seven campgrounds. Most of these campgrounds are beautiful, safe, comfortable, and developed campgrounds, but a few are small, primitive campgrounds with limited amenities.

Other federal-agency campgrounds. In a few states, campers will find more public campgrounds managed by other federal agencies. In Tennessee and Alabama, for example, the Tennessee Valley Authority (TVA) manages six nice campgrounds along the Tennessee River with a total of 355 campsites. In southern Illinois, the US Fish and Wildlife Service (USFWS) manages two nice campgrounds in the Crab Orchard

National Wildlife Refuge. One of these campgrounds has fifty-five campsites in a stand of pine trees with a nice sandy beach, while the other is a small campground specifically designed for basic tent camping. In addition, the refuge has two more campgrounds that are managed by other organizations. In several western states, the Bureau of Land Management (BLM) manages dozens of rustic campgrounds and remote campsites.

Campgrounds managed by other federal agencies are extremely difficult to identify because different federal agencies manage campgrounds in each state and these campgrounds are rarely noted on state highway maps or well advertised. Campers typically learn of their existence by word of mouth, and then once they know the name of a particular campground, they can find additional information about it on the web. But campers who do not first know specific campground names will have considerable difficulty identifying them. *Woodall's North American Campground Directory* identifies many of these campgrounds but is painfully difficult to use.

Some of these agencies and properties may accept reservations, but many do not. Neither the TVA nor Crab Orchard National Wildlife Refuge accepts reservations. Before planning a camping trip to one of these campgrounds, families should visit the property or agency website and perhaps call the district office to determine site-occupancy procedures, safety levels, and probable campsite availability.

County and municipal park campgrounds. A final group of public campgrounds that should be considered when planning summer camping trips are those located in county and municipal parks. Many of these campgrounds offer excellent places to camp near popular tourist attractions and relatives' homes. For example, Point Mallard Park managed by the city of Decatur, Alabama, has a large campground with nice shower buildings, a golf course, ice-skating rink, water park, recreation center, and baseball fields. Many of these county and municipal campgrounds offer Wi-Fi areas, TV rooms, and varied recreational activities. Wisconsin has over one hundred county and municipal parks with campgrounds, and some of these campgrounds have been named as among the best tent-camping destinations in the state. Iowa, with its long history of county conservation boards, has over 310 county parks, and many of these parks offer beautiful campgrounds with overnight security and nice shower facilities. The prices of campsites in these campgrounds range from twenty to thirty dollars depending upon amenities. Some campgrounds accept advance reservations, while others do not. When considering one as a possible camp, call ahead and ask about safety and amenities.

The best way to identify these county and municipal campgrounds varies from one state to another. In Wisconsin, they are listed on a page within the state DNR website. In Iowa, they are listed along with all other public and private campgrounds in the *Iowa Annual Travel Guide* published by Travel Iowa. For Wisconsin, Michigan, Illinois, and Indiana, they can be found, organized by geographic region, in my book *The Family Camping Guide to Wisconsin, Michigan, Illinois & Indiana*. In other states, they are included in *Woodall's North American Campground Directory*, but, as previously stated, finding them in this directory is painfully difficult.

Unfortunately, a significant number of small county and municipal parks across the country do not have adequate overnight security and have experienced occasional problems with drunkenness, loud music, and inappropriate behavior. Before deciding to spend the night in one, campers should visit the park's website, view photos of buildings and other amenities, read descriptions and reviews, and perhaps call the park office to ask questions about safety.

Destinations and Routes

For each trip, campers must decide upon the route they will drive to the destination, the route they will drive back home, the places they want to visit along the way, and the number of overnight camps they must make along the way. To begin this planning process, campers should obtain highway maps for the states through which they will pass and visit MapQuest.com or similar website to determine possible routes, distances, and driving times. For both safety and enjoyment, campers should plan to drive no more than three hundred to four hundred miles a day and never exceed five hundred miles. For example, Eva's and my July camping destination, Door County, Wisconsin, is about nine hundred miles from our home. Accordingly, we must plan at least one overnight camp up to our destination and one overnight camp on the way back home.

To identify possible day and overnight stops, campers can search the Internet and books such as *1,000 Places to See Before You Die* to learn about popular tourist attractions along their routes. Each state has dozens of interesting museums, geological features, ethnic villages, festivals, theme parks, historical sites, hiking trails, fishing spots, canoeing rivers, bike trails, scenic vistas, and restaurants that offer interesting stops for every family regardless of their particular interests. State tourism brochures offer a good starting point for finding interesting attractions, but these brochures are poorly organized to fit typical vacation plans and travel routes. Tourist attractions and overnight accommodations are organized around clusters of counties rather than along major highway routes.

Campsite Reservations

The last step in planning a future camping trip to a particular destination is to determine the best way to secure a campsite for the dates of the planned vacation. Campers must determine how to secure campsites before departing from their homes to assure that sites will be available after driving 100 to 400 miles. Larger parks and campgrounds typically accept reservations, and campers should make these reservations as soon as possible to ensure a good selection of available campsites.

To reserve campsites in most state DNR properties, campers must go to www.reserveamerica.com, select a state, select a property, and enter relevant details about the day of arrival and length of stay. First-time users will have to register before making their reservations. Once they enter the site, campers can find campground maps showing available sites and links to each site. Clicking on a particular site link will open a description of the site and frequently show one or more photos of the site. Users can use the campground map, site descriptions, and site photos to select the best-available sites. Once users have selected their sites, they must enter payment information and get confirmation numbers. Some states, such as Michigan, use their own reservation system rather than the ReserveAmerica system. Families that want to camp in these states must go to the state DNR website to make their reservations.

To reserve campsites in most federal campgrounds, campers must go to www.recreation.gov and enter the relevant details about the trip. Like ReserveAmerica, Recreation.gov requires first-time users to register before making reservations.

To reserve campsites in county and municipal parks, campers should go to the park's web page, find the telephone number, call the park office, and ask about reservation policies. Some county and municipal parks accept reservations, while others do not. After selecting the destination and making the reservations, campers can relax until a couple of weeks before the day of departure.

When planning trips to smaller campgrounds, plan to arrive as early in the week as possible, when few campers are likely to be there. Sunday through Thursday arrivals will almost always find a good selection of available sites, but Friday, Saturday, and holiday arrivals may have very few, if any, choices.

Companions

As Holding (1908) observed many years ago, taking a good chum on a camping trip can make the trip more enjoyable. Having a camp companion facilitates social conversation and provides extra hands to share routine chores such as cooking, cleaning, and breaking camp. Unfortunately, many nice people (including friends and family members) do not make good camping companions. Some are unwilling to do their fair share of the work, while others try to take control of the trip and make important decisions. In either case, a well-planned trip can quickly turn into an unpleasant experience. A one- or two-week trip with a poorly chosen companion can turn into a seemingly endless nightmare. To avoid as much misery as possible, campers should select their companions with care and initially plan short one- or two-night trips to nearby destinations to evaluate compatibility and define the division of labor. After a few trips, they can try a longer trip or two until they are convinced that they have found good companions.

I was very fortunate when I met my wife Eva. As a child, she spent many years living in rural Mexico and acquired many outdoor-living skills. She has considerable experience cooking meals on an open fire, washing clothes on a rock in the river, fishing for dinner, and more. When we took our first camping trips together, we seemed to be perfectly compatible. Now we are taking our grandchildren on progressively longer camping trips and watching them explore new tourist attractions and learn practical camping skills.

Whenever possible, adults should take children and grandchildren on camping trips. Although children typically require extra work and limit mobility, they can greatly benefit from getting away from home and friends, closely associating with family members, learning about the environment, and visiting novel attractions. When taking children on a camping trip, parents should always keep it simple. Plan short trips; plan simple meals, such as oatmeal, sandwiches, and hot dogs; and plan simple activities, such as swimming or riding bikes in the park.

Activities

After determining the destination, reserving a campsite, and identifying the travel route, basic tent campers should begin to plan daily activities for the trip. State tourism brochures and the Internet provide a good starting point for exploring these possible activities. For example, people who plan camping vacations in the Shawnee National Forest in southern Illinois may want to search for livery stables located near the forest. People who plan to spend a week camping in Muskegon State Park in Michigan may want to investigate fishing charters and guide services in the area. Others who want to ride bikes or paddle canoes may want to search for liveries near their destination. Families who plan to visit festivals, amusement parks, museums, and other attractions should check the web to determine hours of operation, costs, schedules, and other details. Whatever the particular interest, families may occasionally have to make advance reservations to ensure that they will be able to enjoy their planned activities during their vacation time.

Resource Materials

When planning future camping trips during the winter months, families may want to obtain a few resource materials that will help them identify some of the best public campgrounds in each state they plan to visit and nearby activities. The following resource materials are useful for most trips:

- State department of transportation (DOT) maps.
- State department of tourism brochures—These brochures are available by request and in most highway rest areas.
- *Woodall's North American Campground Directory*—This is an oversize paperback book with over 1,650 tissue-thin pages. It provides basic information about most campgrounds in each state but is painfully difficult to use.
- The Best in Tent Camping series—Menasha Ridge Press has published a series of small books that describe fifty small campgrounds in selected states. It includes books for Tennessee, Georgia, Kentucky, North Carolina, Illinois, Wisconsin, Michigan, and several other states.
- State park guidebooks—Several publishers have published guides to selected states. While some of these guides are over ten years old, they provide useful information about state park campgrounds and amenities.
- National Geographic books—In 2010, National Geographic revised their *Guide to National Parks of the United States* and *Guide to State Parks of the United States*. These books provide considerable detail about some of the most scenic and historically significant state and federal parks in each state. They typically select four to six parks in each state and describe many excellent

basic-tent-camping destinations. But they omit many other popular camping destinations.

- *Camping with the U.S. Army Corps of Engineers*—This book lists all Corps of Engineers properties and campgrounds in each state.
- *National Park Service Camping Guide*—This book lists and briefly describes camping areas managed by the National Park Service in every state.
- *The Family Camping Guide to Wisconsin, Michigan, Illinois & Indiana*—This book provides basic details about over eight hundred public state, federal, county, and municipal campgrounds in the four Lake Michigan states. For more information, please visit www.BasicTentCamping.com.

Site #A-6 in the Elkmont Campground (Great Smoky Mountains National Park) is an excellent campsite. Like many others in the park, it has an elevated tent pad that prevents flooding during heavy rain.

Site #46 in the Tippecanoe River State Park in Indiana is exceptionally large, level, and shady.

Site #27 in the Union Bay Campground in Porcupine Mountains
State Wilderness Park in Michigan is one of eight sites that
are directly on Lake Superior. Although it is too rocky to
swim here, a nice beach is located a few miles away.

Like many sites in South Higgins Lake State Park in Michigan,
site #323 is large and level but provides no privacy.

11

PACKING

About two weeks before a trip, basic tent campers should begin organizing their equipment and clothing. When packing, campers should consider their destination, planned activities, length of trip, probable weather, and vehicle storage capacity. Trips to Florida Gulf Coast beaches in hot weather, for example, require less clothing and, thus, can accommodate more personal items such as beach shelters and toys. After considering relevant factors, campers should begin packing early so that they have time to remember everything they want to take, purchase needed items, and organize these items so that they can be packed in the available space. A packing guide, such as the one at the end of this book, can be helpful.

Over the past forty-five years, I have packed my camping gear in many different bags, boxes, and other containers. In the 1980s, I made two wooden cube-shaped boxes to pack clothing and personal items and then used these boxes as stools in the campsite. I also made a small wooden cabinet with hinged doors to pack all my kitchen gear and nonperishable foods. But after a few trips, I wearied of lugging these heavy boxes around. In the 1990s, I packed my clothing and personal items in soft-sided and hard-sided coolers and then used the coolers to store perishable foods purchased after setting up my base camp. In the 2000s, I used a variety of plastic tubs and cargo boxes, but most of these containers had curved sides and wide tops that required more packing space than I expected. After using each one and becoming dissatisfied,

I bought another smaller or larger size only to become dissatisfied with it too.

In 2010, I began organizing our camping equipment and clothing into duffel bags and milk crates. After setting up camp, Eva and I use the smaller duffel bags as pillows and the milk crates as kitchen-storage shelving. This system allows us to pack a considerable amount of equipment into a small space and provides essential comforts after setting up camp. We'll probably stick with it for a long time to come.

Shelter

About two weeks before departure, Eva and I decide which particular tent we want to pack for the upcoming trip and pull it out of its storage tub. Our favorite tents are the Eureka Timberline 4 and the REI Camp Dome 4 because both tents are easy to set up and take down and are well ventilated. We prefer these particular tents because neither has a full-coverage rain fly or vestibule that accumulates more condensation and requires extra packing space, extra setup space, extra setup time, extra effort to enter and exit, and extra take-down time. For motorcycle trips, we select the Mountain Hardwear Lightwedge 3. We also use this tent to accommodate our older grand children when they join us. If the weather will be windy and stormy, we pack our Marmot Den 4 with a full-coverage rain fly. And when one of my sons or Eva's son joins us with his family, we may also pack our Eureka Headquarters 8 for them. Regardless of the tent selected, we loosely fold each piece and pack the pieces into a lightweight duffel bag with the ground sheet on top so it is ready to spread out when we arrive at our campsite.

After packing our tents, we pack our kitchen-canopy tarps along with their guy lines and support poles plus our tablecloth and extension cord in another duffel bag. Once all our shelter items have been packed, we place the duffel bags in the garage near the door so that they are ready to load into our vehicle when the time comes to pack up the car.

Tools

After packing our shelter, we open our tool bag and inspect all our tools. We first check the sharpness of our knives and hatchet. If they need sharpening, we sharpen them at home where we have time and equipment to do it right. We examine our ropes for signs of rot and other tools for signs of rust. We also count our tent and tarp stakes to be sure we have at least ten for each tent and ten for the kitchen canopy. When necessary, we replace tools that are no longer serviceable. Once all tools have been inspected, we repack them into their small tool bag. Once packed, we place our tool bag with our shelter near the garage door so that it is ready to be packed in our vehicle when the time comes to load up.

Furniture

After packing our shelter and tools, we turn our attention to our furniture. For motorcycle trips, we just take a plastic tablecloth and a tie-down cord and pack these items in the same duffel bag with our shelter. But for most car-camping trips we add two folding armless quad chairs, two hammocks (each packed in a small nylon stuff sack along with its straps or ropes), two bath mats for picnic-table benches, and a fifteen-foot extension cord. For short trips, we may pack only one small folding table but for extended base camps, we also tie a five-foot tabletop on our rooftop carrier and pack two adjustable-height sawhorses in the vehicle.

Most of these furniture items can be packed into an XL heavy-duty military-style duffel bag or Kelty Basecamp Duffel Bag. In the past, we used an ultralight Outdoor Products Basic Duffel that folded into a small space when empty, but its lightweight material was easily torn by accidental mishandling. Once packed, we place our furniture duffel bag with our shelter and tool bags near the garage door so that it is ready to be packed into our vehicle when the time comes to load up.

Protection and First Aid

About ten days before departure, we examine our first aid kit, which is packed in a small red Cordura bag that always remains in our car. Eagle Creek's Quarter Cube bags are ideal for small first aid kits. Economy-minded campers could use a one-quart food-storage bag. We examine the contents of the kit to be sure it has sufficient bandages and medicine for the trip. If the kit does not have enough ibuprofen or antiseptic ointment, for example, we replace partly filled containers with full containers. Then we pack sunscreen, insect repellent, hand sanitizer, and lip balm in storage compartments or under a seat so that we can easily access all these items at any time while traveling or camping.

Kitchen

When packing the kitchen gear, we must consider the amount of available packing space and the length of the trip and then decide how many kitchen items to pack. When traveling by motorcycle, we only have space to pack the essentials plus perhaps a small pot for boiling water, but when traveling by car, we can pack many more optional items—depending upon our meal plans. On most car-camping trips, we pack a full kitchen in three milk crates so that we are able to prepare almost any meal we may want. We stack four large dinner plates, a ten-inch frying pan, a four-quart pot, four small salad plates, our Bugaboo cook set, a plastic Tupperware bowl, four plastic salad bowls, and assorted lids together into one milk crate along with two dishrags, four dish towels, and several plastic garbage bags stuffed into the corners. Next we pack our fuel cylinders, cups, utensil containers, paper towels, dishwashing detergent, butane lighters, can opener, and folding knife into a second milk crate. Our utensils are organized into two Duluth Pack canvas water-bottle pouches but my sister uses empty coffee cans. In addition, we usually fill two water jugs at home because our city water tastes better than potable water available in some campgrounds and pack these bottles in a third milk crate along with a bottle of charcoal lighter fluid and some canned goods.

Clothing

About a week before departing, we begin selecting and packing our clothing. We need to consider available packing space, the length of the trip, probable weather, and planned recreational activities. For motorcycle trips, for example, we can only pack essential garments and must plan to wash them often. For car-camping trips we can take more optional garments. For some trips we will need extra shorts and bathing suits, while for other trips we will need long underwear and insulated jackets. Most of the time, we only select garments made from polyester, nylon, or wool because these garments are warm, compressible, moisture wicking, and fast drying. We know we can pack these garments into a small space and expect to find them unwrinkled several days later. These garments can be washed often and dried quickly and will keep us warm even when still damp. For hot-weather trips, we may pack a few light-colored cotton shirts because these shirts are cooler than polyester shirts. Regardless of predicted weather, we always pack wool socks and nylon or polyester underwear. Four additional clothing-related items we pack are a dirty clothes bag, a small travel-size bottle of Woolite or some other liquid detergent, raincoats, and hats. When we first start selecting our garments and shoes, Eva and I lay all of our selected garments out on a bed so that we can view and critique and revise our selection. After inspection, we may add one or two forgotten items or cut back one or two.

Once all our garments have been assembled, we set aside the clothing we plan to wear on the first day of our trip, pack a T-shirt and pair of shorts into our shower bag, and pack the rest of our clothing into small soft duffel bags and/or backpacks. When we arrive at our campsite and set up our sleeping quarters, we cover these bags with pillowcases and use them as pillows. Currently, I pack my clothing into a small Outdoor Products Basic Duffel and a REI Flash 18 day pack. Both these bags make great pillows when partly filled with clothing and covered with nice pillowcases. Eva prefers to pack her clothes in a larger duffel bag and rolls a small fleece travel blanket for her pillow. Once these bags have been packed, we place them in one corner of our bedroom at home so that we can add any items that we may have initially forgotten.

Personal Items

As soon as we finish packing our clothing, we begin assembling our personal items. When traveling by motorcycle, we are only able to take a few personal items, but when traveling by car, we typically pack many more. In general, we divide these items into those that will be brought into the tent and those that will stay outside. Personal items that will come into the tent are packed in a small backpack that can be used as another pillow if needed.

Perhaps the most important item brought into the tent is our prescription medicine. When packing, we must determine whether or not we have sufficient prescription medicine for the entire trip. Both Eva and I take medicine to lower cholesterol, and I need medicine to control high blood pressure. Other campers may need medicine for diabetes or some other medical condition. From painful experience, we have learned that obtaining this prescription medicine from a new pharmacy along our travel route is much more difficult than obtaining it from our local pharmacy. Other personal items that will be brought into the tent include our bath supplies, grooming kits, portable music players, books, games, and headlamps.

Some personal items that will stay in the car or outside the tent include bicycles, beach toys, and balls. After assembling these personal items, we place them near the garage door so that they are ready when the time comes to load up the vehicle.

Nonperishable Foods

About a week before departure, we begin thinking about the meals we intend to prepare in our campsite and then begin to pack the nonperishable food items. On motorcycle trips or short beach trips, we only pack a few simple breakfast foods, such as hot chocolate packs, oatmeal packs, and instant grits packs. After arriving at the campsite, we can purchase cold cereal, sweet pastries, bagels, and fresh fruit, such as bananas, blueberries, and strawberries, to supplement our breakfast menu. When traveling in a car, we pack several more nonperishable food items so that we will have a variety of meal choices every day. We repackage many of these items into smaller containers to save packing space. We typically pack these nonperishable food items:

- salt, pepper, and garlic salt repackaged into small dispensers
- pepper sauce
- honey in a small plastic container
- hot chocolate, coffee, or tea packs
- tortillas
- instant oatmeal packs
- instant grits packs
- pancake mix repackaged into a one-quart food-storage bag
- bread or buns packed in a plastic bread container
- cookies, chips, and snacks repackaged into one-gallon food-storage bags
- corn oil repackaged into a ten-ounce plastic juice bottle
- canned beans and other vegetables
- canned tuna or chicken breast
- dried rice or pasta meals, such as Rice-A-Roni, Zatarain's, and Knorr Pasta Sides
- McCormick food mixes divided in half for two people and packed in snack-size food-storage bags
- Hamburger Helper mixes divided in half for two people and packed in snack-size food-storage bags

Bedding

A few days before departure, we pack our bedding. First, we stuff our sleeping bags into a pillowcase-size stuff sack. Then we roll secure each mattress with a two-foot length of cord and pack these mattresses along with our ground blanket, sheet, and pillowcases into a large duffel bag. When traveling with our lightweight summer sleeping bags, we can also squeeze our two bags into this duffel. Presently, we are using a thirty-inch Outdoor Products Basic Duffel. We like this particular bag because it folds into a very small package when empty and can be easily stored in one of our tent storage pockets. In cold weather, we may not be able to squeeze our sleeping bags into the large duffel bag and, thus, may have two bags with our bedding. When traveling by motorcycle, we pack our mattresses and sleeping bags into our shelter duffel. Once packed, we place our bedding duffel bag in the corner of our room near our clothing so that it is ready to carry to the vehicle when the time comes to load up.

Perishable Foods

Two or three days before departure, we begin to assemble and repackage the perishable foods we plan to take on our trip and place these items together in our refrigerator. We need to repackage many items because the large packages sold in stores require much more space than we have available in our cooler. When repackaging, we use plastic, rather than glass, containers for safety reasons. A broken glass food container in an ice cooler can be especially hazardous. We frequently pack these perishable foods:

- milk and juice repackaged into Ocean Spray juice jugs
- butter (one and a half sticks) repackaged into a plastic soap dish
- eggs (six) packed in a plastic egg holder with handle removed
- pancake syrup and Italian salad dressing repackaged into ten-ounce plastic juice bottles
- mayonnaise, jelly, pickles, and pickled jalapeño peppers repackaged into four-ounce Lexan jars
- small containers of mustard and ketchup
- fresh-cut vegetables such as carrots, radishes, celery, cucumber, and broccoli packed in one-quart food-storage bags
- cream cheese in an eight-ounce tub
- sliced American cheese packed into a plastic sandwich container
- bacon cut in half and packaged in a one-quart food-storage bag

- steaks, pork chops, bratwurst, and ground beef packed in one-quart food storage bags

After packing each individual item, we pack all the meat and egg containers into one four-quart plastic food-storage container, and all the pickles, jelly, mayonnaise, and cheeses into a second four-quart container. After packing them, we place them in our refrigerator until the day before our departure. The reason for packing these small items in larger plastic containers is to keep them from getting soaked by melted ice water after they have been placed in the cooler.

On the day before departure, we transfer these plastic containers to our cooler along with our milk, juice, ketchup, mustard, pancake syrup, salad dressing, and fresh vegetables plus plenty of ice. This packing system will allow us to easily drain water from the cooler each day without having to remove several small food packages. For some trips, we may also pack a second smaller travel cooler with cans of pop and juice to drink during our highway travel and for later daytime excursions.

In addition to the above-named items, we typically pack whatever fresh vegetables and fruit that may be in our home kitchen. We frequently pack these fresh food items:

- onions
- potatoes
- bell peppers
- jalapeño peppers
- tomatoes
- bananas
- apples

We pack each type of vegetable or fruit in a separate mesh bag saved from previous grocery store purchases and then pack these mesh bags into a bucket or reusable shopping bag.

Final Details

During the week before departure, we attend to a few more details:

- Get vehicle serviced and checked by a mechanic.
- Pack extra keys in case the primary key gets lost or locked inside the vehicle.
- Check driver's licenses to be sure they have not expired.
- Be sure current insurance and registration documents are inside the vehicle.
- Obtain cash, debit cards, and credit cards needed for the trip. Be prepared to spend more than budgeted.
- Copy itinerary and give to family members or friends in case of emergency.
- Fill vehicle with gas.

In addition to the above tasks, campers should consider purchasing emergency highway service such as offered by AAA.

On the day before departure, we begin loading all of our camping equipment into our car. We pack our clothing and kitchen equipment first and then pack our shelter, bedding, tools, furniture, non-perishable foods, and perishable foods last so that they are easily accessible when we stop. The next morning, we awake about 4:00 a.m., dress, eat a light snack, and get on the road before 5:00 a.m.

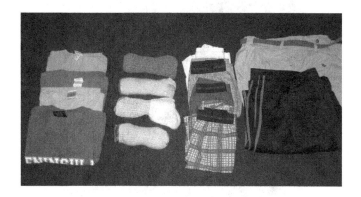

We lay all needed garments on a bed about a week before our departure date. We use the packing guide at the end of this book to be sure we don't forget anything.

Once all clothing and personal items have been secured, we pack them in small duffel bags and day packs that can be used as pillows after our sleeping quarters have been set up.

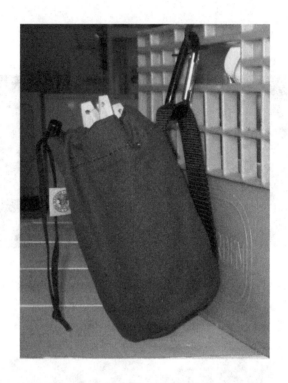

We organize our eating utensils into this canvas
water-bottle bag sold by Duluth Pack.

We pack a variety of food staples from our home cabinets
and plan to buy more food after setting up camp.

We load our equipment, clothing, and food into the car one day before our departure so that we can get an early start the next morning.

Our car has been packed, and we are ready to go.

12

TRAVEL-DAY ROUTINE

Every camping trip involves at least two travel days—one driving to the ultimate destination and a second day driving back home. Trips to more-distant destinations may involve more travel days. For example, when Eva and I travel to Wisconsin and Michigan every summer from our home in Alabama, we spend at least two days traveling up to our ultimate destination and two more on the way back home. Over the past few years, we have spent more time traveling to and from our destinations so that we can visit more campgrounds and attractions along the way. Each travel day is organized around four basic objectives: breaking camp in one location, driving to the next destination, setting up camp, and exploring amenities and attractions at the new location. Each of these four basic objectives includes several specific tasks, such as setting the GPS receiver, eating meals, visiting parks and tourist attractions, exploring the new place, preparing for bed, and sleeping well. The amount of time spent for each task will vary each day due to specific circumstances. For example, on some travel days Eva and I may only drive a short distance to the next destination so that we have more time to spend at a particular tourist attraction along the way or at the ultimate destination. On other travel days, we may not visit any tourist attractions so that we can drive longer distances. On the last travel day, campers will arrive home late in the afternoon and must unpack their gear rather than set up another campsite. Further details about these routine basic activities are discussed in this chapter. Specific camping skills and strategies will be discussed in the next five chapters.

Break Camp

Each travel day, campers should try to rise as early as possible so that they can get to their day's destination early in the afternoon and still have time to register, set up camp, enjoy local activities, eat supper, and bathe before ten o'clock in the evening. On the first day of a trip, campers can get on the road very early. Since their vehicle was packed the night before and they do not have to break camp, they can rise about four in the morning, eat a light snack, attend to a few last-minute packing details, and pull out of the driveway before five o'clock. Passengers in the car can continue to sleep for a few more hours.

On subsequent travel days, campers should observe campground quiet hours and enjoy sleeping until about six thirty in the morning. When they awake, they should first organize their clothing and personal items, visit the bathroom, eat a light snack, strike the tent, and pack the car in about an hour. If it rained the previous night, these activities may take a little longer as campers dry the equipment as much as possible before packing.

Organize clothing and personal items. The first thing to do after waking in the morning is to repack clothing and personal items into their respective ditty and duffel bags. When organizing these items, campers should specifically make a point to pack their shower bags so they will be ready for the coming night. Each camper should pack a clean T-shirt and pair of shorts in the shower bag along with a headlamp, grooming kit, soap, washrag, towel, and shower shoes. Packing the shower bags early in the morning, before exiting the tent, makes it easy to find needed items and organize them so that they will be ready for the evening visit to the showers. At the end of the day, campers can easily grab the bags, even in the dark, without having to rummage through several hastily packed stuff sacks to find individual items.

After packing shower bags, campers should reorganize and pack their clean clothes into one or more duffel bags, personal items into another bag, and dirty clothes into a dirty-clothes bag. Once everything has been packed, place these bags outside the tent so they are ready to be carried to the car or the motorcycle in a few minutes.

Pack sleeping bags. Next, campers should turn their sleeping bags inside out to air and stuff them into storage bags. When traveling in a large vehicle with ample space, it is not necessary to compress sleeping bags. Unnecessary repeated severe compressions will gradually damage synthetic fibers and, consequently, diminish the bag's ability to keep users warm on cool nights. Just loosely stuff each bag into a large pillowcase-size ditty bag. When traveling on a motorcycle or in a small car, campers will have to compress their sleeping bags into smaller stuff sacks so that they can be squeezed into a small space. After packing the sleeping bags, put them into the bedding duffel bag.

Roll mattresses. After packing the sleeping bags, campers must pack their mattresses. When traveling in a larger vehicle, campers may be able to lay these mattresses flat on top of their camping gear. If not, loosely roll them and secure them with two-foot lengths of cord. When traveling by small car or motorcycle, it is necessary to squeeze as much air as possible out of them to reduce their packing space. After securing the mattresses with small cords, pack them in the bedding duffel bag along with the sleeping bags.

Fold sheet, ground blanket, and pillowcases. After rolling mattresses, one person should finish dressing and exit the tent so that he or she can begin carrying clothing and personal items to the car. The other camper should stay in the tent and attend to the remaining chores, such as folding the sheet, ground blanket, and pillowcases and packing these items into the bedding duffel bag. This person should then place the bedding duffel bag outside the tent for the other camper to carry to the car. Before exiting the tent, this person should also sweep dirt and trash out of the tent.

Relax, eat a snack, and visit the bathroom. Once all clothing, personal items, and bedding have been packed, campers can relax for a few minutes and eat a light snack to stave off hunger until they can stop for breakfast. Snacks typically include breakfast bars, doughnuts, fresh fruit, and juice. If necessary everyone can leisurely walk together to the bathroom and enjoy the fresh morning air.

Strike, dry, and fold tent. Once everything has been removed from the tent, campers must begin to strike, dry, and fold it. First, wipe surface moisture away with a microfiber towel, remove ground stakes, and remove and fold poles. If it rained, plastic buckles or tent-pole tips near the ground may be clogged with sand and difficult to disassemble. In this situation, simply pour a little water over the joint to wash the sand away. Once disassembled, hang the tent, rain fly, and ground cloth on a line to dry while attending to other packing chores. After the tent has dried five to ten minutes, loosely fold each part (canopy, rain fly, and ground cloth) and place all three parts in their duffel bag. This bag should be the last thing to pack so that the tent can continue to dry during travel and is readily accessible after arriving at the next destination. When traveling by motorcycle, campers must tightly fold and roll the tent so that it can be crammed into the smallest possible packing space.

When folding long dome tent poles, most camping books and a few tent makers recommend that campers initially separate poles in the middle and then fold sections from each half together to preserve the life of the shock cord. Presumably, this procedure lengthens the shock-cord life by placing equal stress on each end rather than excessive stress on the last folded end. My personal experience does not support this argument. Since buying my first dome tent about twenty-five years ago, I have always folded poles from one end to the other and have never noticed a problem. After some camps I started with one end, and after other camps I started with the other end. At first, I intended to fold my poles according to the recommended procedure but forgot in the haste of breaking camp. Upon remembering the recommended procedure, I vowed to follow the correct procedure the next time—only to forget it again in my haste to get on the road. Now, as I reflect back and think about the many years that my tent poles have lasted, I'm not convinced that the recommended procedure adds significant life to the shock cords. The shock cords in my old REI Family Dome 4 were almost as strong when I sold it after eleven years as they were when they were new. The shock cords in most other dome tents I have owned have remained strong for dozens of camping trips over five or more years. In fact, the only stretched shock cords I have seen were in an economy tent owned by family member, and this tent was only a year old. I've concluded that the shock cords stretched because the tent maker used an inferior-grade shock cord rather than because the poles were folded incorrectly.

Strike, dry, and fold kitchen shelter. If a kitchen shelter was set up, campers must take it down and pack it along with their tents. The first step to taking down a kitchen tarp is to remove and pack the poles. Then use pliers to pull guy-line stakes, fold guy lines, and pack guy lines and stakes in the tool bag. Wipe away surface moisture from the tarp, and then loosely fold it and place it in its duffel bag. This bag, along with the tent duffel bag, will be the last things to pack in the car.

Pack furniture, kitchen equipment, and tools. While the tent and kitchen tarp are drying, campers can fold and pack their chairs and place them into their duffel bag. Then disassemble the table and pack it in the car. Kitchen items must be packed into their respective milk crates and then packed into the car along with nonperishable foods and the cooler. Finally, inspect camp tools, pack them into the tool bag, and then pack the bag in the car. Once all clothing and equipment has been packed in the car, place the tent and kitchen shelter duffel bags on top of the equipment so that they can be easily accessed when you arrive at the next campsite.

Clean campsite. Before leaving the campsite, ethical campers should systematically walk around the site looking for items such as tent and tarp stakes, guy lines, or tools that may have been inadvertently left on the ground. Make a point to look under the picnic table and around the fire ring. Also check nearby trees to be sure all ropes have been removed. After you are certain all equipment has been packed, walk around the campsite one more time to pick up any trash that you or previous campers may have dropped on the ground. Also inspect the fire ring to be sure that the fire has been extinguished, trash has been removed, and the fire ring is ready for the next campsite occupant.

Travel to New Destination

Each travel day, campers will typically drive about 100 to 450 miles and make two to six stops along the way. A good time to make the first stop is after an hour on the road. During this first stop, campers can fill the car with gas, visit the bathroom, eat breakfast or snacks, buy ice, and repack the cooler. During subsequent stops they may visit museums and other tourist attractions, eat lunch, and tour public campgrounds along the route. By midafternoon, travelers should start looking forward to arriving at their day's destination, setting up their camp, and exploring recreational opportunities in or near the park.

Set GPS or smartphone. Before departing from a campsite, campers may want to look at the highway map to determine the approximate route to the final day's destination and the places they want to visit along the way. Then set the GPS receiver or smartphone for the first stop. Ideally, GPS coordinates have been determined for each planned stop in decimal degrees that can be easily entered into the receiver. When these coordinates are unavailable, campers can program a street address or search for an attraction's name. Once the receiver has been set, it will give turn-by-turn directions to each planned destination—but when following these directions, campers must also keep the highway map handy because sometimes receivers give incorrect directions or the operator may have entered the wrong numbers. For example, one day our GPS receiver led us to a point just a few hundred feet south of the Indiana campground entrance we planned to visit. Unfortunately, the point was on the opposite side of the Ohio River, and no bridge was located nearby to cross the river. Moreover, campers must be alert to the fact that GPS receivers occasionally take bad routes.

Learning how to use a GPS receiver can take a little time because GPS coordinates are still given in four different formats and users must learn how to reset their receiver to the specific format matching a given set of coordinates and/or convert coordinates from one format to another. These formats are UTM coordinates; degrees, minutes, seconds (DMS); degrees and decimal minutes (DM), and decimal degrees. Different camping and tourism books, articles, and websites use different formats, so GPS users must become familiar with all four formats. For example, *The Best in Tent Camping: Illinois* gives both UTM coordinates and DMS information, while *Camping with the Corps of Engineers* only gives decimal-degrees information.

Over the past five years, the decimal-degrees format seems to be evolving as the preferred format. It is certainly the easiest to understand and use. Any destination will have a number for the latitude (distance north of the equator) and a second number for the longitude (distance west of the prime meridian). For all destinations in the United States, the longitude will be a negative number, but frequently this negative sign is omitted. For example, the coordinates for the entrance to the Kentucky Dam Village State Resort Park campground are 37.01304 latitude and -88.28154 (or just 88.28154) longitude. Once these coordinates have been obtained, they can be entered into a GPS receiver and the receiver will provide turn-by-turn directions to that location.

Visit tourist attractions. It is always nice to break up a long trip by visiting local tourist attractions. For example, while driving from Alabama to Wisconsin and back home over the past thirty-five years, we have visited dozens of tourist attractions along the way. Some memorable stops include Mammoth Cave National Park, Tippecanoe Battlefield, various Lincoln sites, Chicago's Art Institute, Wrigley Field, Pictured Rocks National Lakeshore, Tahquamenon Falls, Mackinac Island, and Mounds State Park.

Eat meals. Since traveling will usually require several hours, campers will usually have to stop for breakfast and/or lunch. Campers can stop at restaurants or can save money by stopping at a highway rest area and eating sandwiches or snacks from their cooler.

Visit public campgrounds. When traveling to distant locations, Eva and I frequently visit at least one new campground along the way so that we can determine whether or not it is suitable as a future overnight camp. When visiting a new campground, campers must first stop at the park office or entrance-control station and ask permission to drive through the campground. Some campgrounds will not allow visitors to drive through the campground but will allow them to walk through it. Indiana and other states require visitors to pay an admission fee, making it rather expensive to visit two or three different parks on a trip. While getting permission to drive through the park, campers should request maps and information about local attractions, activities, and restaurants. After entering the park, drive through each family campground, and visit the swimming area, visitor center, and other recreational areas. Also visit the bathrooms, take pictures, and make notes that will help you decide whether or not you may want to camp in this park on a future trip.

Set Up Camp

When campers arrive at a new campground destination, they must register at the office or registration station before setting up their campsite. Most of the time, campers should have reserved a specific site before arriving at the campground. In these cases, registration merely involves (1) informing park staff that you have arrived; (2) providing personal information such as type of camping unit (tent), names of people on the site, and vehicle make, model, and license plate number; (3) receiving an orientation to the park and its rules; and (4) signing a form indicating that you will abide by park rules and regulations. In Michigan, registration can be accomplished without exiting the car. Campers who arrive after the office has been closed should look for an envelope with their name or instructions regarding how to secure their site after hours. Sometimes campers will be instructed to visit the campground host site. If campers decide that their reserved site is not as nice as expected, they may be able to pick out one or two alternate sites, return to the park office, and request a site reassignment. Most parks will honor these requests as long as the sites have not been reserved by other campers.

When campers do not have reservations, staff in most parks will usually explain how to identify available sites and then allow campers to drive through the campground to pick their first three or four choices. After identifying their choices, campers must return to the office and complete the registration process before setting any equipment on the site. If a previous arrival claims an empty site while you are still riding through the campground, you have to settle for your second or third campsite choice. Unfortunately, a few parks, such as Rock Cut State Park in Illinois, no longer accept walk-up campers without reservations. To avoid unnecessary delays, call the park office before arriving without reservations.

Some campgrounds, particularly in national forests and county parks, do not accept advance reservations and have unmanned registration stations. In these campgrounds, campers should stop at the registration station and follow instructions for securing a campsite. In many cases, campers will be instructed to ride through the campground, find an unoccupied site, set up a tent, and return to the registration station to complete the registration process. In some campgrounds, such as Deep Creek campground in Great Smoky Mountains National Park, the registration station has a machine that will process the registration information and accept credit or debit cards. Some small campgrounds only accept cash so have it available just in case.

Plan campsite layout. After registering, campers should drive to their assigned campsite and then take a few minutes to decide how to set up their camp. Every campsite presents specific conditions that should be considered before deciding where to set up a tent and kitchen canopy. The first task is to determine the best place to set up the tent. If it is a drive-in site, park the vehicle as close to the road as possible so that you can evaluate all possible setup possibilities. If the campsite has an elevated crushed-stone or sand tent pad, the task of deciding where to set up the tent has been settled. The remaining tasks are to decide where to position the tent door and where to set up the kitchen canopy. If the campsite does not have an elevated tent pad, campers must evaluate the lay of the ground and identify the best place to set up the tent. In general, the tent should be set up on the highest level spot in the campsite so that it will not flood if heavy rain occurs. Furthermore, the tent should be set up several feet away from the fire ring so that hot embers will not drift over and burn holes in the tent material.

If the campsite has a dirt, grass, or sand surface with a little slope, plan to set up the tent and kitchen canopy near the high edge. Beware of campsites that have a large packed-down or dark spot in the center because previous campers may have repeatedly pitched their tent on that spot and packed the ground down, making it a small bowl that will hold rainwater. Also beware of small valleys in the campsite that might drain rainwater from adjacent areas. Finally, beware of campsites that have elevated paved or gravel parking pads built to support heavy vehicles and RVs because the remaining areas of these sites may be low dirt or grassy areas that could easily flood after moderate rainfall. In these later campsites, you may have to set up the tent on the paved or gravel parking pad.

After identifying the best place to set up the tent, the next task is to decide whether or not to set up the kitchen canopy. In short overnight base camps, Eva and I typically do not set up a kitchen canopy unless afternoon or early-evening rain is predicted. If we plan to stay in this campsite for several nights, we almost always set up a kitchen canopy because we enjoy the shade on hot summer days and know that it usually rains once or twice a week in the eastern United States.

If setting up a canopy, campers must determine the best place for it. Ideally, it should be set up on the highest possible ground, but specific circumstances may not allow this placement. For example, in campsites that have immovable concrete picnic tables, campers may have to set up the canopy over the table, wherever it is located. If campers are traveling light and do not have enough poles to fully support the canopy, they must set it up near whatever trees are available near the campsite. In small sites, campers may have to set up the canopy over the paved parking area.

When planning the campsite layout, also look for things that could cause injury. In particular, look for partially exposed roots or rocks, yellow jacket nests, and poison ivy. Also look up for dead tree limbs (widow makers) that could fall on the tent. Also look for abandoned firewood, plastic sheets, large pieces of wood, or other items on the ground near the site that could possibly attract snakes or spiders.

Set up kitchen canopy and table. After planning the camp layout, the next step is to set up a kitchen canopy and clean table. Once the canopy has been set up, campers will have a shady and dry place to stand, open their tent and bedding duffels, and relax. The procedure for setting up a tarp canopy is described in chapter 14, "Ropes and Knots." After the canopy is set up, the general procedure to prepare the table includes the following steps:

- Move the picnic table under the canopy.
- Use a microfiber towel, cloth rag, or whisk broom to clean the table of old food crumbs, twigs, leaves, and other debris. If the table is sticky, use water and paper towels to clean the area. Also look under the table and benches. Clean away dirt, sticks, spiderwebs, wasp nests, and other debris.
- Cover the table with a clean plastic tablecloth.
- To secure the tablecloth to the table, wrap an cord around the table and tablecloth, insert the distal end of the cord through the permanent loop tied on one end, pull it tight, and tie a slippery half hitch (bow knot).

Once the table has been covered, it can be used as a working area for organizing tools and shelter parts.

Set up tent. After setting up the kitchen canopy and table, the tent can be easily set up. Ideally, campers should already be familiar with the setup procedure and be able to move efficiently. Campers should set up new tents at home to ensure that all parts were included in the package and to familiarize themselves with the setup procedure. Each tent design (cabin, dome, modified dome, tunnel, A-frame) has its own unique steps, but the general procedure for setting up most tents includes these steps:

- Remove sharp rocks, pinecones, and twigs on the ground that might damage the tent floor, puncture air mattresses, or cause discomfort while sleeping. Remove embedded rocks with the crowbar, and fill in the depression with dirt, sand, or gravel.
- Remove the tent stakes and hatchet from the tool bag, and bring them and the tent duffel bag to the setup location.
- Place the ground cloth flat on the ground. It should be smaller than the floor of the tent.
- Open and spread the tent or tent canopy on top of the ground cloth. Position the tent so that its door faces the kitchen canopy.
- Carefully assemble the main support poles and place them near their position on the tent canopy.
- For dome tents, poles can be attached before staking the corners. Gently slide main support poles through their sleeves, if any, bend them over the tent, and insert their tips into their respective corner seats.
- For tunnel tents, spread the floor tight, double-wrap corner loops around tent stakes, and drive each corner stake into the ground with the cheek (or side) of the hatchet. When the stake head gets close to the ground, use the hatchet poll (or butt) to drive them deeper.
- If the tent must be set up on a concrete parking pad or other hard surface, drive stakes into the ground just beyond the concrete slab, and use cords to secure corner stake-out loops to the stakes. If the tent has been set up on sandy soil, use deadman anchors to secure corner loops.

- Place additional support poles into their positions, and attach all plastic clips.
- Deploy the rain fly and attach the hook-and-loop (Velcro) strips under the fly to the tent poles. These attached points increase overall support and integrity.
- Pull rain fly taut, and stake all stake-out loops.
- Attach at least one guy line on each side of the tent. Attach more guy lines if storms or winds are predicted.
- Throw out the welcome mat.

These steps go much faster when two people work together. Additional details about tying knots, rigging guy lines, digging trenches, and rigging deadman anchors are described in chapter 13, "Base-Camp Chores," and chapter 14, "Ropes and Knots."

Set up sleeping quarters. Once the tent has been set up, campers must set up their sleeping quarters. When Eva and I are traveling together, she enters the tent to arrange our bedding and clothing while I bring bedding, clothing, and personal items from the car to the tent. Campers should generally follow these steps to set up sleeping quarters:

- Place a fleece or wool ground blanket on the floor. This blanket provides extra protection from sharp rocks or sticks, softens the sleeping surface, absorbs moisture, and insulates the tent interior from the cold ground.
- Unroll mattresses on top of the ground blanket. If they are self-inflating Therm-a-Rest mattresses, open the valves so they will begin automatically inflating. Depending upon the temperature, each mattress will inflate in five to ten minutes. This time can be used to begin setting up other areas of camp.
- After the mattresses have fully inflated, blow extra puffs of air into them to provide an extra measure of firmness, and then close the valves.
- Place a fitted sheet over two pads. Although many campers sleep on bare pads, Eva and I prefer to sleep on a cotton sheet.

A full-size fitted sheet fits two large mattresses perfectly and is very comfortable—especially in hot weather when we cannot get inside our sleeping bags. Furthermore, the sheet is easy to remove and wash every week.

- Place each person's sleeping bag on his or her mattress.
- Cover clothing-filled duffel bags or day packs with pillowcases, and place one at the head of each person's bed.
- Arrange each person's personal items along the side of the tent and in the corner near his or her head.
- Place shower bags with headlamps near the door so that they can be easily located later in the dark.
- If not in bear country, place one Bounce fabric softener sheet near the tent's door to create a fresh smell and discourage insects from entering the tent, but do not use these sheets in bear habitats.

The objective is to set up beds and sleeping quarters early so that campers can come back at the end of the day, easily find everything they need after dark without having to fumble around through multiple bags, and relax without having to prepare beds when tired.

Set up kitchen. Campers may want to set up a kitchen and dining area on the table under the kitchen canopy. Our procedure for setting up the kitchen is outlined below.

- Set up additional table, if available, and put stove and milk crates on top of it.
- If you didn't pack another table, designate one end of the picnic table as the cooking end and the opposite side as the dining end. Place stove on the cooking end and the milk crates on their sides on the benches to serve as shelves and extra counter space.
- Attach cooking and eating utensil bags to a milk crate.
- Set out a garbage bag. Many campers simply place a garbage bag on the ground, but a better procedure is to hang it from a tree or tarp support pole so it is handy and away from ants and

bugs. See chapter 14, "Ropes and Knots," for my method for hanging a garbage bag.

- Check the fire ring and remove any trash left by previous campers so that it is ready whenever you decide to start a fire.
- Draw potable water in water jugs and bucket. This water will be used to wash hands, wash dishes, and cook.
- Plan to wash dishes on the additional table or on the dining end of the picnic table.

Explore Local Attractions

After setting up camp, campers should usually have a few hours to explore the area and enjoy local recreational activities. On hot summer days, Eva and I especially enjoy swimming in nearby lakes or pools. Almost every Michigan state or federal park has a nice beach, but parks along the Lake Michigan shore are our favorites. When camping on the Florida Gulf Coast, we usually spend a few hours on the beach after setting up our camp and sometimes go out to a nice seafood restaurant. When camping in Mammoth Cave National Park in Kentucky, we try to take one of the cave tours. At Turkey Run State Park in Indiana we tour the visitor's center and hike one of the trails. In Wisconsin, we look for ethnic festivals. In other locations, we can find interesting museums, galleries, and theaters.

Eat Supper and Retire

On most travel days, we usually return to our campsite about six o'clock and begin preparing supper. After eating, we must clean up the campsite and bathe, and then we retire to the tent. Before drifting off to sleep, we frequently play a game of dominos, read a book, or listen to music.

Prepare supper and clean up. The particular food we typically prepare on travel days varies considerably from hamburgers, steak, or pork chops cooked on the grill to fresh vegetables, rice, and beans cooked on a stove. Whatever the meal plan, everyone should work together to make the fire, chop the vegetables, cook the food, and set the table. Additional information about meals is presented in chapter 15, "Meals." Immediately after eating, campers should clean up. Draw some fresh water, and heat it on the campfire or stove. One person can clear the table and repack food staples while another person begins to wash and rinse dishes. Then the first person can dry the dishes and repack them in their respective milk crates. After cleaning up, pack all food back in the car, and take the garbage to the trash receptacles.

Relax. After supper, campers may occasionally go out for a concert or play, but most of the time they just settle in to the campsite and relax for an hour or two before bedtime. Some nights they may want to read books or local tourism materials. Other nights they may want to sit by the campfire and roast marshmallows, play games, or watch a movie on a tablet or portable DVD player.

Batten down. Before going to bed, campers should focus their attention on a few details around the campsite to avoid overnight weather and animal-scavenger problems.

- Store all foods properly so that animals cannot get to them. When traveling by car, pack all food items inside the trunk. When traveling by motorcycle, discuss food-storage options with park rangers during the registration process. Some campgrounds, such as those in Great Smoky Mountains National Park, provide metal food-storage lockers. If suitable storage is not available, campers may have to hang their food from a tree limb as described in chapter 14, "Ropes and Knots."
- Pack all gear lying on the picnic table and around the campsite to ensure that it does not get wet or damaged by animals, wind, or rain during the night. This gear includes chairs, books, cookware, and other things lying on the table or about the site. Properly packing this gear is important because many calm evenings can turn into stormy nights. Nobody wants to wake

the next morning to find their gear wet or damaged from being blown off the table.

- Consider the weather forecast to decide how to best secure the kitchen tarp. On most nights, retighten guy lines and make sure one corner is lower than the other three so that dew or light rain will drain off the tarp. If storms are predicted, unhook the tarp for the night, use it to cover tools, furniture, and kitchen gear on the table, and secure it with a couple of ropes, heavy rocks, filled water bottles, or firewood. Leave ground stakes and guy lines in place so that the tarp can be easily redeployed the next morning after the storm has passed.

- If storms are predicted, formulate an emergency plan. If high winds develop, campers should move to a bathroom or shelter to wait out the storm. Planning where to go before going to bed makes it easier to move quickly if hazardous weather develops during the night.

- Extinguish the campfire. The recommended procedure is to pour water on the fire, stir the ashes, pour water again, stir again, and repeat until the fire is completely out. Make a special effort to avoid accidentally starting a forest fire.

A few years back, while traveling to Wisconsin, some friends and I camped overnight at Moraine View State Park near Bloomington, Illinois. After finishing our evening meal, I wanted to go to bed early, but my friends wanted to stay up a little longer. I assumed they would batten down the site before going to bed, but they did not get all the food and garbage securely packed away. During the night, a dozen raccoons must have invaded our site. I slept through the whole affair, but when I awoke the next morning, I was shocked to see that our site was littered worse than a garbage dump. Tiny shreds of paper were strewn far and wide. We had to spend a considerable amount of valuable travel time to get everything cleaned up before we could get on the road.

Bathe. Most large public campgrounds have bathrooms with hot showers. About nine o'clock every night, after eating supper, cleaning the campsite, and attending an evening program or relaxing, campers should put on shower shoes, reach inside their tent to grab their previously packed shower bags, and walk to the shower building. Not only do showers rinse away sweat and dirt accumulated during the day, but they also rinse away food smells acquired while cooking, refresh the body, help the body to retain heat during the night, and help to keep sleeping bags clean by reducing the amount of dirt and body oil that can transfer from one's body to the sleeping bag liner.

Campground showers vary considerably in terms of their overall quality. Some showers are nice, while others are cramped or dirty with poor temperature control or insufficient water pressure. In fact, showers in the same facility may vary. If several showers are available, check each one to find the best one. Shower areas should have a bench and several hooks for hanging shower bags, towels, and dirty clothes. When undressing, put your watch, glasses, and headlamp in your shower bag, and keep your shower shoes on.

When showering, campers should try to conserve water. When possible, take a fast shower, but if you like to take longer showers, wet your entire body first, and then turn off the water, lather up, turn the water back on, rinse, and turn the water off. This procedure will conserve a valuable natural resource that is becoming scarcer every year. Conserving water helps to ensure that our children and grandchildren will have the same water resources that we take for granted.

In campgrounds without shower buildings, such as those in Great Smoky Mountains National Park and many national forest campgrounds, campers can wait until dark, put on a bathing suit, fill a bucket with warm water, and take bucket baths in the campsite. Campers who are unable to bring a bucket could take a sponge bath at a bathroom sink, but these baths can be messy. Extra time will be needed to clean the sink area after a sponge bath. After bathing, brush your teeth, shave, and attend to other grooming matters. Some women may want to apply facial cream before going to bed. When finished in the bathroom, couples can meet outside the building, turn on their headlamps if necessary, and walk together back to their campsite. Before retiring for the day, hang towels on a clothesline, on chairs under the kitchen canopy, or on the backs of car seats, and place smelly shoes, dirty clothes, and personal grooming kits inside the car.

Sleep well. Inexperienced campers frequently report that they have difficulty sleeping in tents because they are afraid that bad things could happen to them during the night. Some fear that evil people or animals will come to their campsite or tent to harm them. Others fear that snakes, spiders, or other critters will crawl inside their tent. Because sleeping poorly is a common problem, many inexperienced campers become discouraged and decide to either stop camping altogether or purchase expensive RVs.

After camping in tents for over forty years in over two hundred different campgrounds, I can confidently assert that all these fears are unfounded. In large developed campgrounds I have found that the biggest problems are (1) difficulty adjusting to a different sleeping routine, which may cause one or two sleepless nights; (2) noise from people, birds, and animals, which may take a day or two to adjust to; and (3) the inconvenience of having to get up and walk several yards to a bathroom in the middle of the night. However, with the right bedding and a little experience, campers can sleep better in their tents than they can in their beds at home. Here are a few tips to help those who experience sleep problems:

- Buy a good mattress and sleeping bag to maximize comfort.
- Eat well, exercise during the day, and limit caffeine consumption.
- Avoid alcoholic beverages and sleeping pills.
- Eat the last meal of the day at least four hours before retiring, and drink a glass of water about thirty minutes before retiring.
- Take a shower or bath before retiring to refresh the body and keep dirt and body oil from soiling bedding.
- Wear warm clothes. In hot weather wear a T-shirt and pair of shorts. In cool weather wear a T-shirt, long-sleeve shirt, and pair of athletic pants. In cold weather wear a T-shirt, long-sleeve shirt, fleece or insulated jacket, thermal pants, fleece pants, wool socks, and a knit wool cap.

- Use clothing-filled duffel bags and day packs covered with pillowcases as pillows.
- Read books or listen to music to relax before turning off lights.
- Take aspirin or ibuprofen for aches and pains.
- Consider packing ear plugs to block ordinary campground noise.

In summary, travel days can be very productive and enjoyable when planned well, but they also can be very tiring. At the end of the day, most campers look forward to going to bed early and sleeping well.

To strike the Eureka Timberline 4 and similar tents, first remove the rain fly and unhook the peak bungee cords.

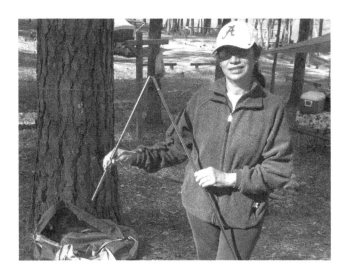

To fold tent poles, gently remove each section and fold it back upon the remaining pole sections.

A GPS receiver makes travel to an unfamiliar destination much easier.

The first task of setting up a new campsite is to set up the kitchen canopy and table.

13

BASE-CAMP CHORES

After setting up a base camp, campers will have plenty of time every day to enjoy various recreational activities, but they must also attend to a few chores each day. Typically, Eva and I arise around seven thirty each morning, eat a leisurely breakfast, and discuss the chores that must be completed that day. We always have to wash breakfast dishes, drain melted ice water, buy fresh ice, and repack the cooler each morning. We also have to plan meals for the rest of the day. Some days we must go to the store and buy groceries, and other days we must repair damaged equipment. Once a week we must find a self-service laundry and wash clothes. Several common base-camp chores are described in this chapter. Making things with ropes and knots is discussed in chapter 14, "Ropes and Knots," and preparing meals is discussed in chapter 15, "Meals."

After completing our chores for the day, we usually have time to enjoy a wide range of recreational activities. For example, when we camp in Elkmont Campground or Cades Cove Campground in Great Smoky Mountains National Park, we try to hike a different trail every day, go shopping in Gatlinburg at least once, attend a few naturalist programs, tube down the Little River, and swim in the swimming hole near Townsend. We also enjoy relaxing in our hammocks, reading books, listening to music, sitting by the campfire, and roasting a few marshmallows.

Organize Clothing and Personal Items

After arising in the morning, the first thing to do is organize clothing and personal items. Depending upon predicted weather and planned activities, lay out garments that you will wear during the day. In hot weather, select shorts, a T-shirt, a hat, socks, and hiking shoes. Refold and repack any clean garments that may have been removed from their bags. Then repack electronic devices into their bag and place the bag on the side of the tent. Next be sure that one headlamp is in the corner of the tent nearest your head, and repack your shower bag with a second headlamp so that it is ready at the end of the day. Then turn sleeping bags inside out to air out during the day, and take dirty garments out to the dirty-clothes bag in the vehicle. Once clothing and personal items have been organized, campers can easily grab what they need later in the day without having to rummage through their bags.

Prepare Meals

Every day campers must spend a few hours preparing meals and cleaning up. The first steps of meal preparation are to decide what food to cook and how to cook it. Sometimes campers will cook their meals with a camp stove, other times with a charcoal grill, and yet other times with a wood campfire. When cooking with charcoal and sometimes with wood, campers should use a cooking grate. Many campgrounds provide cooking grates as part of their fire rings, but these cooking grates are frequently too high, broken, or otherwise unusable. Michigan state parks do not provide cooking grates. Consequently, basic tent campers should consider packing a cooking grate in their camping gear.

When cooking on a stove, campers may have to make a windscreen to block the wind and cook effectively. Perhaps the best way to make a windscreen is to attach a second tarp or bedsheet as a wall to the upwind side of the kitchen canopy. After attaching this wind wall, campers can further block the wind by placing large objects, such as coolers, milk crates, and water jugs, around the stove. Backpackers, who do not have tarps or sheets to make wind walls, can use a larger pot or aluminum foil sheets to make a ring around the stove.

Additional suggestions for preparing meals are presented in chapter 15, "Meals."

Clean Up

Although some people may not always clean up their kitchen immediately after eating at home, basic tent campers should clean up immediately after meals to avoid serious insect and animal problems. In bear habitats such as Great Smoky Mountains National Park, campers must keep their campsites clean to avoid attracting bears. To enforce this rule, rangers and campground hosts constantly patrol the campground looking for unattended coolers and food containers. If they see one in a campsite, they confiscate it and require the owner to come to the office to claim it. When claiming the container, the owner will be issued a warning, and if his or her food is confiscated a second time, he or she may be fined seventy-five dollars.

Other campgrounds may not be as strict, but delayed cleanup can bring other animal problems in a hurry. Fitzgerrell State Park in southern Illinois, for example, has skunks that roam the campground at night looking for food. Myakka River State Park in Sarasota, Florida, and many midwestern campgrounds have herds of raccoons that pillage through the campsites at night. In other parks, armadillos, porcupines, opossums, and coyotes visit campsites as soon as occupants leave or retire for the night. Consequently, campers should never leave their campsites for any reason (not even to go to the bathroom) until all dishes have been cleaned, leftovers have been properly stored in a bag or cooler and placed in car trunks, and the garbage has been placed in garbage containers. Pet food should never be left overnight or unattended in a campsite. Always clean up immediately after every meal to avoid animal problems. Do not procrastinate!

Store leftovers. After finishing a meal, campers should pack leftover foods in plastic bags or containers and pack these bags in appropriate storage containers. Perishable foods should be packed in food-storage bags and packed in the cooler. Nonperishable foods can be packed in various plastic bags and containers and stored in the milk crate with other nonperishable foods. Once packed, all food should be placed in the car trunk or in a metal food-storage locker, if available in the campground. In a few parks, other food-storage methods are recommended. Campers should ask whenever in doubt.

Bag garbage. While storing leftovers, campers should also place food scraps and other garbage into plastic garbage bags. Plastic grocery bags make excellent garbage bags. They can be hung from a tarp support pole with a small cord and carabineer. When a bag gets full, remove it from the carabineer, tie the two handles together, and attach an empty bag to the carabineer. Since many parks provide separate recycle receptacles, campers should also separate glass, plastic, and aluminum items.

Wash dishes. To wash dishes, campers only need a medium-size pot or bowl to hold a little warm water, dish detergent, and a bucket to catch soapy rinse water. They do not need large dishpans or portable sinks. As they finish eating their meal, campers should draw a pot of water and place the pot on the fire or stove to heat. After a few minutes, the water should be warm enough to begin washing dishes. Also make sure sufficient water is available for rinsing all the dishes.

Once the water is warm enough, place it on an insulated pad at one end of a table. Put a few drops of liquid dish detergent (ideally environmentally safe detergent) into the pot, and begin washing dishes, glasses, utensils, and cookware with a dishrag. After washing each piece, place it on the table, which is hopefully covered with a plastic tablecloth. To rinse dishes, draw a jug of water, pour the water over the soapy dishes and collect the soapy water in a bucket. Then place the clean dishes on a clean spot on the table. After all dishes have been washed and rinsed, the two workers can dry the dishes, pack them back into their proper storage container, and place them in the car trunk.

Dispose garbage. After washing dishes and packing them in the car along with all leftovers, campers should take their garbage bags to the nearest disposal station. Glass, aluminum, and plastic containers should be placed in appropriate recycle receptacles.

Dispose gray water. Finally, campers should return to their campsite and carry the bucket full of soapy water to the designated gray water disposal station. If the campground does not have a grey water disposal station, pour the grey water down flush toilets (but not in pit toilets). Campers should avoid pouring grey water on the ground. Although a few camping books suggest using grey water to extinguish campfires, this practice can ultimately harm the environment since soapy phosphate-based detergents will eventually enter the ground water or nearby rivers, reduce the water quality, and could lead to extinction of certain wildlife species. In addition, this practice can leave food scraps on the ground that may attract animal scavengers. After dumping the grey water, campers should wash the bucket and refill it with fresh water for the next meal.

Apply Sunscreen

Each morning before starting the day's activities, campers should apply sunscreen to protect their skin from sunburn and potentially harmful ultraviolet radiation. When camping with children, adults should also supervise children to ensure that they apply it to all exposed skin. For me, this is one of the least pleasant routine chores of camping. Typically, I am anxious to start cooking, repairing equipment, riding bikes, or engaging in more-exciting activities and overlook the importance of taking ten or fifteen minutes to apply my sunscreen. When I hurriedly apply my sunscreen and fail to cover all my skin, I sometimes suffer unpleasant sunburn at the end of the day.

Wash Tablecloth

Each morning, campers should wash their tablecloth with soap and water because raccoons, birds, squirrels, and other animals may have walked on the table overnight and left fecal material or germs on the tablecloth.

Dry Equipment

On many days, clothing and equipment will get wet from routine washing, water activities, dewfall, or rain. When items get wet, campers must take time to dry them to prevent the growth of mold and mildew. Some common items that must be dried are described below.

Tent. When staying in a base camp for several days, campers should dry their tent after each heavy rainfall. A wet tent sitting several days in the hot sun is a prime target for mold and mildew. The procedure for drying a tent is summarized in these steps:

- Wait until the sun comes out.
- Remove all bedding, clothing, and personal items from the tent, and temporarily store them in the car or on the table.
- Wipe the rain fly with a microfiber towel.
- Remove the rain fly and hang on a line to dry.
- Remove stake-out loops from stakes, leaving stakes in place.
- For freestanding and semifreestanding tents, lift the tent canopy up from ground, with poles in place, and gently lay it on its side in a dry spot so that the bottom of the tent can dry.
- Secure the tent in place with rope so that it cannot be blown away by wind.
- Lift the ground cloth from the ground and dry with paper towels. I use paper towels because the ground cloth is typically muddy.
- Hang the ground cloth on a line to dry.

- Allow the ground under the tent to dry for thirty minutes. During this time, campers can read books, relax in hammocks, draw potable water, or perform other base-camp chores but should not leave the campsite to ensure that the tent is not damaged by sudden wind gusts.
- After drying for thirty minutes, replace the ground cloth, tent canopy, rain fly, bedding, clothing, and personal items.

Sleeping bags. Frequently, sleeping bags will get wet from body moisture, spilled water bottles, or rain. For example, campers must deal with soaked sleeping bags when they set their tents up in sunken spots that collect rainwater. On one trip to Great Smoky Mountains National Park, Eva's and my bags were soaked after a strong thunderstorm collapsed our cheap department store tent. On another trip, my sleeping bag, tied to the outside of my motorcycle luggage, became completely soaked when I rode through what I thought would be a brief summer shower.

Whenever sleeping bags get soaked, campers should handle and move them gently to avoid tearing delicate insulation, covers, and linings.

Drying synthetic-insulated sleeping bags is relatively easy. Gently lay them out on a warm rock or paved surface until most of the water has drained out, and then gently hang them lengthwise on a line until completely dry. In low humidity, synthetic-filled bags should dry within three hours. On rare occasions when they cannot be completely dried, do not worry. Damp synthetic-insulated bags will provide adequate warmth at night and continue to dry from body heat.

Drying down-filled bags can be more difficult. Ideally, wet bags should be set out in partial sun all day to air-dry. Unfortunately, wet down bags require much longer drying time than synthetic bags, and damp down will provide very little warmth at night. Every hour, campers should turn and fluff the bag to ensure complete drying. This chore will reduce the day's recreation options. If air-drying is not an option, commercial dryers can be used. But before putting a down-filled bag into a commercial dryer, the owner should consult the bag maker's recommendations. When a commercial dryer is used, the heat should be set as low as possible, and the dryer door should be periodically opened to be sure that the heat level is not melting the cover and liner materials. REI recommends adding a few tennis balls to the dryer when the bag is almost dry to break up down clumps in the bag.

Shoes. When hiking shoes get wet, campers should dry them as quickly as possible. Shoes that stay wet for several hours can develop bad odors. To dry them, remove the insoles, insert crumpled newspapers to draw the moisture out, and hang upside down. If the campground has hot-air hand dryers, campers can intermittently use them to speed up the drying but should not rely upon them to provide complete drying. Shoemakers advise people to avoid overheating wet shoes with campfires, clothes dryers, or other artificial heat sources because excessive heat can dry leather and plastic materials and lead to cracking. While their hiking shoes are drying, campers can wear their shower shoes or casual camp shoes.

Clothing and towels. Almost every day, campers will have to dry a few wet swimsuits, bath towels, beach towels, dish towels, dishrags, and garments. Ideally, most of these items should be made from fast-drying nylon or polyester fibers rather than cotton so that they will dry quickly even on cloudy days. To dry these items, campers should set up a clothesline as described in chapter 14, "Ropes and Knots," and use small spring clips from the tool bag to keep dishrags and other small items from blowing away.

Repair Equipment

On a few occasions, campers may have to repair an item or two that has been damaged. To make common repairs, campers will need a knife, a roll of duct tape, several feet of cord, a pair of small pliers, a small flathead screwdriver, a small Phillips-head screwdriver, and perhaps a sewing kit in their tool bag. Additional items such as screws, bolts, and nails can be purchased in a store near the campground.

Some common maintenance chores and temporary repairs are described below. Permanent repairs will be discussed in chapter 18, "Equipment Maintenance."

Bent or broken poles. Occasionally, tent or tarp poles may be damaged by carelessness or high wind. Several years ago, I moved my REI Family Dome tent canopy with its aluminum poles to a dry spot after a rain and failed to secure it in place. While I was attending to other matters, a strong gust blew the canopy about thirty yards over the ground to a row of understory vegetation near the campsite. After my initial shock, I was pleased to find that the tent canopy was not damaged, but one aluminum pole section was significantly bent. At the time I did not have a tent-pole repair tube, and so I tried to bend it back and support it with duct tape until I could get back home to repair it. Fortunately, this procedure worked, but campers should have a tent-pole repair tube in their tool bag to support bent or broken poles. If they do not have a tent-pole repair tube, they can tape two popsicle sticks or similar stiff wooden sticks on either side of the bend to support the pole until permanent repairs can be made.

Fiberglass and aluminum poles can be damaged when campers are in a hurry to set up or take down their tent. When poles are hurriedly and carelessly snapped together, pole-section tips and seats can accidentally bend or break. To prevent this type of damage, campers should carefully open each pole section and place it into its seat. Fiberglass poles are especially fragile and are frequently damaged by age, cold weather, and rough treatment. When fiberglass poles are damaged, they can be temporarily patched for a few days but ultimately need to be replaced.

Torn tent, tarp, and tablecloth. On occasion, tents, tarps, and tablecloths may tear. For example, tents and tarps can develop small holes from hot embers from nearby campfires. They can be torn by children running and jumping in or nearby them or by splinters on a picnic table where they may have been opened or folded. Tablecloths can be damaged by accidentally cutting them with knives or by tight ropes used to tie them down. For whatever reason, tablecloths, tents, rain flies, and tarp fabrics occasionally need to be repaired. To repair poly tarps and plastic tablecloths, campers can simply apply a piece of duct tape under the tear, and this repair will last for several years.

The best way to repair tent and rain fly fabrics in the campsite has been debated by camping authorities. Some books advise campers to live with a tear or hole until they can return home to make a permanent repair. They argue that the adhesive material of duct tape will stick to the tent fabric and will be difficult to remove when the time comes to make a permanent repair. While this advice may be reasonable for short, dry trips, I'm not so sure about longer trips. For long trips to rainy destinations where it rains almost every day, campers must make some type of repair. Ideally, Tear-Aid patches should be applied, but when these patches are not available, duct tape may be the only option. When applied to dry material, the duct tape repair will provide a secure waterproof fix for several weeks. When campers return home, they can call the tent maker's technical support department and ask for advice as to how to make the best permanent repair. Frequently, makers will suggest applying isopropyl alcohol to clean the adhesive materials. Additional information about permanent repairs is provided in chapter 18, "Equipment Maintenance."

Garments and duffel bags. Clothing, backpacks, and duffel bags frequently get torn on camping trips. For example, Eva and I used a lightweight duffel bag to carry our camp furniture to Mexico on two different trips, and airline luggage handlers tore the bag both times. On the first trip, they ripped out a seam, and on the second trip they tore a large L-shaped hole in one end. After each trip, we had to get a needle, thread, and a patch to sew the bag back together again.

On some trips, campers may have to repair or splice nylon straps that were torn or too short. When making these repairs, always burn the ends of the nylon straps to prevent them from unraveling before proceeding with the repair. On other trips, campers will have to replace buttons or repair ripped seams. To make these repairs, use medium-diameter (69 or 92) black bonded upholstery thread, which is available in most department stores. Before departing on a trip, wind about a hundred feet of thread on a bobbin or small stick and pack it in a small plastic case with a few upholstery needles. Then pack this small sewing kit into the tool bag. When repairs are needed, use a small pair of pliers, such as those on multi-tools, to push the needle through thick materials such as nylon straps. If upholstery thread and needle are not available, campers can use dental floss and the awl of a Victorinox Swiss Army Tinker knife to make emergency repairs.

Torn tarp grommets. Although corner grommets rarely tear out of good tarps, tarp grommets are occasionally pulled out by heavy water sitting on the tarp or high wind. When a grommet is pulled out, campers can go to a department or sporting goods store, buy a grommet-replacement kit, and insert a new grommet near the damaged one. Or they can buy a new tarp since poly tarps are inexpensive. Campers who do not have the option of going to a store can easily repair the tarp in the campsite with a little extra time and no extra cost. They can use a marble from their tool bag or find a small stone and make an emergency tarp attachment point as described in chapter 14, "Ropes and Knots." This simple repair will last for the lifetime of the tarp.

Punctured air mattress. Fortunately, Eva and I have never had to deal with a punctured air mattress, because we take several precautions to protect them and camp in the eastern states where thorns are rare. We usually set our tent up on specifically constructed gravel or sand tent pads, brush away sharp twigs and pinecones before setting it up, place a thick ground cloth under the tent floor, and deploy a wool ground blanket on top of the tent floor under our sleeping pads. Nevertheless, many other campers apparently have had to repair their sleeping pads in camp. If they have a tube of Seam Grip and a small box of Tear-Aid patches, this repair is relatively simple. Campers should follow these steps to repair a punctured air mattress:

- Find the hole by inflating the pad, submerging it in water, and looking for air bubbles.
- Draw a circle around the hole with a felt-tip pen.

- Deflate the pad and allow it to dry.
- Clean the area around the hole with isopropyl alcohol.
- Apply Seam Grip, spread around the hole, and dry for eight hours.
- Apply Tear-Aid patch.
- Apply pressure on the patch with a heavy object for four hours.

If campers do not have Seam Grip and Tear-Aid patches, they can use duct tape to provide a quick fix but will have to clean the tape's adhesive residue from the pad when the time comes to make the permanent repair.

Improve Campsite

After initially setting up a campsite and spending a few hours in it, campers frequently decide to change the camp setup in some way. Sometimes they decide to move the tent or the kitchen canopy and table to a different place. In sites with full sun, campers may decide to deploy a second tarp or bedsheet as a sunscreen or windscreen. Occasionally, campers may have to move the entire campsite because of flooding problems or obnoxious neighbors. Three common campsite improvements are summarized below. Other campsite improvements are described in chapter 14, "Ropes and Knots."

Reposition guy lines. A common camping problem is to initially set up tent and tarp guy lines in places that ultimately block normal traffic-flow routes. When initially setting up the camp, the position of these guy lines may have seemed appropriate, but when people start moving around the campsite, they trip or occasionally get clotheslined by poorly placed guy lines. After one or two such encounters, most campers will realize that they need to reposition one or more guy lines or, sometimes, the entire tarp canopy. Adding ten or twenty feet to a guy line can make it easier to walk around tarp support poles, and tying guy lines to trees can reduce clotheslining risks. When a single guy line needs to be moved, remove the ground stake with a pair of channel lock pliers, add extra feet of line, and anchor the longer guy line to new stake driven into the ground with the hatchet or to a distant tree about six feet high.

Add a sunscreen. On hot, sunny days, campers may decide to add a sunscreen to the kitchen canopy to provide more afternoon shade and protection from light rain. To make this sunscreen, Eva and I use a lightweight eight-by-ten-foot poly tarp, but campers can also easily use a full-size bedsheet. Position this tarp along the western edge of the kitchen canopy. Specifically, place corner grommet holes of the sunscreen tarp onto the tips of the two western corner tarp-support poles of the kitchen canopy, pull the bottom edge of the sunscreen out like a lean-to, and anchor the two bottom corners with guy lines and stakes. If using a full-size bedsheet without grommet holes, place a marble or small stone in each corner and secure them with short cords tied with double-reversed half hitches. Then add figure eight loops on the distal end of each cord, and use these loops as the grommet holes. See chapter 14, "Ropes and Knots," for additional details.

Dig trenches. In the early 1900s, trenching around tents and kitchen shelters was considered to be a necessary chore of tent camping since early tents did not have sewn-in floors. Campers staying in long-term fixed camps (base camps) had to trench around their tents and kitchen shelters to prevent rainwater runoff from running under the edges of the shelters. Today, trenching is no longer necessary for several reasons and sometimes is considered to be environmentally unfriendly.

Trenching is usually unnecessary because modern tents have waterproof bathtub floors that prevent rain runoff from entering under the tent. In addition, many developed campgrounds have elevated crushed-stone pads or areas that drain water away from tent and living areas. Leave No Trace guidelines discourage trenching because it can disturb the ground where tiny microorganisms low on the food chain live and feed. When microorganisms lose their habitat, other organisms up the food chain lose their food supply. Trenching is also considered to be undesirable in wilderness areas because it can promote soil erosion and leave unsightly scars on the ground that will prevent subsequent campers from enjoying the natural beauty of the land. As a matter of fact, many conservationists consider the word *trenching* to be a dirty word and sometimes react emotionally when other people use it in connection with camping.

While I generally follow Leave No Trace guidelines and would never dig a trench in wilderness settings, I argue that digging a small trench in developed campsites can be acceptable. Developed campsites are typically constructed by dumping crushed stone or sand on the ground to make elevated campsite areas. In some campgrounds, asphalt and concrete are used to build parking pads for cars and RVs. These camping pads are built to keep heavy vehicles and RVs from sinking down into soft mud after rainy days. In addition, many of these developed campsites also have fixed concrete tables and benches. Over time some of the gravel settles more than other places, leaving small depressions and channels that collect rainwater runoff. When I set up my tent and kitchen tarp in these artificially constructed campsites, I may not notice these depressions until rainy weather creates small lakes and rivers in the middle of the campsite. Several years ago, a giant lake developed in front of my tent door until the park staff had time to dump more crushed stone to fill the depression. In these situations, I argue that digging trenches to reroute and drain water is an acceptable practice.

Another occasion when I had to dig a trench occurred several years ago while camping in a private campground near Great Smoky Mountains National Park. Our assigned campsite was a small spot on the banks of the Oconaluftee River. On the first day of a five-day camp, it rained heavily, and a small river draining water from nearby mountains began to flow through the center of our site and through the only place we could set up our kitchen canopy. Since we did not want to move to a less desirable site, I dug a new channel along the boundary between our site and our neighbor's site and used the dirt and gravel from the channel to fill in the channel through the middle of our site. Digging the channel proved to be a good decision because it continued to rain almost every day for the next four days. Furthermore, future occupants of the site also did not have to contend with frequent rivers running through their site.

To dig a trench, I typically use the small crowbar in our tool bag. My general procedure for digging a trench is summarized below:

- Put on camp gloves to protect hands form sharp rocks.
- Hold the straight end of a small crowbar and drag the curved end through the gravel or dirt like a plow.
- Once the gravel has been loosened, remove the soil with gloved hand.
- Smooth the edges of the trench with gloved hand.
- Use the crowbar to remove embedded large stones.
- Fill in large holes with loose gravel.

In 1908, Holding described an environmentally neutral method for trenching tents. Although this procedure may no longer be needed, I decided to include it in this book so that this wisdom will not be forgotten.

- Position the tent on a slight incline with the head on the high side of the slope.
- Dig a trench across the head end of the tent about a foot away from the tent wall and three inches deep.
- Curve the trench around the tent corners and continue about a foot down each side.
- Further trenching down each side and across the bottom end of the tent is unnecessary because water will naturally run downhill away from the tent.
- Save the grass and dirt so that it can be replaced when the time comes to break camp.

Draw Potable Water

Having ample amounts of potable water in the campsite is an important factor that makes basic tent camping much more comfortable than backpacking or canoe camping. While backpackers must repeatedly filter or purify water drawn from nearby creeks and ponds, basic tent campers can usually find potable-water spigots within a few feet of their campsite. Every day, these campers can easily draw sufficient water to wash their hands, prepare food recipes, wash fresh fruits and vegetables, wash food-preparation areas, wash dishes, rinse dishes, brush teeth, wash clothes, and, occasionally, take bucket baths. Having plenty of fresh water in the campsite allows campers to perform these chores almost as easily as in their homes. Depending upon the amount of time spent each day in the campsite and number of meals cooked, basic campers can easily use two to three gallons of water. As previously mentioned, Ocean Spray juice jugs or one-gallon milk jugs and a two-gallon bucket make excellent water containers.

Purchase Supplies

Almost every day, basic tent campers must go to a store and buy ice and other supplies. Many campgrounds have small convenience stores in the campground. Other campgrounds usually have small stores located within a few miles. On the first few days of a trip, campers may only have to buy ice to keep their perishable foods cold. When the temperature soars above eighty-five degrees, they may have to buy ice twice a day. After buying ice, they must remove perishable foods from the cooler, drain the water, replace the perishable foods, and repack the cooler with fresh ice. After camping a few days, campers may also have to buy food, batteries, charcoal, and other supplies.

On many days, campers may want to buy fresh fruits and vegetables. Fresh watermelon, cantaloupe, tomatoes, and corn taste especially good on hot summer days. Occasionally, campers will have to buy a bag of charcoal to grill meats or vegetables and to start campfires. I like Kingsford Match Light charcoal even though it is more expensive than other brands because it is easy to light without purchasing lighter fluid and burns evenly. When campers want to prepare packet meals on the campfire, they can buy fresh potatoes and onions plus a fifty-foot roll of heavy-duty aluminum foil. Since most campers will use a lot of paper towels, they may have to purchase another roll every three to four days. If the campsite does not have a grill, campers can buy disposable aluminum lasagna pans, put the charcoal in one of these pans, and then place the grill grate on top. Motorcycle campers may want to buy disposable aluminum loaf pans to heat water or warm canned foods on a grill or campfire.

Wash Clothes

After a few days on the trip, campers may have to wash a few garments. When traveling by car, campers can pack enough clothing for a week and wash clothes in a Laundromat. Several larger campgrounds have nice laundry facilities in the campground, while other campgrounds have Laundromats located within five miles of the park. Campers who travel by small car or motorcycle may not be able to pack as many clothes and, thus, may have to wash underwear and socks every day or two. Try to wash early in the morning on sunny days so the garments can dry on a clothesline. Motorcycle riders can tie wet garments to the outside of their luggage so they can dry while riding.

Although most Laundromats sell detergent, I prefer to pack a small amount of liquid detergent in a travel-size bottle before leaving home because it is handy for washing clothes in the campsite and more economical than buying detergent in a Laundromat. In particular, I prefer liquid Woolite because it is concentrated, gentle for delicate nylon and polyester garments, and environmentally friendly. Other campers prefer biodegradable detergents, such as Seventh Generation Natural 2X or Arm & Hammer Essentials. After putting a few drops of detergent in the washer, set the control to gentle cycle. Sometimes campers may want to dry their clothes a few minutes in a dryer, but they must be careful to monitor the heat to prevent accidentally damaging delicate fabrics, especially polypropylene. On sunny days campers can just bring their clean garments back to the campsite and dry them on a line. Garments made from silk, polyester, nylon, and wool will dry within a couple of hours. If they are hung on the line in the morning, they should be dry by noon.

When washing machines are not available, campers can wash most garments in a bucket or bathroom sink. First fill the bucket with water, add a few drops of detergent, and wash each garment. Then dump the soapy water in an approved gray water disposal station and refill the bucket with clean water. Rinse each garment to remove as much soap as possible, pour the rinse water into the gray water disposal station, refill the bucket, and rinse again. If a bucket is not available, campers can use a bathroom sink but should not hog the sink when other people need to wash their hands, shave, or brush their teeth. After washing the clothes, be sure to clean up the sink area so that it is ready for the next user.

Find Firewood

In the past, finding firewood was a simple matter. After setting up a tent and kitchen canopy, campers just walked through the woods and picked up dead wood lying on the ground. If it was a little too long, they cut it with a camp axe or saw. But those days of gathering firewood from the surrounding area are almost over. Many developed campgrounds no longer have firewood lying on the ground. The wood was either already gathered by previous campers or, more likely, by park personnel who bundle it and sell it as firewood. Furthermore, many parks now forbid gathering firewood because it removes habitat for small plants and animals that live in the park. As firewood became increasingly difficult to find, some campers began loading firewood from their homes or previous campsites and bringing it to their new campsites. But this practice is now forbidden by virtually all public parks east of the Mississippi River to slow the spread of the emerald ash borer and other harmful pests. Most park rules now require campers to obtain their firewood within twenty-five miles of the park.

Because of these pests, basic tent campers must purchase bundles of firewood from the camp store or a local vendor. Purchasing firewood from the camp store is usually the most convenient way to get it back to a campsite, especially when riding a motorcycle, but firewood sold in campground stores frequently costs more than firewood sold outside the park. Plus, it seems to have smaller pieces and lots of knots that prevent splitting. Over the past few years, I have found that grocery stores usually offer the best firewood at the most-reasonable prices. Convenience stores also offer good firewood at reasonable prices.

Before purchasing firewood, campers should check it to be sure it is dry or seasoned. Most firewood vendors only sell dry or seasoned wood, but some vendors sell wet or green wood. The best way to identify wet wood is to examine its weight and appearance. Green wood will feel heavier than dry wood due to its moisture content, will have bark that is firmly attached, and will not have cracks or checks. Its cut ends may also feel damp. When campers try to use green wood to make a fire, the fire will not start burning naturally, will require constant effort to keep going, will produce considerable smoke, and will produce very little heat. Green wood will also produce small water bubbles on each end when burning. Cooking a meal with green wood is impossible. If a person discovers that he or she has purchased a bundle of green wood, the best thing to do is lay it aside and buy another bundle of wood from a different vendor.

Several types of wood are sold as firewood. As a general rule, soft wood (such as southern pine, cedar, and cottonwood) can be used to start fires but should be avoided after fires are burning well. These woods produce low heat value plus considerable smoke and soot. They will deposit a gum residue on food or pots. Instead, campers should look for hardwood such as oak, ash, hickory, maple, hornbeam (ironwood), and birch to maintain hot and relatively smokeless campfires. Many experts claim that oak, ash, and hickory make the best firewood because the wood is easy to split, produces few sparks and little smoke, and has high heat value.

Campers do not have to buy firewood every day. Sometimes the weather is too hot for a campfire. Other times, evening programs, concerts, plays, or guided hikes are available. Yet other times, campers may want to play games, read books, or listen to music. Campers may not want to have a campfire on the night before a travel day so they can get to bed early and get an early start the next morning. And campers may not be allowed to have campfires during periods of high fire danger. But on cool base-camp nights and early mornings, campfires can be very comforting. They warm the hands, feet, back, and soul. Furthermore, they can be used to heat water for hot chocolate, cook meals, and roast marshmallows. Therefore, campers staying in a base camp for several days should purchase two or more bundles of firewood and be ready for the right moment.

At the end of their stay, campers should leave any unused firewood in the campsite for the next occupant or give it to a friendly neighbor.

Split Firewood

Accomplished woodsmen have sometimes said that building a campfire warms you twice—once when cutting the wood and again when burning it. This observation also applies to basic tent camping despite the fact that basic tent campers do not have to cut their firewood. Typically, they just buy bundles of five to eight precut logs that range from three to seven inches in diameter and then split these logs into smaller pieces that can be used as fuel for cooking and campfires. Splitting several logs with a hatchet will quickly generate a lot of body heat.

Some hardwoods can be easily split with a camp hatchet, while other woods are more difficult to split. Red oak and ash, for example, are easy to split, while elm and butternut are very difficult to split. Birch, which is frequently sold for firewood in northern Wisconsin, requires some effort but can be split by striking the log parallel to the growth rings rather than in the center of the log perpendicular to the rings.

Splitting firewood with a hatchet or axe is one of the more dangerous camping chores. Many people have sustained severe lacerations to their legs and feet from careless hatchet swings. To reduce the risk of injury, campers should observe several safety measures. For example, never attempt to split logs after consuming alcoholic beverages or taking other mind-altering drugs, and do not allow children to handle hatchets. When available, use a tree stump as a splitting block. Other woodsmen recommend kneeling while using a small-handled hatchet, setting up a safety log between the person and the splitting block, and confining swings to the frontal zone. My procedure for splitting firewood includes these steps:

- Put on a pair of leather gloves, protective eyewear, and sturdy shoes or boots. Do not wear shower shoes or sandals.
- Focus all attention on the task. Be extremely cautious. Move slowly and deliberately. Do not hurry!
- Set up a wooden splitting block. It should be relatively flat so that logs will stand upright on it. If necessary, improvise one from available pieces of firewood.
- Stand individual log upright on the splitting block. If a log will not stand upright on the splitting block, use a small-diameter stick to hold it upright while swinging the hatchet. Never hold the log with your hand.
- Stand back from the splitting block as far as possible and spread feet as wide as comfortable.
- Bend at the waist until the upper body is almost parallel with the ground.
- While holding the hatchet, lock the wrist so that the hatchet bit is parallel to the splitting block or ground.
- Keeping the wrist locked, make a short swing with the shoulder and elbow. The wrist must remain locked to prevent it from pivoting the hatchet bit back toward the body.
- If the hatchet bit sticks in the wood but fails to split it, leave the bit in place and use it as a wedge. Pound the hatchet poll with another piece of wood, or turn the log upside down and drop the hatchet poll on the splitting block.
- If a piece of wood splits easily, split it several times to make many small pieces for starting the fire and cooking. To split small pieces, put the hatchet bit in the place to be split, and then drop both the hatchet and the wood piece together on the splitting block.
- Sometimes it is possible to tie the whole bundle of wood together and split individual pieces one at a time. Being bundled with other logs will keep small logs from falling off the splitting block and allow you to split several at one time without having to stop and bend over to pick up small pieces. A rope and bungee cord can be used to hold several logs together.

If a log is difficult to split, position it across the front or by the side of the campfire to serve as a windscreen until it is dry enough to burn as fuel. After sitting next to the hot fire for a half hour, the large log will begin to flame up. When it does, move it onto the fire as needed. These larger logs can be used after cooking meals when the fire has become very hot with a good bed of coals.

Build Campfire

When fires are permitted in a campground, campers should build them in the fire ring and keep them small enough to keep under control. Fires should be kept small so they can be easily extinguished when the time comes to leave the campsite or go to bed. A bucket of water and a few water-filled jugs should be readily available in case the fire gets too big.

To set up a good cooking campfire, most accomplished woodsmen make keyhole fire pits. To make one of these keyhole fires in a fire ring, campers could place several large stones in two lines about twelve inches apart and perpendicular to one edge of the fire ring to support the cooking grate. Then they should start two fires—one in the small confined area under the grate and a second one in the larger fire ring. When the small fire burns down to coals, it is ready for cooking. To maintain high heat levels in the cooking area, move coals from the larger fire under the grate as needed. If stones are unavailable in a particular campground, campers can use two or three large pieces of firewood to support the cooking grate, but these pieces of wood will have to be replaced often. After using stones and logs to support cooking grates for several years, I made a folding campfire stove that was described in chapter 9, "Kitchen." Procedures for preparing different meals with different types of kitchen equipment will be discussed in chapter 15, "Meals."

Two basic methods can be used for safely starting a campfire—the textbook method and the easy method.

The *textbook method* is described in most camping books and scouting handbooks and is briefly outlined below:

- Place *tinder*, such as dry newspaper, fat pine, cotton balls soaked with Vaseline, or commercial fire starter, in the center of the fire ring.
- Gently lay *kindling*, such as small, dry wood twigs or shavings cut from larger pieces of firewood, on top of the tender.
- Gently place small *sticks* about the size of large pencils on top of the kindling in the shape of a tepee. The wood should be arranged such that plenty of air can get to the base of the fire.
- Once this mound has been built, light the paper or tinder at the bottom of the mound.
- As the smaller pieces of wood and sticks begin to burn, add more sticks. Start with small sticks.
- Once a bed of coals develops, gradually work up to larger sticks.
- After the fire is burning well, add small two-inch-diameter *logs* in the shape of a teepee.
- When a good bed of coals has developed and the fire is under control, a combination of smaller sticks and larger sticks can be added across the coals to maintain the desired heat level.

The *easy method* for starting campfires is an alternative method that works well—even when dry tinder and kindling are unavailable:

- Place about ten Kingsford Match Light charcoal briquettes in the center of the fire ring.
- Light the bed of coals with a butane lighter.
- As the charcoal begins to burn, place small pieces of split firewood on top.
- Add firewood as needed to maintain heat level.

With this easy method, there is no need to mess with tinder or kindling, and there is no need to worry about the placement of small sticks. The wood will begin burning immediately and quickly make coals suited for cooking within a few minutes.

Enjoy Rainy Days

Brief summer showers can be refreshing, but long spring and fall storms can be miserable—especially when camping in a small tent several hundred miles away from home. To endure long periods of rainy weather, campers should follow ten important principles when planning trips and setting up their campsites:

- Purchase good-quality sleeping bags, tarps, and mattresses that provide maximum rain protection.
- Pack a variety of fast-drying nylon, polyester, silk, and wool garments that can be layered to maintain core body temperature in a wide range of daytime highs and nighttime lows. Don't forget hats and gloves.
- Pack books, dominoes, personal music players, portable DVD players, cards, and compact board games to pass time in the campsite.
- Select campsites with elevated tent pads or good drainage. If an assigned site does not have proper drainage, request an alternate site.
- Integrate the tent and kitchen canopy so that they provide a dry entryway into the tent plus a place for standing, sitting, cooking, eating, dressing, and playing board games.
- Secure the tent and kitchen canopy to the ground with guy lines to withstand moderate wind.
- Plan activities such as scenic drives, museum tours, plays, movies, and shopping that get you away from the campsite several hours each day.
- Eat simple foods that require little preparation and no heating. Better yet, eat meals in restaurants.
- Seek shelter if lightning is close.
- Dry the tent, sleeping bags, mattresses, and other equipment when the sun comes out.

Prepare for Bed

At the end of each day, campers must bathe, batten down, snuggle into their beds, and sleep well. Details about these activities were discussed in the previous chapter, "Travel-Day Routine."

Although this list of base-camp chores may seem daunting, most basic tent campers will only have to perform a few of these chores each day, and the amount of time required to complete each one will be relatively short. In other words, despite having to perform a few chores, basic tent campers will have several hours every day to enjoy their favorite recreational, educational, and leisure activities.

After breakfast, apply sunscreen to prevent sunburn and block cancer-causing UV radiation. Reapply often during the day.

While camping in the Big Muskellunge Lake campground in the Northern Highland–American Legion State Forest in Wisconsin, we bought our ice and supplies in this store.

Basic tent campers staying in developed campgrounds should purchase their firewood from local stores. To make efficient fires, most pieces will have to be split several times.

When possible, use a tree stump or log section as a splitting block.

14

ROPES AND KNOTS

To live comfortably in a campsite for several days, basic tent campers should learn how to use ropes and knots to perform a variety of camp chores. In 1911, *The Boy Scouts Handbook* described camping skills and included several useful knots. Since then, several other camping books discussed the value of knots for camping. Kephart (1917), for example, devoted a full chapter to knots, hitches, and lashings. As early as 1968, I began using ropes to deploy a tarp over my table and continued to experiment with various rope diameters and lengths for many years. Recent camping books have recommended clothesline cord or parachute cord, but these products do not work as well as one-eighth-inch utility cord. After trying different diameters of rope and cutting random lengths, I have devised a system for packing an ample amount of rope that can be repeatedly used to perform a wide range of basic-tent-camping chores.

Preparation

Several weeks before departing, campers should buy two hundred feet of three-millimeter- or one-eighth-inch-diameter nylon utility or tarp cord. This cord can be purchased in most hardware, department, or camping stores. This particular size seems ideal for basic tent camping because it is strong enough to handle most camp chores yet small enough to pack two hundred feet of it into a small tool bag. This cord is frequently sold in fifty-foot packs for about five dollars, so the total expense for two hundred feet is about twenty dollars. Hardware and department stores may only have white cord, but REI and other camping outfitters typically offer several bright and reflective colors.

After purchasing a package of cord, precut it into standard lengths that will be useful for a wide range of future camp chores. Begin by cutting thirteen five-and-a-half-foot (sixty-six-inch) sections. One fifty-foot package yields nine of these sections, so the second package will have leftover cord after cutting just four sections. Each time the cord is cut, immediately burn the ends with a butane lighter or candle to prevent them from unraveling. For each length of cord, bend six inches of one end back to make a bight, and then tie a small permanent overhand loop at the end. Once the loop has been tied, the cord should be about five feet long. Hereafter, this loop end of the cord will be called the loop end. The other end of the cord will be called the distal or working end.

To pack these thirteen cord sections and prevent them from tangling, hook all the loop ends with a small carabiner and fold the cord sections in half two times until they are about twelve inches long. Then secure the bundle of cords with a short one-foot length of cord and a square knot. This procedure allows a camper to carry sixty-five feet of five-foot cord lengths in a small tool bag without them tangling.

After preparing the five-foot sections, cut ten ten-and-a-half-foot-long pieces and prepare them in the same manner to make ten-foot sections. Pack in the same way with a carabiner as well. These ten-foot sections will be used to make the kitchen-canopy guy lines, clothesline, and table cloth tie-downs. If another ten-foot section is needed in a particular campsite, two five-foot sections can be joined using a sheet bend knot.

Basic tent campers should also prepare three other useful cord sections. *Leverage loops* can be made by cutting two-foot sections and tying small permanent overhand loops on both ends. Campers will need eight of these leverage loops—one for each canopy guy line. Then cut two more two-foot sections to secure rolled air mattresses during travel. Finally, cut about four one-foot sections to be used to secure cord bundles during travel, make longer tent stake-out loops, or solve unique problems in each particular campsite.

When campers arrive at a particular campsite, they can combine the long and short cord sections with sheet bends to make longer lines for specific applications. Leverage loops can be used along with taut-line or trucker's hitches to tighten guy lines and clotheslines. The exact number of cords needed in a particular campsite depends upon the number of trees available and their location. To be prepared for all situations, basic tent campers should have plenty of cord available. When the time comes to break camp, untie all the knots except the permanent loops, hook similar-length cords together with carabineers, fold them several times, and tie them together with one-foot cords.

Useful Knots

To use cord effectively, campers must learn how to tie the best knot for each specific application. Some knots should hold strong without slipping, while other knots should slide easily. Regardless of their intended function, good knots are those that can be easily untied at the end of the camping trip. Being able to tie good knots that can be easily untied will greatly enhance a camper's overall mobility and enjoyment. The knots that are frequently used are summarized below. A few photos of these knots are included at the end of this chapter. More photos and video how-tos can be found on the Internet.

Overhand loop. The overhand loop is a simple knot that creates a permanent loop in a rope. It is used to hold tarp pole tips or make lassos around trees or other large objects. The knot can be difficult to untie, so it should be used when campers want a knot to stay in place forever, or until the cord becomes unserviceable. Follow these steps to tie an overhand loop:

- Fold six inches of one cord end back on itself to make a doubled cord called a bight.
- Make a small loop with the doubled cord.

- Pass the bight end over (or under) the doubled cord and back through the loop.
- Pull tight.

Figure eight loop. This knot is used to make a temporary loop. It adds an extra turn to the overhand loop that allows it to be easily untied when the time comes to break camp. Follow these steps to tie a figure eight loop:

- Fold eight inches of a cord end back on itself to make a bight.
- Make a loop with the bight.
- Pass the bight end around the back of the doubled cord twice and back through the loop.
- Tighten.

Slippery half hitch. This knot is used to make a clothesline or tight line between two fixed objects (such as trees) that can be easily untied, tightened, and retied. It is a simple bow knot that will hold tight against considerable pressure but can be easily untied by pulling the distal end. Follow these steps to tie a slippery half hitch:

- Anchor the loop end of the line to a stationary object such as a tree.
- Pull the distal end to a second object, such as another tree or tent stake-out loop.
- Pass the distal end of a rope through the stake-out loop or around the small tree and pull tight.
- The line section running from the anchor to the second object will now be called the lower part and the section running from the second object back toward the anchor will be called the upper part.
- Pinch the upper and lower parts of the distal end together and hold.
- Make a bight on the lower part.
- Pass the bight over the lower part and back through the loop.

- Pull tight.

Double-reversed half hitch. This is a useful knot when campers need to tie the distal end of a cord to a tree or some other large object. It is two half hitches combined. When pulled, the hitch will tighten but will not fail. When the time comes to break camp, the knot can be easily untied. To tie a double-reversed half hitch follow these steps:

- Anchor the loop end of the line to a stationary object such as a tree.
- Pull the distal end to a second object, such as another tree or tent stake-out loop.
- Pass the distal end of the line around or through the second object.
- Pull the line tight, and pinch the upper and lower parts together.
- Pass distal end over fingers, *over* and around the lower line, and back through the loop. This step completes the first half hitch.
- Move an inch or two up the lower line and pass the distal end *under* and around it a second time.
- Pass the distal end through the second loop. This completes the second half hitch.
- Tighten.

Taut-line hitch. This is perhaps the best-known Boy Scout knot that has been used to secure tent guy lines for many years. It is similar to a double-reversed half hitch but with an extra pass around the upper part of the line (called a round turn). This knot is a good choice for guy lines because it is a friction knot that will hold tight in windy conditions but can slip around the tent stake-out loop when the time comes to tighten the line. The correct application of this knot for securing guy lines will be described later in this chapter. To tie a taut-line hitch follow these steps:

- Anchor the loop end of a cord to a tree, tent stake, or some other fixed object.

- Pull the distal end out to and around a tent guy-out loop or some other object and back up the side of the cord until tight.
- Pinch the upper and lower lines together with fingers while tying the knot.
- Pass the distal end over finger, around the lower line, and back through the loop to make a half hitch.
- Pass the distal end around the upper line a second time to make a round turn.
- Move down the lower line, pass the distal end over and around the guy line a third time, and pass it through the second loop to make a second half hitch.
- Tighten.
- The hitch should hold tight but slide up and down the guy line with a little pressure.

Trucker's hitch. This knot is frequently used by truck drivers to tie heavy loads on top of their trailers. Basic tent campers can also use it for several packing and camping applications. When traveling by motorcycle, campers can use it to secure duffel bags onto back seats or luggage racks. When traveling by car, campers can use it to tie equipment or cargo boxes on the top luggage rack. In the campsite, it can be used to rig tent guy lines. In general, it can be used anytime tight lines are needed to hold items in place securely. This knot will hold tight as long as needed but can be easily untied when the time comes to break camp. To tie a trucker's hitch follow these steps:

- Anchor the loop end of the line to a stationary object, such as a luggage rack rail or tent stake.
- Make a small loop a few feet before a second stationary object, such as the opposite luggage rack rail or tent guy-out loop. The exact position of this loop can vary depending on the length of cord.
- Immediately past the loop, make a bight, pass it through the first loop, and pull tight to make a second loop.

- Run the distal end of the cord around the second luggage rack rail or guy-out loop.
- Bring the distal end back to and through the second loop, cinch it tight, and pinch the line at the loop.
- Tie a slippery half hitch (bow knot) that can be easily untied when the time comes to remove the load or break camp.

Sheet bend. The sheet bend is used to join two shorter cords to make a longer line. For example, it can be used to join two five-foot cords to make a ten-foot guy line or clothesline. This knot is helpful when trees are more than ten feet apart. It can also be used to make a long line needed to hang a food bag from a high tree limb. The sheet bend is perfect for these applications because it will not slip or give way when the line is pulled tight but can be easily untied when the time comes to break camp. To tie a sheet bend follow these steps:

- Run the distal end of one cord through the permanent loop of a second cord.
- Pass the distal end of the first cord around the back of the loop and then back under itself.
- Tighten.

Bowline. This is a popular knot that is used to make a loop that will not slip under extreme pressure. It is a good knot for hanging hammocks because it will hold the weight of a person's body without slipping but will be easy to untie when the time comes to break camp. To tie a bowline follow these steps:

- Pass the distal end of a rope around a tree and back through its own loop to make a lasso around the tree.
- Make a small loop a few feet below the lasso.
- Bring the distal end of the rope down to the hammock, through its attachment ring or loop, and back up to the rope loop.
- Pass the distal end through the small loop, around the back of the rope, and back down through the loop.

- Tighten.
- If the hammock strap needs to be shortened, loosen the knot and pull the distal end further around and back through the loop and retighten.

Clove hitch. This knot is described in almost every camping book but has very few practical uses. The only application that I use this hitch is when hanging a food bag from a high tree limb using the Pacific Crest Trail method. This method is discussed later in this chapter. To tie a clove hitch follow these steps:

- Wrap the cord around a stick one time.
- Pass the distal end over the round turn, and wrap it once again around the stick.
- Tuck the distal end under the last pass around the stick and pull tight.

Square knot. This knot is useful for securing bundles of folded cord together for travel. To tie a square knot follow these steps:

- Cross two cord ends.
- Pass the upper end over and around the lower end.
- Cross the two ends again.
- Pass the upper end over and around the lower end, and then pull it through the newly created loop.
- Tighten.

Clotheslines

When trees are available, campers usually set up clotheslines in most base camps and many overnight camps. Clotheslines can be used to dry swimsuits, dishcloths, dish towels, bath towels, washrags, and other wet items. In the morning they can be used to air out sleeping bags and other bedding. When breaking camp, campers can hang their tent on a clothesline before packing it into the car. To rig a clothesline follow these steps:

- Lasso a length of cord around the larger of two trees. Use five-foot cord sections for small trees and ten-foot cord sections for large trees.
- Tie a figure eight loop on the distal end. A figure eight rather than an overhand loop is preferable in this application because the figure eight will be easier to untie when the time comes to break camp.
- Lasso a second length of cord around the second tree. The best cord length will depend upon the distance between the two trees.
- Run the distal end of the second cord through the figure eight loop of the first cord, cinch tight, and pinch the loop to keep it from slipping.
- Tie a slippery half hitch (bow knot). The slippery half hitch is the best knot for this application because it can be pulled very tight but will be very easy to untie when it is necessary to retighten the line or break camp.

Alternatively, follow these steps:

- Lasso one cord around the larger of two trees.
- Add additional cord sections as needed using sheet bends.
- Pull the line tight, and pass the distal end of the cord around a second tree two times (round turn).
- Tie a half hitch and a slippery half hitch.

Guy Lines

Most tents, tarps, canopies, and other shelters require a few guy lines to prevent them from being inadvertently blown away or damaged by strong wind. To accommodate these guy lines, most tents have one or two guy-out loops on each side, and most commercial kitchen shelters have one or two guy out loops on each corner.

For almost a hundred years, tent makers and camping authorities such as the *Boy Scouts Handbook* recommended a specific procedure for rigging these guy lines. The procedure involves first tying a length of rope or cord to each guy-out loop with an overhand loop. Once the ropes have been attached to the tent loops, a small piece of thin wood, plastic, or metal with three small holes (called a slide) was used to make an adjustable loop on the distal end to be placed around a stake. In the early years, these slides were made at home from wood but, after a few years, equipment manufacturers began making them from steel, aluminum, or plastic. The cord was attached to the slide by passing it through a hole on one end, then through the middle hole, then through the third hole, and finally tied with a knot. When setting up a tent, campers make each guy line by pulling the first loop of the slide out and around a tent stake. When properly set, the slide holds the guy line firm against strong wind gusts but easily slides when necessary to adjust the tension of the guy line.

Sometime during the mid-1900s, camping authorities began using taut-line hitches rather than slides because hitches did not require small pieces of wood or plastic that could get lost or damaged. In 2013, *Backpacker Magazine* suggested using a trucker's hitch instead of the taut-line hitch. Regardless of the specific knot used, the overall strategy of this traditional procedure is to anchor one end of the cord to the tent and adjust it around the stake.

After using this method for several years, I realized that it was backward. When a stake is driven deep into the ground, its guy line will not slide around the stake to permit tightening because the cord becomes wedged into the ground. To adjust the guy-line tension, the soil around the stake must be loosened, and consequently, the stake will become loose. I realized that the cord should be anchored to the stake or tree—rather than to the tent—and adjusted around the tent or tarp guy-out loop. In this later configuration, tent or shelter stakes with attached cord ends can be driven deep into the ground or even buried in the ground as deadman anchors while still allowing easy adjustment of guy-line tension. Either a taut-line hitch or trucker's hitch can be used to make the adjustable line. Both hitches will hold tight during strong winds and be easy to untie when the time comes to break camp. To rig a guy line follow these steps:

- Anchor the loop end of a cord to a stake or tree. To secure a guy line to a stake, wrap the loop twice around the stake head and drive the stake deep into the ground. To secure it to a tree, lasso the line around the tree.
- Run the distal end through the tent guy-out loop and back down the upper end.
- Cinch the line tight.
- Tie a taut-line hitch or trucker's hitch.

Emergency Tarp Attachment Points

Most tarps have grommets placed in each corner and along the sides to serve as attachment points for guy lines. But occasionally, grommets pull out, or campers want to use a flat sheet as a sunscreen. In these cases, marbles or small stones can be used to improvise tarp attachment points. To make an emergency tarp attachment point follow these steps:

- Prepare a short length of cord with a double-reversed half hitch on one end and a figure eight loop on the other end.
- Place a marble or small stone in a corner of the sheet about two inches from each edge.
- Pull the tarp material around the marble, and secure with the double-reversed half hitch. This knot is best for this application because it will hold the marble and tarp tightly as it is pulled but can be easily untied when the time comes to break camp.
- Pull tight.
- Use the figure eight loop to secure the tarp corner to a pole or stake, or anchor with a guy line.

Deadman Anchors

In sandy or muddy soil, campers may have to use deadman anchors to secure their tarp guy lines and tent stake-out loops. The procedure for making and using a deadman anchor is summarized below.

- Buy a wooden closet pole and cut it into ten-inch lengths—one for each anchor.
- Cut a two-and-a-half-foot length of rope for each anchor. After cutting the rope, burn both ends to prevent unraveling.
- Drill a three-quarter-inch hole in the center of each pole, insert one end of the cut rope through the hole, wrap around the pole, tie a double-reversed half hitch, and pull tight.
- Tie a simple overhand loop at the other end. After tying this knot, the loop should be at least one foot from the wooden piece.
- Dig a ten-inch-deep hole in the sand or mud with a crowbar. Then lay the wooden piece flat, pull the rope up out of the hole, and fill in the hole with sand or mud so that a few inches of rope and the loop extend above the ground level.
- For sand, pour water onto the filled hole to provide weight and adhesion.
- Tie the guy line to tent or shelter loop.

When traveling to the Florida Gulf Coast beaches, campers could use these deadman anchors with a full-size flat bedsheet, four marbles, two six-foot poles, some guy lines, and a garden trowel to make a sun cabana. One marble can be placed in each corner of the sheet and secured with a double-reversed half hitch to make guy-line attachment points. If campers have not made deadman anchors at home, they could improvise by lassoing a cord around a stick, sand-filled stuff sack, or some other object and then burying this object about a foot into the ground.

Kitchen Canopy

Each campsite has certain features that determine the relative ease or difficulty of setting up a kitchen canopy. Campsites with movable tables are the best because the canopy can be set up wherever convenient and the table can be moved under it. To set up the tarp, campers will need one eight-by-ten-foot (or ten-by-twelve-foot) tarp, three eight-foot poles, one six-foot pole, eight ten-foot guy lines, and eight stakes. To set up a kitchen-canopy tarp follow these steps and reference the diagram at the end of this chapter.

- Lay tarp flat on the ground in the place where it is to be set up.
- Drive two stakes into the ground for each corner. Each stake should be positioned five to six feet away from the corner and in direct line with one tarp edge. See diagram at the end of this chapter.
- Attach the distal end of a guy line to a leverage loop using a taut-line hitch (or trucker's hitch).
- Double-wrap other end of leverage loop around a stake.
- Lay each guy line on ground with the permanent loop near its respective tarp corner.
- Assemble one eight-foot pole, insert its tip through a corner tarp grommet, place two guy loops on the pole tip, and slowly raise the corner until the guy lines are taut enough to hold the corner up.
- Repeat the above step for each remaining corner, using the six-foot pole for the low corner.
- If trees are present in the campsite, they can be used to support one or more guy lines.
- Once the tarp is partially erect, readjust poles, stakes, and guy lines until tarp is fully upright and taut.
- Move the picnic table under the tarp.
- For longer base camps, add a second tarp or sheet as a lean-to wall on the western side of the kitchen canopy to provide afternoon shade and additional wind and rain protection.

Unfortunately, a few campgrounds have installed fixed tables to discourage vandalism. The worst table is a concrete table (ugh!), but with a little more effort, a tarp canopy can be set up over these tables using this modified setup procedure:

- Lay one end of the tarp flat on the ground about two feet beyond the edge of the table. This step is necessary for determining the positions of the four stakes for that end.
- Drive in the four stakes, attach the distal end of a guy line to a leverage loop using a taut-line hitch (or trucker's hitch), and attach the leverage loop to its respective stake.
- Spread the tarp over the table.
- Ask a companion to hold the opposite side of the tarp and pull tight.
- While your companion is holding the opposite side, assemble one eight-foot pole, insert one of its tips into a corner grommet, attach guy lines to two corner stakes, place guy line loops over the pole tip, raise the corner, and adjust the guy lines until they are taut enough to support the tarp corner.
- Assemble and position the second eight-foot pole with guy lines.
- Move to the opposite side of the tarp, and insert the third eight-foot pole into one corner grommet.
- Drive in two stakes for the third pole, attach guy lines, place permanent loops over the tip in the grommet, and tighten until the guy lines hold the corner upright.
- Insert the six-foot pole into the last corner grommet, and follow the same steps as for the third pole.

Having three high corners is perhaps the most practical way to set up a kitchen canopy. It is simple to set up, easily handles heavy rain, and is easy to take down. Tarps that are merely tied to trees without support poles typically do not drain well and will collect water in the center of the tarp that will eventually split the tarp, pull the guy-line stakes out of the ground, or snap the ropes. Tarps that are set up with two high sides and two low sides like a lean-to will have much less usable space and will collect water along the lower edge.

Garbage Bags

A common problem for many campers is where to put the garbage bag. Placing it on the ground or tabletop will likely spill its contents when accidentally bumped and will attract ants. A good solution to this problem is to hang the garbage bag from a tarp support pole or tree. To hang a garbage bag follow these steps:

- Place the loop end of a five-foot cord over the tip of a tarp support pole.
- Allow the distal end to dangle beside the pole.
- Tie a figure eight loop about three feet down.
- Use the remaining distal end to tie a double-reversed half hitch around the pole.
- To make a paper towel holder, run the cord through a paper towel roll before tying the distal end to the pole.
- Attach the handles of a standard plastic grocery store bag to the loop with a carabineer.
- When the bag becomes full or when battening down, unclip the bag from the carabineer and attach a new bag.

In this position, the garbage bag is about chest high and accessible without having to stoop. It is off the ground and away from bugs and small animals, and it will not accidentally fall over and spill its contents. Alternatively, campers could tie the distal end of a cord around a tree with a double-reversed half hitch and attach the bag to the dangling loop with a carabineer.

Food Storage

Campers must always protect their food from animal scavengers, especially during the night and when they are away from the site.

When registering in a campground, always ask the park rangers or personnel about the best food-storage procedures. In many developed campgrounds, campers can store their food inside their locked vehicles. Campgrounds in bear habitats frequently provide metal storage lockers located around the campground for motorcycle riders and other people who cannot store their food in an enclosed vehicle. In a few campgrounds, campers are advised to use bear-proof barrels or bags or to hang their food in bags from high cables or tree limbs. Several methods for hanging food bags have been proposed in different camping and backpacking books. The Pacific Crest Trail method is an easy but effective method:

- Find a cable or high tree limb that is located several yards away from the tent or sleeping quarters. The limb should be approximately fifteen feet high and strong enough to hold the food bag yet small enough that it would not support a bear's weight.
- Connect several cord sections using sheet bends to make a forty-foot line.
- Tie the loop end of the long line to a heavy object, such as a rock or dirt-filled stuff sack.
- Throw the heavy object over the cable or high tree limb and allow it to fall back to the ground.
- Remove the heavy object, and hook the loop end of the cord to the food bag with a carabineer. The food bag should be relatively heavy for this to work properly.
- Insert the distal end of the line through the carabineer.
- Pull the distal end of the line through the carabineer until the bag has been lifted up to the limb.
- Tie a small but strong twig about the length and diameter of a pencil as high as possible on the cord using a clove hitch.
- Gently lower the bag until the twig catches on the carabineer. The bag should be hanging about ten to twelve feet above the ground.
- Tie the loose end of the line to a nearby tree.

- To retrieve the food bag, pull the distal end until you can reach the twig, remove it, and then lower the bag.
- To remove the line, pull the loop/carabineer end of the line to keep it from getting hung on the high limb.

Hammocks

When selecting a specific campsite, campers should look for sites that have at least two trees suitable for hanging hammocks. Better yet, look for sites that have three or more trees. The easiest way to hang a hammock between two trees is to use a pair of Eagles Nest Outfitters (ENO) nylon SlapStraps or SlapStrapPROs, which can be purchased at most outdoor outfitters. These straps have a large loop at one end that can be used to lasso the strap around a tree and smaller loops spaced about every ten inches that can be used with a heavy-duty carabineer to adjust the height of the hammock above the ground regardless of the distance between two trees. Campers who cannot find these straps or do not want to buy them can easily make hammock straps from about thirty feet of nylon static (nonstretch) rope rated to hold about three hundred pounds. To hang a hammock follow these steps:

- Cut the nylon static rope into two equal fifteen-foot sections, and burn each end to prevent unraveling.
- Tie a simple overhand loop at one end of each rope. The simple overhand loop is ideal for this application because it is strong and will never need to be untied.
- In the campsite, select two trees that are about twelve to twenty feet apart. Avoid poison ivy.
- Lasso one rope around each tree as high as possible. Ropes should be placed at least seven feet high to achieve the best hammock position.
- Loosely tie a bowline with a large loop on the distal end of each rope. The bowline is ideal for this application because it can support considerable weight, can be easily retied to adjust

hammock height, and can be easily untied when the time comes to break camp.

- Adjust the hammock height by loosening the knot and pulling the distal end of the rope through the small loop.
- Use a strong climbing-quality carabineer to attach the hammock to the large bowline loop.
- When first hung, the hammock should be about four feet above the ground because it will sag closer to the ground under a person's body weight.

In summary, having ample amounts of rope and knowing how to tie useful knots are two important factors that help to make basic tent camping more comfortable than backpacking and more mobile than luxury tent camping. Using cord to rig various amenities eliminates the need to pack many bulky items.

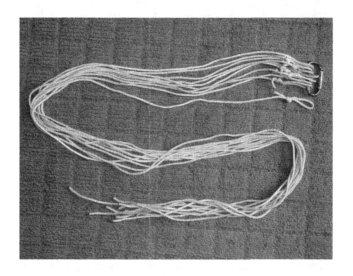

Before leaving home, cut and prepare five- and ten-foot lengths of cord so that they are ready for any camping chore.

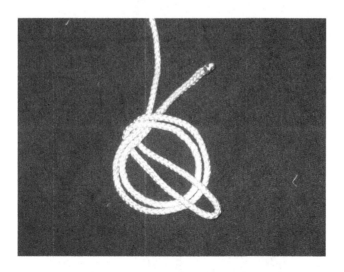

Tie a simple overhand loop at one end of each length of the five- and ten-foot sections.

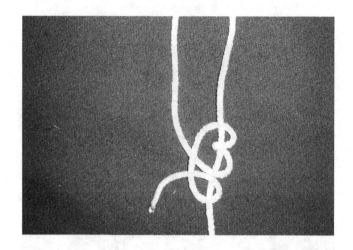

The taut-line hitch is traditionally used to make tent and tarp guy lines because it can be easily tightened when necessary.

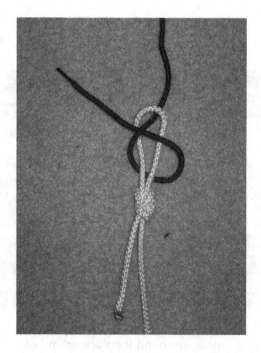

A sheet bend is used to temporarily join
two cords to make a longer line.

To rig clotheslines and guy lines, I frequently
begin by lassoing one cord around a tree.

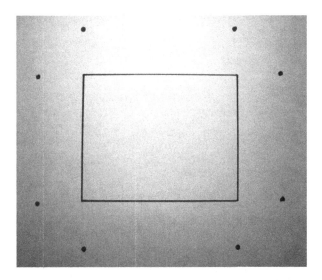

This drawing shows the overall setup plan for a kitchen-canopy tarp.
Each dot represents the placement of a guy-line stake. Note that
each stake should be placed directly in line with one tarp edge.

15

MEALS

Being able to eat a wide variety of simple, good-tasting meals is an important factor determining the overall comfort and enjoyment of a basic-tent-camping trip. Good food provides energy for daily activities and comfort at the end of the day. The variety of meals that can be prepared while camping depends primarily upon the amount of kitchen gear, coolers, and food boxes that can be packed in the vehicle. Individuals and couples riding motorcycles with limited packing space, for example, will have the fewest meal options because they only have space to pack a few kitchen items and food staples. Families traveling in small cars with more packing space for small coolers and food-storage containers will have more meal options. And families traveling in larger cars with ample packing space for medium-size coolers and food boxes will have the most meal options.

Holding (1908) emphasized the importance of eating well in his book and discussed food options in six chapters. In total, almost a third of his book deals with cooking and eating while camping in the outdoors. The first food chapter begins with a discussion of fresh fish, game, poultry, eggs, fruits, and vegetables that could be easily acquired near the campsite most of the time. The next chapters describe how to find or cook stewed rabbit, porridge, sweets, jellies, fresh fruit, tapioca pudding, quick lunches while away from the campsite, breads, cheese, milk, butter, eggs, lobster salad, and tinned (or canned) foods, such as salmon, Irish sausages, soups, potted meats, fruits, and vegetables, that could be brought from home. Kephart (1917) also recognized the importance of eating well during a camping trip. In the *Camping* volume of his two-volume book, he devoted nine chapters (103 pages) to describing different types of foods that could be prepared in a campsite. An underlying assumption was that fish or game could be obtained near the campsite most days. Individual chapters discuss cured meats, breads, vegetables, and desserts. Moreover, most early camping books and magazine articles assumed that campers could secure some of their food near their campsite and needed to pack basic staples that would increase the variety of meal options.

Recent camping books, on the other hand, spend very little space discussing fresh staples that can be packed at home and how to obtain additional food after setting up camp. Backpacking books do not discuss fresh-food options because backpackers cannot carry much weight. Thus, backpacking books focus upon lightweight, high-calorie snacks and dehydrated foods that can be packed into a small space. In fact, backpacking books encourage campers to plan meals by determining the minimum number of pounds of food per person per day. After setting up camp, backpackers typically must collect water from nearby creeks or lakes, boil it, and then pour it into a small package of dehydrated food to rehydrate it. Although a few of these meals are tolerable, they certainly are not as good as meals made with fresh ingredients that basic tent campers can easily cook.

Other camping books seem to be unduly influenced by backpacking procedures and assume that other campers will eat a lot of dehydrated foods too. The few books that do discuss meal options typically give a few exotic recipes that require lots of spices and unusual ingredients. Some examples of these exotic meals include curried chicken and peppercorn roast. Although some of these recipes are reasonably tasty, most are no better than simple foods that can be prepared with fewer ingredients and less effort. Basic tent campers may want to try one or two of these exotic recipes but should consider Holding's opinion expressed over a hundred years ago: "The average, every-day camper has no time for all that." Oddly enough, virtually no camping books explain how to cook simple, good-tasting meals that ordinary tent-camping families typically eat.

On travel days, campers may want to select quick and easy meals so that they can get to their planned destination as early as possible. Campers who plan to get an early start could stop at a fast-food restaurant after an hour on the road to eat breakfast sandwiches with hash browns and drinks. Around noon, they could stop at a rest area and make sandwiches with ham, chicken salad, tomatoes, or pimento cheese—or look for a Mexican taqueria or other fast restaurant. When traveling in the Upper Midwest, Eva and I plan to eat at least one meal in a Culver's restaurant.

After arriving at the day's destination and setting up camp, campers must decide what they want to eat for supper. When traveling by car, they may have several meal choices packed in the cooler and nonperishable-food box. When traveling by motorcycle, campers may have to run to a local store to buy a bag of charcoal and enough food for the evening meal and the next morning. On a few occasions, they may decide to eat supper in a local restaurant.

After arriving at the ultimate destination and setting up a base camp, campers are able to ride to the store every day and prepare many economical, good-tasting meals in the campsite. Some options require cooking, but others do not. Some options require a few kitchen items, but other options can be prepared with very little kitchen equipment. On days when a full schedule of activities is planned, campers can eat a light breakfast, such as instant oatmeal, cold cereal, fresh fruit, cheese, bread, or pastries. When more time is available to cook and clean up, campers can cook pancakes with bacon or egg burritos with sausage. For lunch, many families eat sandwiches or buy meals in fast-food restaurants. For supper, basic tent campers can prepare steak, pork chops, or bratwursts, paired with fresh Idaho potatoes, sweet onions, corn, and a tossed salad. The meat can be grilled over charcoal, and the potatoes and onions can be cooked by boiling them in a small pot or roasting them in an aluminum foil packet in the coals. On other occasions, campers can prepare rice or pasta dinners when a stove and pot are available. Dozens of simple meal suggestions that can be prepared in a campsite are presented throughout this chapter.

Since food cost can be one of the most expensive parts of a family camping vacation, basic tent campers may want to consider setting a budget. By cooking most meals in the campsite, campers can eat very well for several weeks and still keep the total meal costs low. In 2013, for example, Eva and I took a twenty-one-day trip through Illinois, Wisconsin, Michigan, and Indiana, and our total food cost was $525 (less than $25 a day or $12.50 per person per day). Based upon this trip, it seems reasonable to set a goal of keeping food costs under fifteen dollars per day per person for future camping trips.

Takeout Meals

When traveling by motorcycle or when too busy to cook, campers can drive to local restaurants, grocery stores, or convenience stores and buy a variety of tasty but economical takeout meals. These meals offer good-tasting food that requires no kitchen gear and little effort. Some good takeout meals include pizza, Chinese food, and Kentucky Fried Chicken meals. When traveling near Ludington, Michigan, campers should try to buy at least one takeout fried-fish dinner from Bortell's Fisheries. This market has a variety of fresh-fish selections and will deep-fry each customer's choice and serve it with french fries and slaw. In Traverse City, Michigan, campers may want to try Scalawags. In other geographic locations, campers may want to ask about local restaurants or just buy hamburgers or taco takeout meals from chain restaurants. Many grocery stores also offer nutritious, economically priced takeout meals—such as meatloaf with two vegetable sides; fried chicken; or beef tips with potatoes, rice, and vegetables—in their deli area. A few convenience stores also offer economically priced takeout breakfast sandwiches, lunch sandwiches, and fried chicken.

Prepackaged, Ready-to-Eat Foods

Another easy meal option to consider when traveling by motorcycle or when too busy to cook is prepackaged, ready-to-eat foods such as potato chips, crackers, nuts, trail mix, muffins, bagels, bread, peanut butter, jelly, honey, cakes, cookies, doughnuts, fried fruit pies, cereals, cereal bars, gummy fruit snacks, dried fruit, tossed salads, pickles, sauerkraut, summer sausages, jerky, beef sticks, smoked salmon, and shrimp cocktails. A small pound cake combined with some fresh strawberries, blueberries, or peaches and a little milk makes a nice breakfast or evening dessert. All these foods can be purchased in grocery stores, and many of them can be found in convenience stores at a little higher price.

Dairy Products

A third easy meal option is to buy butter, cheese, cream cheese, cottage cheese, or milk to combine with crackers, bread, or fruit. Sharp cheddar cheese combined with Gala apples makes a good light meal, as does butter and fresh homemade bread. For dessert, a large glass of milk and a few cookies is a tasty option. Cream cheese goes well with bagels, and cottage cheese goes well with fresh or canned fruit. To preserve these dairy products for a few days, campers will need a cooler. When traveling in larger vehicles, campers can pack a few dairy products in a medium-size cooler. When traveling by motorcycle, campers can pack small quantities of dairy products in personal coolers, such as the REI Go Box or REI Lunch Cooler.

Oils, Spices, and Condiments

For most trips, basic tent campers should pack a few spices. In particular, salt, pepper, garlic salt, and crushed red pepper are basic staples that can add flavor to many foods. These spices can be packed in small containers, such as the GSI Outdoors Salt and Pepper Shaker. People with limited packing space could obtain several individual-serving packs of salt and pepper like those available in fast-food restaurants and store these packs in small medicine vials.

Mayonnaise, ketchup, and mustard can be packed into small Lexan containers and can be used to make tuna and chicken salad for sandwiches and salads. Spicy mustard goes well with bratwursts; ketchup is frequently needed for burgers. All these condiments can be obtained in small packets like those available in fast-food restaurants. Italian salad dressing, vegetable or olive oil, and pancake syrup can be packed in small ten-ounce juice bottles. In addition to dressing salads, Italian dressing can be used to marinate grilled chicken or fish. Other spices mentioned in various camping books are rarely needed and may cover up the natural flavor of most well-prepared foods.

Grains

According to the USDA, grains should comprise about one-quarter of a person's daily diet, and most of these grains should be whole or unrefined. Bread is perhaps the most commonly eaten source of grain. Homemade bread is especially nutritious and should be purchased as often as possible. It tastes great with butter and can be used to make many good-tasting sandwiches. When good homemade bread is difficult to find, campers may have to settle for multigrain or Swedish rye bread, dinner rolls, brat buns, or hamburger buns. When traveling, bread should be packed in plastic bread boxes so that it does not get crushed during the trip.

Bread can be used to prepare a variety of sandwiches with a minimum of kitchen equipment. Sandwiches can be made with peanut butter and jelly, tomato and cheese, deli-sliced ham or turkey with butter and lettuce, tuna or shredded chicken mixed with mayonnaise, and pimento cheese. In camp, bread can be used to make grilled burgers, bratwursts, or chicken breast sandwiches. For breakfast, bread can be fried in butter to make toast or egg and cheese sandwiches.

Grilled cheese sandwiches are especially popular with both children and adults. To make these sandwiches, campers need a small stove (or fire), a frying pan, and a spatula or pair of tongs. Melt a little butter in the frying pan, soak a slice of bread in the butter, melt some more butter, soak a second slice of bread, put two slices of American cheese between the two bread slices, and fry until each bread slice is toasted golden brown. Another tasty sandwich option is an open-faced sloppy joe made with ground beef and McCormick Sloppy Joe mix. With a stove and frying pan, campers can make garlic toast for spaghetti, fettuccini Alfredo, and other meals. To make garlic toast, melt butter with garlic salt in the frying pan, place a slice of bread in the butter to soak it up, and then fry the butter-soaked bread until toasted golden brown.

Pancakes are a good meal choice for breakfast. Campers will need a nonstick aluminum frying pan, a spatula, and a medium-hot fire. When using a small backpacking stove and frying pan, campers must be very careful to avoid tipping the pan off the burner. Having a large camp stove and frying pan makes the job much easier. Follow these steps for making pancakes:

- Select a good pancake mix. (Eva and I use Bisquick.) Sometimes it can be found in small two-serving packs in grocery stores, but most of the time it is only available in larger boxes.
- When packing, scale the recipe for however many people are in your group, and then measure out that much mix into a one-quart food-storage bag. You can also cut the recipe off the box and bring it with you if needed.
- Assemble the mix according to the directions. With Bisquick, to serve two people that means blending one egg, three-quarters cup of milk, and one cup of mix (this is half of the box recipe with a little extra milk).
- Warm nonstick frying pan with medium heat. Do not add oil.
- Pour small amount of pancake mixture into the center of the pan.
- Wait a few minutes until several bubbles appear on the surface.
- Flip the pancake, and wait a few more minutes until the pancake rises.
- Press down with the spatula, and allow pancake to cook another thirty seconds or so.
- Sometimes the pancake must be flipped back to the first side to cook a little longer.

- Move the pancake to a plate, and place a pat of butter on top.

Other foods made with grains include cold cereal, which only requires some milk and a bowl; Quaker Instant Oatmeal and Instant Grits, which require a stove and pan to heat water; Stove Top stuffing mix, which only requires a little hot water; and tortillas, which require a stove and frying pan or a grill to heat. Corn tortillas are especially popular in southern Mexico and can be used as a substitute for breads with many meals; flour tortillas can be used to make several different good-tasting burritos. Finally, packaged rice and pasta meals combine grains with vegetables and meat to make complete meals.

Fresh Fruit and Vegetables

The USDA suggests that fruit and vegetables should comprise half of a person's diet, and campers must make a concerted effort to include several servings of these foods every day. Some easy options are prunes, apples, grapes, cherries, blueberries, kiwis, bananas, tomatoes, onions, lettuce, baby carrots, celery, radishes, broccoli, cucumbers, bell peppers, and jalapeño peppers. Tomato, lettuce, and cheese sandwiches are especially tasty when tomatoes are in season. Once at their base camp, campers can frequently find watermelons, cantaloupes, and pineapples in nearby stores.

In addition to eating raw fruits and vegetables, campers can easily cook several vegetables with their meals. Fresh corn, in particular, can be easily cooked in a pot or in the coals of a campfire. Shuck it and boil it for eight minutes on the stove, or soak it in water in its husks and then cook it on the grill or in a bed of coals for fifteen to twenty-five minutes, depending upon the heat level. Alternatively, it can be shucked and wrapped in aluminum foil for grilling.

Potatoes are easy to cook and go with most meats and vegetables. One large baking potato or three small red potatoes make a nice serving for two people. One way to cook them is to chop them into small pieces and boil them with onions for about ten minutes with a camp stove. Sometimes, boiled potatoes can be used to make mashed potatoes by adding a couple of butter pats, salt, and one tablespoon of milk and then mashing everything together with a fork. Potatoes can also be mixed with onions with a little mayonnaise, diced pickles, and salt to make potato salad. Adding a diced hardboiled egg further enhances the flavor. Another way to cook potatoes is to wrap them in aluminum foil packets with onions and butter and steam them on hot campfire coals for about thirty minutes.

Other fresh vegetables that can be easily cooked include green beans, carrots, zucchini, and broccoli. Fresh tart apples like Granny Smith apples make a great dessert or treat. Cut them into small pieces, wrap them in aluminum foil with raisins, butter, and sugar, and cook them in the campfire coals for about fifteen minutes.

Aluminum Foil Packets

One way to cook fresh vegetables and fruit with little kitchen equipment is to make meals in aluminum foil packets. The packet-meal method allows campers to cook many foods, such as potatoes, onions, squash, broccoli, carrots, zucchini, rice, and apples, without a stove or pot. The following steps make up the general procedure for preparing packet meals:

- Tear fifteen-inch sheets of heavy-duty aluminum foil, and place sheets on a flat surface with shiny side up.
- Cut food into small, bite-size pieces, and place an individual serving on the foil.
- Add one teaspoon (pat) of butter, salt, pepper, and a small ice cube or spoonful of water.
- Pull the long ends of the foil sheet up together, roll together several times, and squeeze tight.
- At each end, pull the two edges together, roll together several times, and squeeze tight.
- When completed, the packet should be sealed with a small air space so that the liquids cannot leak out.

- Roll the packet in a second piece of aluminum foil to protect it from accidental puncture.
- Prepare similar packets for each person in the camping party.
- Use camp gloves and tongs to place packets on the grate of a hot fire or in a bed of coals.
- Listen for the sizzle, which signals the start of the cooking time, and turn every three to five minutes.
- Depending upon the heat level, broccoli will steam in five to six minutes. Steam it three minutes, turn, and then steam it two more minutes. Cook corn about ten to twenty minutes. Cook potatoes and onions about thirty to forty minutes.
- Use gloves, tongs, or pliers to carefully open packet to determine if food is completely cooked. The aluminum foil will be hot, and the steam inside the packet can cause serious burns.
- If not fully cooked, reseal the packet, and cook five to ten minutes longer.

Once the food has been cooked, it can be eaten right out of the foil. No plate or bowl is necessary. When finished, simply throw the foil in the trash, and wash utensils. Several websites, including the ones for Reynolds Aluminum, Kraft Foods, and the US Scouting Service, provide dozens of simple packet-meal recipes. Basic tent campers should browse these sites and look for appealing suggestions. When they find one, they should copy it and stash it with their kitchen gear. When the time comes to pack for the next trip, the recipe will serve as a reminder. The more campers cook with foil, the easier it becomes.

Canned Foods

Canned foods offer a wide range of simple meal options. Some canned foods, such as peaches, pears, fruit cocktail, V8 Vegetable Juice, and tuna can be consumed right out of the can, but most canned foods require brief heating. These foods can be easily heated on a campfire with a disposable aluminum loaf pan, on a backpacking stove with a small one-quart pot, and on a two-burner camp stove with a two-quart pot. In addition to the equipment needed for heating the food, campers will need a can opener, bowls, and spoons for eating it. Examples of canned foods suited for basic tent camping include green peas, green beans, corn, spaghetti, ravioli, soups, beef stew, chili, chicken breast, potted meats, and sardines. Although canned pinto beans are technically classified in the protein food group with meat, Eva and I think of them as vegetables and eat them often with our meals.

Rice and Pasta

Several companies make a variety of rice and pasta meal mixes that can be easily cooked in a base camp with a stove and pot. Ramen noodles and Kraft macaroni and cheese are two easy options to prepare. But many more tasty rice and pasta meal mixes can be found in grocery stores. For example, Hamburger Helper makes several pasta-based meals, such as Cheeseburger Macaroni and Beef Stroganoff. To make one of these meals for two people, cut the recipe in half, and use only a half pound of ground chuck. Knorr makes several rice sides, such as Creamy Chicken Pasta and Cheddar Broccoli Rice, that could be combined with two or three other vegetable sides and bread. McCormick makes mixes for spaghetti sauce and fettuccini Alfredo. Rice-A-Roni, Uncle Ben's, and several other companies make other rice sides. And Bertolli makes a variety of frozen pasta meals that can be cooked in a frying pan.

One of Eva's and my favorite pasta meals is spaghetti with meat sauce. To make this meal for two people, we boil two servings of spaghetti in a pot and brown half a pound of ground chuck in a frying pan at the same time. Next, we drain the grease from the meat, add half a pack of McCormick Thick & Zesty Spaghetti Sauce Mix, water, tomato paste, and chopped onions. Then we stir the meat mixture together, cover, and cook for fifteen minutes. In addition, we frequently include a tossed dinner salad and garlic bread to complete this meal.

Our favorite rice meal is Zatarain's red beans and rice. We begin by dividing the contents of a box in half to make just enough food for two people. Then we add a few onions, green peppers, and kielbasa.

After simmering all the ingredients for about twenty minutes, we have a great-tasting meal.

Meat, Eggs, and Fish

Meat, eggs, and fish can be cooked in a variety of ways with or without kitchen equipment. Campers who are unable to pack many kitchen utensils can cook many meat entrées on a charcoal grill or in aluminum foil packets in the campfire. For example, hamburgers, steaks, pork chops, bratwursts, Polish kielbasas, thin pieces of boneless chicken, and other meats can be easily cooked on a charcoal grill. Sometimes we grill thinly sliced steak and make carne asada tacos or sandwiches.

Meat, eggs, and fish can also be cooked in aluminum foil packets on the grill or in the coals. For example, scrambled eggs with onions and polish kielbasa or country ham can be cooked in foil packets for breakfast. Sloppy joe meat can also be easily cooked in homemade aluminum bowls or disposable aluminum pans for lunch or supper. With a stove and frying pan, campers can easily cook several other meats, including bacon. When buying bacon, Eva and I prefer Oscar Mayer brand. After buying a package, cut the bacon in half so that it will fit into a one-quart food-storage bag. This size is easy to cook in a small frying pan and seems to curl less than longer strips. To cook crispy bacon, cook it over low heat, and flip often until brown on both sides. Using a pair of tongs, remove the bacon from the pan, and place it on a paper towel to drain excess oil.

Many campers enjoy fishing and especially enjoy eating freshly caught fish for any meal. Fish can be cooked on a grill but is much easier to fry in a pan. To cook thin fish, heat a small amount of olive oil in a frying pan, and fry the fish for about three minutes per side. Alternatively, butter and blackened seasoning can be used instead of the olive oil. Small rock bass plentiful in the waters near Peninsula State Park in Door County, Wisconsin, are very tasty. Although other fishermen throw them back into the lake, they are easy to clean, easy to cook, and good to eat. Thin fish filets, such as trout, tilapia, and orange roughy, can also be cooked in foil packets with some butter and

Chef Paul Prudhomme Blackened Redfish Magic or with Italian salad dressing. Depending upon the thickness of the filet, total cooking time will be ten to fifteen minutes.

Roasts and stews are two other meat options, but basic tent campers will rarely have the time to cook them. They require considerable amount of kitchen equipment, long preparation time, and long cooking time. Most camping families prefer to spend their time engaging in recreational and educational activities.

Freeze-Dried Backpacking Meals

Several companies offer a variety of freeze-dried backpacking meals in small aluminum pouches. When a person is ready to eat a meal, he or she pours boiling water into the pouch and waits about twelve minutes until the food has rehydrated. Mountain House, for example, sells single-serving pouches for $6.40, double-serving pouches for $5.50 to $7.50, and four-serving pouches for $12. Entrées include eggs with bacon, beef stew, beef stroganoff, chicken Alfredo, turkey tetrazzini, chili mac with beef, lasagna, rice, and vegetarian dishes. Backpacker's Pantry sells a variety of two-serving breakfast entrées, such as Huevos Rancheros and Scrambled Eggs with Bacon Bits; meal entrées, such as Kung Pao Chicken and Hawaiian Chicken; vegetable dishes, such as Green Beans Almondine; and desserts, such as Hot Apple Cobbler and Dark Chocolate Cheesecake. Other companies making freeze-dried backpacking meals include Richmoor (Campmor) and AlpineAire. Most of these meals are available in camping outfitters and online.

Basic tent campers may want to consider a few backpacking meals because they require little packing space; offer meal options, such as lasagna, that would otherwise be difficult to prepare in a campsite; require no cooking skills; require few kitchen items; are quick to prepare; and are easy to clean up after eating. Two limitations of these meals are that they do not taste as good as other meal options and cannot be found in most grocery and department stores.

Meals Ready to Eat (MREs)

A few campers, especially those with past military experience, like to pack US military meals ready to eat (MREs) for their camping trips. An MRE is a medium-size, olive-colored plastic bag that contains one hot entrée, a heating system, several individually packaged cold foods, and a package of disposable utensils and spices. A carton of twelve MREs can be purchased from military surplus stores and Amazon.com for about sixty-five dollars ($5.42 per meal). Some hot entrées include beef stew, sloppy joes, chicken tortellini, chicken noodle stew, macaroni with beef, chili with beans, and vegetable lasagna. To heat the entrée, one must first slide the entrée box into a specially designed bag with a heating unit, pour a small amount of water into the bag, and mix. The water activates the heating unit, and the food heats in few minutes. Cold foods include nuts, trail mix, pretzels, peanut butter, jelly, hard crackers, and powdered juice mix. One complete MRE should give a person 1,200 calories needed to perform strenuous outdoor activities during the day.

People who like MREs cite several reasons for taking them on camping trips. For example, MREs eliminate the need to plan meals or shop in grocery stores since all the food needed for one meal is neatly combined into one package. In addition, MREs have a long shelf life, do not require extra kitchen equipment other than a cup, and do not require any cooking skills. Cleanup after eating an MRE is a snap—just throw everything in the trash.

While I was in army basic training, I ate MREs every day for about four weeks, and more recently I have tried a few newer entrées. Based upon this experience I have concluded that these meals are poor choices for basic tent camping for at least four reasons. First, several of these meals needed for a multiday camping trip require much more packing space than other foods and a small kitchen kit. Second, MREs do not include fresh fruit and vegetables, which campers should routinely eat almost every meal. Third, they are more expensive than many other good meal options. And finally, they do not taste as good as foods made with fresh ingredients. While one meal is tolerable, a regular menu of MREs over several days would get old in a hurry! In addition, individual

MREs are difficult, if not impossible, to find during most camping trips. They are not sold in local department or grocery stores and, thus, cannot be obtained near most camping destinations.

Beverages

Campers living in the outdoors should try to drink several glasses of water every day. In addition, they may want to drink milk, tea, or hot chocolate. During the day campers may want to consider powdered fruit drinks or bottles of fruit juice instead of pop. As a general rule, caffeinated beverages should be avoided because caffeine can cause sleeplessness, nervousness, and other mild health problems. Alcoholic beverages should also be avoided because they are expensive, can cause many health and behavioral problems, and are forbidden in many state parks.

In summary, basic tent campers can save hundreds of dollars by eating simple but good-tasting meals during their camping trip. They can find a wide range of good-tasting foods regardless of their vehicles, available packing space, and destination. The general strategy is to pack as much kitchen gear as space allows and buy foods from local restaurants and grocery stores every two to three days.

Tortillas heated over a wood fire are especially tasty and can be eaten for any meal.

Packet meals can be cooked on the grill with other food or in the coals of the campfire.

Pancakes, bacon, and fruit provide plenty
of energy for morning activities.

Jambalaya with shrimp and corn makes a nice evening meal.

16

SAFETY

Despite the fact that many camping books describe shocking life-or-death survival stories about flash floods, bear and mountain lion attacks, venomous snakebites, broken bones, severe lacerations, and other worst-case scenarios, basic tent camping in developed public campgrounds is an exceptionally safe recreational activity. I have taken hundreds of recreational camping trips over the past forty-plus years and have never been seriously injured in my campsite during all this time—thanks be to God. Friends and family have accompanied me on many of these trips, and only one has ever gotten injured on a trip—she stepped in a small hole one night and broke her ankle. Furthermore, I have never been aware of other campers being seriously injured or killed in a campground. On the basis of this personal experience, I think it is safe to conclude that the risks of injury while camping in developed campgrounds are extremely low.

Research studies on camping-related injuries and fatalities are difficult to find but generally support this conclusion. A few national parks and states publish search-and-rescue (SAR) statistics, and some publish hospitalization statistics. Examples of such studies include a ten-year retrospective study of 1,912 SAR missions in Yosemite National Park by Hung and Townes (2007) and a five-year retrospective study of 516 recreational injuries and 19 deaths in Mount Rainier National Park and Olympic National Park by Stephens, Decoma, and Klein (2005). One study by Flores, Haileyesus, and Greenspan (2008) examined factors related to approximately 500,000 admissions to sixty-three hospitals scattered across the United States and attempted to determine specific factors related to 212,708 injuries sustained while engaging in outdoor recreational activities.

When considering the results of these and other studies, readers should understand that most statistics are based upon all park users and not specifically upon campers. Most serious injuries and fatalities usually occur when campers or day users hike, climb, or wander away from the campground and engage in dangerous activities. Males are more likely to be injured and killed while engaging in outdoor recreational activities than females, and males under thirty-five years of age are more likely to be injured and killed than males over the age of thirty-five. Furthermore, many injuries and fatalities are associated with the use of alcohol or other drugs. Most of these injuries could have been prevented had the victims obeyed park rules and used a little common sense.

Flores and his colleagues (2008) used data taken from a sample of hospitals to estimate the rate of outdoor recreational injuries as 72 per 100,000 participants. Data from this study were also used to estimate injury rates related to several specific outdoor recreational activities. The rate of injury related to camping was estimated to be less than 1 percent of the total, and many of these injuries were burns and lacerations sustained by young children. The rates of injury related to other outdoor recreational activities were as follows: 18 percent from snowboarding, 8 percent from sledding, 4.6 percent from hiking, 2.6 percent from personal watercraft, 2.4 percent from fishing, and 1.5 percent from swimming. Another study by the National Park Service reported 872 injuries and 136 fatalities during 2007 in all the national parks combined (www.NationalParksTraveler.com).

All the studies cited above, plus many more, agree that falling from high places is the primary cause of serious outdoor recreational injuries and fatalities. Stephens and his colleagues (2005) found that falls accounted for 37 percent of the 535 injuries in Mount Rainier National Park and Olympic National Park between 1997 and 2001. Hung and Townes (2007) reported that falling was the most common cause of fatalities in Yosemite National Park between 1990 and 1999.

And the October 2008 issue of *Backpacker Magazine* reported that falls caused 4,616 mountaineering disasters between 1951 and 2006, while the second-highest factor (falling debris) caused only 971 disasters. Searching the web for "hiker falls" will usually yield half a dozen stories about deaths and serious injuries sustained by hikers in state and national parks during the past few years.

When hikers fall, they are likely to incur broken bones, lacerations, internal injuries, and head injuries. Furthermore, they frequently fall down into places where rescue and evacuation is difficult and, thus, incur further injury due to delayed medical treatment. On the basis of these separate studies, it seems reasonable to conclude that falling from high cliffs, bluffs, or ridges causes over a third of all serious injuries and fatalities in state and national parks.

After falling, the next most frequent causes of outdoor recreational injuries and deaths are drowning, heart attacks, hypothermia (usually caused by getting lost in caves or in the forest at night), and heat stroke. Other occasional causes of injuries and death in wilderness areas are lightning, avalanches, bee stings, mosquito-borne viruses, and assaults by other people (The National Park Service reported twelve murders in national parks for 2007.) At the bottom of the list of risks are snakes, spiders, mountain lions, bears, and alligators. More information about these dangers, including their *Backpacker* Terror Indexes, are presented in the October 2008 issue of *Backpacker Magazine*.

To prevent most injuries, basic tent campers should adopt a few commonsense practices. First, repair or replace damaged equipment that could lead to injury. Broken tent poles should be repaired, and leaking propane stoves should be replaced. When registering for campsites, people should inquire about potential problems in the park and pay attention to posted signs. For example, many parks advise campers to learn how to recognize and avoid poison ivy. In Governor Dodge State Park in Wisconsin, campers are advised to avoid contact with wild parsnips growing near campsites since these plants cause blisters and rashes. In Great Smoky Mountains National Park, campers are advised to follow food-storage regulations to prevent bear problems. Campers should read and obey posted signs, listen to rangers' advice, ask questions, and follow rangers' recommendations. Finally, campers should avoid taking any mind-altering drugs, including alcohol and marijuana, as these drugs impair judgment, perception, and coordination. Intoxication and drug impairment can cause many serious injuries, such as burns, lacerations, and broken bones. Campers who follow these commonsense practices should have few, if any, problems.

Despite the low probability of injury while camping in public campgrounds, basic tent campers should learn basic principles of first aid and CPR. Campers should be prepared to treat minor injuries and help stabilize more-serious injuries that could occur in public campgrounds. For example, individuals who have sustained broken bones or severe lacerations or who have been stung multiple times by yellow jackets, bitten by a venomous snake, or seriously burned should be stabilized in the campground and transported to a medical facility as quickly as possible. Each specific injury should be stabilized in a different way. For example, severe lacerations should be stabilized by controlling the bleeding with sterile gauze pads and direct pressure and treating for shock if necessary. As soon as feasible, someone should call 911 and contact park personnel. To stabilize an apparent heart attack patient, a certified person should begin CPR until a more qualified medical person can take over, and someone else should call 911. Specific problems that could occur during a camping trip, along with prevention strategies and response guidelines, are discussed in this chapter.

Highway Travel

Every basic-tent-camping trip begins with at least one travel day and ends with another travel day. Longer trips begin with two to five travel days and end with another two to five days with overnight camps along the way. On each travel day, campers may drive anywhere from fifty to five hundred miles on unfamiliar two- and four-lane highways with dozens of potential hazards. To ensure safe trips, campers must learn and apply basic principles of highway safety. Over my lifetime, I have had many conversations about highway safety with acquaintances. From these conversations, I have concluded that a large number of intelligent people fail to understand and observe basic principles of highway safety.

For example, many people know that speeding is a major cause of highway fatalities but believe that they can safely drive five to fifteen miles above posted speed limits. When these people are involved in highway crashes, they blame other drivers and refuse to acknowledge any personal responsibility for their crashes. In particular, many people blame slow, law-abiding drivers for causing highway crashes. A significant number of people believe that they are still good, or even better, drivers after consuming alcoholic beverages or smoking marijuana. Many motorcycle riders think that wearing leather jackets and/or reflective vests will protect them from serious injury and death. Unfortunately, many of these misinformed and overconfident people will eventually have major crashes and experience serious injuries.

According to the National Highway Traffic Administration (NHTSA), over 840,000 injuries and 1,700 fatalities occur every year on American highways, and the primary causes of these injuries and deaths are speeding and alcohol impairment. Most of these people probably thought they were safe drivers before their crashes. States that have significantly higher traffic fatality rates tend to have higher speed limits and/or more relaxed enforcement. Wyoming and Mississippi are two states with high fatality rates (27.48 and 21.58 per 100,000 people, respectively). Massachusetts and New York, on the other hand, have significantly lower fatality rates (4.79 and 6.19 per 100,000 people, respectively), and these states also have lower speed limits and stricter enforcement.

Readers who want to learn more about highway safety should first go to the NHTSA website. The following suggestions can make for safer highway travel:

- Obey posted speed limits.
- Depart early, and take frequent breaks.
- Never travel more than five hundred miles in one day.
- Slow down in congested areas, intersections, darkness, and rain.

- Travel in the far right (travel) lane because it usually offers an exit route to the right and better control over the space between your vehicle and other vehicles in front, in back, and to the left side.
- Increase your visibility by maintaining a four-second space behind the vehicle in front. If another vehicle tailgates you, slow down and encourage them to pass. Also slow down when near larger vehicles, such as tractor-trailers and buses that could obscure you vehicle from the view of other drivers.
- When traveling behind a slow vehicle, be patient and wait until you can execute a safe passing move as described in most state driving manuals.
- Learn to recognize potential highway hazards such as "gators" and "gaggles."
- Signal all turns and lane changes before making them.
- Accelerate and stop slowly and smoothly so that inattentive drivers will have time to react to your maneuvers.
- Wait at least one hour per standard unit of alcohol consumed before driving. For example, after consuming two twelve-ounce bottles of beer, wait at least two hours before driving. Better still, don't drink alcoholic beverages, or wait until the next day to drive.

Campsite Hazards

In general, camping is a very safe recreational activity. Thousands of families spend thousands of hours every year camping in public campgrounds and rarely, if ever, sustain serious injuries. However, basic tent campers should be aware of several potential hazards in some campsites and take special precautions to avoid these hazards.

Widow makers. Although extremely unlikely, high tree limbs have occasionally come crashing down onto tents and injured the occupants. Dead tree limbs (widow makers) are especially likely to fall during thunderstorms. The combination of weight from the rain and wind provides sufficient force to break limbs that have hung in place for several dry and sunny days. To avoid potential injury from widow makers, look up when you first arrive at a campsite. If a widow maker is visible, return to the park office and request a different campsite. In severe storms, live trees and limbs can fall. For example, during a fall camping trip to Unicoi State Park in Georgia a few years ago, a strong thunderstorm blew down several large pine limbs around the campground, and one of them fell a few feet away from Eva's and my tent. Consequently, campers should seek shelter in a bathroom or covered pavilion during thunderstorms until the strong winds pass.

Campfires. Fire seems to fascinate both children and adults. Sitting by a campfire and gazing into the flickering flames is a very relaxing activity for many people. Many children enjoy playing near fires and watching various objects burn. As a result, building campfires has become a traditional ritual for many families. Perhaps because campfires are so popular, campfire burns are the most common type of camping injury. These burns are usually caused by intoxication, carelessness, and horseplay near a campfire. To avoid these injuries, insist that children avoid horseplay in the campsite, especially near the fire ring, at all times—whether a fire is burning or not. Also plan the campsite so that the fire ring is separated from the tent and table to allow wide traffic routes around the site. You can also place folding chairs and tables around the fire ring to serve as a buffer to the potentially dangerous area. When working in or near a campfire, wear leather gloves to avoid accidental burns. Also avoid taking any mind-altering drugs because these drugs impair attention and dexterity and thus could lead to falls and severe burns.

The recommended treatment for a minor burn is to flush the burned area with cold water, pat or air-dry the area, and then apply an aloe cream or gel to reduce pain and excessive tissue drying. For moderate and severe burns, the person should be transported to a medical facility.

Severe burns have occasionally occurred from careless use of gasoline or other flammable materials. Gasoline and other accelerants should never be used to start fires. They can be extremely dangerous.

This fact is strongly etched into my mind because the younger brother of a friend died a few years ago as a result to using gasoline to start a fire. If a person's clothing catches on fire, experts recommend trying to extinguish the flames as quickly as possible by wrapping the person in a blanket or towel and rolling him or her on the ground. Then have the person lie down, and treat him or her for shock. Do not try to remove clothing, and immediately call for emergency medical assistance.

Hatchets and knives. Routine camp chores require frequent use of hatchets to split wood and knives to clean fish and cut food. Unfortunately, these sharp tools can also cause lacerations. To prevent lacerations, be careful and avoid horseplay, alcohol and other mind-altering drugs while using these tools. If a serious laceration occurs, first try to stop the bleeding by applying a sterile gauze pad from the first aid kit and direct pressure. If the gauze pad gets soaked with blood, apply a second pad on top of the first. The first pad should not be removed. If a sterile pad is unavailable, you can use a clean white towel; if a clean white towel is unavailable, you should use any available cloth or towel to stop the bleeding. If considerable bleeding has occurred, treat the victim for shock. Have the victim lie down with the feet slightly elevated and cover him or her with a blanket or sleeping bag. Call 911 or transport him or her to the nearest medical facility.

Tripping hazards. Around any given campsite, objects such as guy lines, tree roots, tree stumps, landscape timbers, stones, fire rings, and holes can cause falls and injuries, including sprains, broken bones, and sometimes soft-tissue injury. To prevent these injuries, survey the campsite before setting up and plan the layout so as to avoid most tripping hazards. Also set up camp several yards away from bluff drop-offs, rivers, and lakes. Tents, fire rings, and tables should be set up several feet apart to allow unrestricted traffic flow through the middle of the campsite. As already stated for other hazards, horseplay, alcohol, and other mind-altering drugs should be avoided in the campsite. When falls occur, abrasions, sprains, and bruises are the most common injuries, and these injuries can be treated in the campsite by washing the injured area and perhaps applying an elastic bandage from the first aid kit.

Broken bones and soft-tissue injury are more serious and require medical attention. Women may be at higher risk for broken bones than men because of osteoporosis. As previously stated, one of my female companions stepped in a small hole one night and broke her foot. In this case, I was able to help her get into the car and drive her to a local hospital emergency room. If more-serious injuries occur, have the injured person lie on the ground, call 911 and park personnel for assistance, and treat for shock. Backpackers who camp many miles away from cars, roads, and assistance are especially concerned about these hazards and should learn how to apply splints to broken bones and fashion crutches from small trees to help an injured person get back to a parked vehicle.

Tent fires. Although many camping and backpacking books suggest that campers can safely use emergency candles in their tents and cook meals in their tent vestibules during cold weather, basic tent campers should *not* attempt these foolish acts! All tent manufactures clearly state that candles, stoves, and other flammable materials should *never* be used in or near their tents because modern tents are made with highly combustible materials such as polyester and nylon. If a flame or spark touches the tent material, it will likely melt the material on contact, and the melted material could cause severe burns to human skin. And a small flame can quickly burn a relatively large area. To avoid tent fires, never use candles or cigarette lighters in or near tents, cook in tents, smoke cigarettes in tents, or use space heaters in tents. If a person is injured by a tent fire, flush the injury with cold water, leaving the melted plastic in place, and transport the injured person to a medical facility.

Carbon monoxide. Several companies, such as Coleman and Mr. Heater, sell portable electric, kerosene, and propane heaters presumably suited for camp use. And on cold fall, winter, and spring camping trips, many families might be tempted to buy these heaters to warm the insides of their tents. The most widely used of these heaters are catalytic

309

and infrared radiant propane heaters. Although these companies claim that their products are safe when used in well-ventilated areas, the US Consumer Product Safety Commission published two reports in 2002 and 2003 that question the validity of these claims.

The first report cited eighteen documented deaths due to carbon monoxide poisoning from portable infrared radiant heaters and tested the CO emissions from eighteen different models on the market. The report concluded that most of the tested heaters failed to comply with US government regulations regarding carbon dioxide emissions and oxygen depletion. The second report cited another documented death due to carbon monoxide poisoning from a portable catalytic heater and tested the CO emissions from the most popular model on the market. The report concluded that this catalytic heater produced marginally high carbon monoxide levels and depleted available oxygen much more than government standards allow. In other words, these heaters are not safe and should never be used. In cold weather, wear warm layers of clothes during the day, take hot showers before going to bed, wear warm layers of clothing at night, and sleep in sleeping bags that are rated at least fifteen degrees lower than anticipated low temperatures.

Intoxicated Neighbors

In my experience, the most common and most troublesome camping problem has been intoxicated neighbors. Frequently, groups of people decide to use a campground for an all-night drinking party. Families who have camped often in public campgrounds have probably endured a few of these drunken parties. Drunken campers frequently play loud music, argue, shout profanities, break glass, urinate in public, and drive recklessly in the campground. If another camper asks the group to settle down or to reduce their noise level, individuals in the group frequently become belligerent and increase the intensity of their obnoxious behavior.

It is not easy to predict who will turn into intoxicated neighbors. The campers in the next site may seem very friendly during the day, but when their friends arrive and they start drinking, a nice, quiet group can change into loud, belligerent drunks after dark. The best way to prevent the problem of intoxicated neighbors is to stay in large campgrounds with strict enforcement of quiet hours and overnight security. Larger state and federal campgrounds have entrance-control stations, campground hosts, and park rangers who can stop disturbances before they get out of hand.

Several years ago, while camping at Deep Creek campground in Great Smoky Mountains National Park, we were impressed with the park rangers who quelled a drunken party before it got out of hand. After setting up our campsite one Friday afternoon, another group arrived and set up tents on several sites near ours. Soon after the first group set up the tents, a second group arrived with cases of beer, a commercial generator, and portable stadium lights on a trailer. Needless to say, we were concerned. But as soon as the lights came on that night, rangers visited their site and convinced the group to turn off their lights and go to bed. The night was quiet. Fortunately, many state parks, such as those in Tennessee, Illinois, and a few in Michigan, prohibit alcoholic beverages in their campgrounds. Other states, like Wisconsin, have stepped up their enforcement of quiet hours. These parks generally have quiet and safe campgrounds that are suited for families and their children.

If a disturbance develops and officials do not come to stop it, you have few options. You could pack up and leave, but packing is hard to do after settling in for the night. If possible, call or visit the campground host or ranger. If they are unavailable, call the local police department or 911. The next morning after a disturbance, file an official complaint in the park office and request a refund. Odds are you will not get the refund, but the written request will draw the attention of park officials. After returning home, write a letter to the park's director and/or to the director of the state department of natural resources giving details of the incident, including the date and description of the disturbance and the lack of official intervention. Then repeat the request for a refund. You may not get your money back, but the documentation may save future campers from having to endure similar experiences.

Animal Scavengers

In many parks, various animals roam through the campground during the day and night looking for food. Unfortunately, many past campers have made food available to these animals and, thus, reinforced their scavenging behavior and increased the number of scavengers that are aggressive toward people. In the Smoky Mountains, Yellowstone, and Yosemite, past campers have provided food for bears, which has made some bears more aggressive toward park users. In fact, some people camp in the Smoky Mountains so that they can take photos of bears, and they take pride in showing close-up photos taken after chasing bears into the woods and giving them food. One recent bear-related death in the Cherokee National Forest in Tennessee was reportedly caused by a child feeding a bear so that her parent could get a close-up photo.

In any given location, several animal scavengers may roam through the campground looking for food. Mice, raccoons, and squirrels are common scavengers in many campgrounds, and the mice may attract snakes. In other campgrounds, opossums, skunks, armadillos, and coyotes may roam at night. My worst experience with animal scavengers was in the Myakka River State Park near Sarasota, Florida. When my companion and I sat down to enjoy our supper, a dozen raccoons crept within five feet of us and did not retreat when we tried to scare them away. In fact, I think that had we done nothing, they would have eventually climbed onto the table and tried to take our food away. After trying several things to discourage them, I threw a glass of water on one, and it retreated. Then we began throwing water on the others, and they all retreated back into the undergrowth. Since then, I have used a Super Soaker water gun to discourage aggressive scavengers.

A common mistake many campers make is bringing food, candy, chewing gum, and snacks into their tents. Children are especially inclined to bring food into the tent and must be constantly reminded and supervised. When told not to bring food in, some will try to sneak it in. The reason for leaving all food outside the tent is to avoid having food smells inside the tent that could attract mice and other animal scavengers. If food smells are in the tent, animals might damage the tent and perhaps injure people inside the tent trying to find the food. While camping in the Fort Pickens Campground in the Gulf Islands National Seashore several years ago, I saw a squirrel rip open the side of a neighbor's tent to get food that had been left inside. In Yellowstone and other bear habitats, bears may be attracted to food smells in a tent during the night and injure anyone inside to get the food. Once food has been brought into a tent, the smell may linger for several future camping trips, possibly continuing to attract other animals. In addition to leaving food outside the tent, campers should never bring clothing worn while cooking, toothpaste, deodorants, or other fragrant cosmetics into their tent. The best practice is to bathe every night before going to bed and leave all food, dirty clothes, shoes, and grooming kits in the car or an approved storage unit.

Perhaps the greatest concern with animals is the unlikely possibility of rabies. If you see a bat, raccoon, coyote, fox, skunk, or some other animal that appears injured or is wandering aimlessly or behaving in an unusual manner, stay clear and notify park officials. Generally speaking, you will not be bitten if you do not attempt to touch or capture animals and do not feed them. Additional details about common scavengers are presented below.

Mice. Several backpacking books and magazine articles report that mice present a potential problem in some backcountry campsites. They seem to gather near campsites where previous campers have left food and garbage around the grounds. They will come out at night and chew through tents, backpacks, stuff sacks, plastic wrappers, and other plastic containers. Once mice move in, snakes will soon follow. The best way to prevent mice is to pack snacks and other food in cars and deposit garbage in garbage stations. Backpackers should pack out garbage until they find a suitable trash receptacle.

Squirrels. These diurnal animals will also eat any food or garbage left around the campsite. Furthermore, they will tear holes in tents to get at food left inside. The best way to prevent these problems is to store food properly and never bring it into the tent.

Raccoons. These masked bandits are, by far, the peskiest animals for campers. They typically sleep in trees during the day and descend into campgrounds shortly after dusk. If raccoons live in the campground, they will visit every campsite during the night looking for food or garbage. They have opposable thumbs that allow them to open many different types of coolers and lockable boxes. They seem to be especially fond of eggs and corn but will eat almost any food they find. When raccoons come to a campsite, they will pick up spoons, plates, and other objects left out. They will also try to open any containers they find. If they find paper or plastic with food smells, they will shred it into a thousand pieces and strew it all about the site.

Raccoons look very cute and seem docile, but do not be deceived. They can be vicious when competing for food. They can easily kill or cripple feral barn cats that are relatively tough fighters. To prevent raccoon problems, never feed them, and never leave food or garbage in the campsite. Do not try to touch or handle them or any other wild animal. If they come too close, throw a cup of water on them or squirt them with a water gun.

Skunks. Skunks also come out after dark and could present problems for campers. They will roam through a campground during the night looking for food. In fact, they may walk right up to your picnic table as one did to me one night at Kentucky Dam Village State Resort Park near Paducah, Kentucky. If they feel threatened, they may spray your gear with an offensive odor that will be very difficult to remove. This is another reason for keeping campsites clean and keeping food packed away. If you see a skunk at night, remain calm and walk slowly away from it.

Porcupines. Porcupines are nocturnal animals that live in northern states east of the Mississippi River (e.g., Wisconsin, Michigan, and New York) and in all states west of the Mississippi River. I have little experience dealing with them, but other campers have experienced a few problems with them. Porcupines seem to be fond of eating salt and hard plastic like that used in coolers and plastic storage containers. When camping in porcupine territory, do not leave plastic containers out at night. The most common reported problem is pet dogs that get too close to porcupines and get quilled. Occasionally campers sleeping in hammocks have reported being quilled by porcupines wandering under their hammocks during the night. These quills have barbs similar to fish hooks and must be removed to prevent further injury. Removal is painful but necessary. Campers who cannot remove them themselves may have to seek medical assistance.

Coyotes. The number of coyotes in the eastern United States has increased significantly over the past twenty years, and these animals are venturing into public campgrounds and suburban neighborhoods looking for pet food, garbage, and small animals. Coyotes are reclusive animals that avoid human contact, but as their numbers rise in a particular geographic area, their attacks on pets and humans increase accordingly. Attacks on adult humans are rare, and the few documented attacks caused only minor injuries. Attacks on unprotected young children and small pets, on the other hand, can be more dangerous. Fortunately, few attacks have occurred in public campgrounds. To avoid possible coyote problems in public campgrounds, observe posted regulations, store food properly, guard young children, and leave pets at home.

Mountain lions. According to Wikipedia, only twenty people have been killed by mountain lions (or cougars) in North America over the past one hundred years. In other words, mountain lion attacks are extremely rare. Several of these fatalities were children, and only one of the fatalities was camping at the time of the attack. Although a cougar attack is extremely unlikely, people camping in mountain lion territory should always be alert to potential problems and ask rangers about risks and recommended prevention methods.

Bears. Many recent camping books and magazine articles have been a little overdramatic when discussing bears. They typically begin by explaining that two basic types of bears live in the lower forty-eight states. Black bears can be found in many states, especially North Carolina. Brown (or grizzly) bears are primarily found in the northern Mountain States. Both types are much more plentiful in Canada and in Alaska. Generally speaking, both types of bears are shy and usually try to avoid human contact. According to Wikipedia, thirty-one fatal bear attacks have been documented over the past thirty years in the United States, and most of these attacks occurred in Alaska. I have personally camped several times in bear habitats, and most of the trips, I never saw a bear. When I did, they were near hiking trails or in Cades Cove. Based upon official statistics and my personal experience, it is safe to conclude that the risk of a fatal bear attack in developed campgrounds in the lower forty-eight states is extremely small. Nevertheless, many camping and hiking books go into lengthy discussions regarding preventing and fighting off bear attacks.

A recent article in *Backpacker Magazine* reported that bears in some western parks (especially Yosemite National Park) have become adept at stealing food from locked cars and campsites in developed campgrounds. And once bears learn to steal food from humans, they can easily injure someone. To keep these bears under control, park rangers tranquillized several that were lingering too close to campgrounds and tagged them with radio wave transmitters. After the bears were released, the rangers could monitor their movements in the dark. When a bear got too close to a campground, the rangers located it and harassed it with loud noise until it left the area. When camping in bear habitat, campers should follow these seven commonly listed rules:

- Never feed bears.
- Keep food in cars or metal lockers, and put garbage in metal garbage receptacles to prevent bear access, especially when leaving the campsite or retiring for the night.
- Never bring food, toothpaste, sunscreen, or other fragrant items into a tent.
- Remove clothing worn when cooking before entering the tent.
- Do not approach or follow bears or their cubs.

- Make noise when hiking to avoid accidentally surprising a bear that may be feeding or resting near the trail. Some hikers attach bells to their clothing or hiking poles.
- Never chase bears into the woods.

In bear habitats, talk with park rangers and follow posted rules. Some people buy cans of bear-repellent spray, but most people do not feel the need to purchase this item.

Hiking Trails

As previously mentioned, a significant number of park visitors are injured every year by falling from high places. Typically, careless people hike to scenic places along the trails, ignore posted signs, venture too far out toward the edge, and lose their balance. Along popular trails hikers will see dozens of careless people who seem to be oblivious to the risks of serious injury and death. Climbing slippery, moss-covered rocks near waterfalls is a common example. Popular waterfalls in the Appalachian Mountains typically have dozens of people climbing these slippery rocks every day. In fact, some parents encourage their children to climb these rocks so they can get good photos. It is a wonder that more people are not injured. To avoid these injuries, be careful, refrain from drinking alcoholic beverages, obey posted signs, and use good judgment.

Food- and Water-Borne Illnesses

According to the Center for Disease Control and Prevention, at least thirty-one different pathogens may cause food- or water-borne illness. Some of the more common pathogens include *Norovirus, C. perfringens, Campylobacter, Salmonella, Listeria, E. coli, Toxoplasma, Crypto,* and *Giardia*. While other camping and backpacking books frequently discuss *Giardia*, they typically fail to mention other more likely causes of food- and water-borne illnesses.

Most of these illnesses are caused by fecal contamination of food or water. Common sources of infection include chicken and other meats, eggs, fresh vegetables fertilized with manure, fresh fruit, and contaminated water. Common symptoms include gastrointestinal discomfort, diarrhea, fever, and muscle aches. The illnesses differ in terms of initial symptom onset, severity of symptoms, and duration of symptoms. Some illnesses, such as norovirus, produce relatively mild symptoms, while others, such as toxoplasmosis, can be fatal. Rehydration and occasional antibiotic medicine may be needed, but most healthy adults will recover from these illnesses with few complications. Children, elderly people, and people with other serious illnesses such as HIV/AIDS could experience more-serious symptoms, kidney failure, central nervous system infection, convulsions, and even death. Follow these basic procedures to help prevent these illnesses:

- Wash hands often. Always wash hands after going to the bathroom and before preparing food.
- Do not prepare food when sick.
- Store chicken and meats in a separate container from other foods.
- Wash cutting boards, knives, plates, and tablecloths with warm soapy water after contact with foods, especially raw chicken and other meats.
- Wash raw fruits and vegetables.
- Cook foods thoroughly, especially chicken and other meats and eggs.
- Package and store leftovers in coolers immediately after finishing the meal.
- Discard leftovers after two days.
- Wash clothes often.
- Backpackers and other people camping in remote wilderness areas should filter and sterilize water used for food preparation and drinking.

People can contract these illnesses in their homes or in restaurants, but basic tent campers spending several days in outdoor campsites with limited clean water may be at greater risk. Tent campers do not have a ready source of hot water, large sinks, reliable stoves, and refrigerators and, thus, must take extra care to follow good kitchen-hygiene practices.

Weather

Many beginning tent campers strike out on their first camping trips unprepared for possible weather problems. In fact, many people may not know how to prepare for these conditions because they spend most of their time in heated and air-conditioned buildings and automobiles. They become accustomed to dressing with a minimum amount of clothes and may not have the extra warm layers needed for extended outdoor living. When they decide to take camping trips, they may bring one or two jackets, but these garments may not be suited for extended periods of time outdoors.

Cold. After a few hours of inactivity in relatively cool temperatures (lower than 60°F) without adequate clothing, body core temperature may begin to drop, especially when clothing is wet from rain or sweat. As a result campers may begin to shiver uncontrollably and could develop hypothermia. When a person develops hypothermia, he or she will likely become a little confused and make poor decisions, which could increase the risk for serious accidents.

The best way to prepare for cold weather is to pack the right type of clothes. Wear moisture-wicking underwear, thermal underwear, and several layers of moisture-wicking polyester or wool garments. Also bring a sleeping bag that is rated at least fifteen degrees lower than the expected low temperature. Cotton garments and leather jackets should be left at home because they will not keep body core temperature within the normal range.

If you begin to shiver, go to a warm building. Hot-air hand dryers in bathrooms are useful for warming. If possible, take long, warm showers when cold. If your clothes get wet, put on dry clothes, and dry the wet clothes as soon as possible. If you do not have warm clothing and bedding, pack up camp and drive to a motel (or to your home) and wait for warmer weather.

Thunderstorms. Thunderstorms are relatively common in many parts of the country, especially during the spring-summer-fall camping season. Most campers in the eastern United States will likely experience thunderstorms on a fairly frequent basis. Most of the time, these storms only create minor inconveniences, such as soaking tents, bedding, and clothing, which then require a little time to dry out. But thunderstorms have the potential for causing serious injury or death. Campers should always recognize this potential and take precautionary actions. One major threat from a thunderstorm is lightning. It kills about eighty people every year in the United States and injures many more. Another threat from thunderstorms is high wind that can cause large trees or limbs to fall onto tents. Heavy rains from thunderstorms can cause flash floods. Sometimes thunderstorms spawn large hail and tornadoes that could injure campers and damage their gear.

The best prevention for thunderstorm-related problems is to monitor local weather forecasts. If strong thunderstorms are predicted during the day, you may want to pack your gear and seek shelter. Any building is better than staying in the open. The best buildings are brick or stone buildings with few glass doors and windows. A basement is an ideal place to go, but many buildings do not have basements. Hospitals, medical clinics, libraries, banks, government buildings, and college buildings are usually good choices. If thunderstorms are forecast for the night, you may want to consider spending the night in a motel.

If you get caught in a thunderstorm, move to a bathroom, park office, recreation building, covered picnic shelter, or similar shelter. You definitely need a solid roof that will keep you dry and protect you from falling limbs, flying debris, and hail. If possible, choose buildings with solid brick or rock walls and few windows, as these buildings can protect you from wind and possible tornadoes.

Poisonous Plants

Several plants, including poison ivy, poison oak, poison sumac, giant hogweed, and wild parsnip, can produce strong allergic reactions. Although a few people may be immune to these plants, most people will have moderate to severe reactions characterized by skin irritation. A few people may experience extreme symptoms such as difficult breathing and swallowing. The way to prevent accidental exposure is to learn how to recognize these plants and avoid contact with them.

Poison ivy and poison oak have distinctive three-leaf clusters. Either plant may grow as a vine on a tree or as sprouts from the ground. Poison ivy leaves tend to be pointed with toothed edges, while poison oak leaves tend to be rounded with smooth edges. Frequently, the stems of poison ivy and poison oak are pink or red. Many campgrounds will have poison ivy near campsites, and campers should be especially vigilant when tying kitchen canopy guy lines and hammock straps to trees.

Poison sumac is a bush or small tree that typically grows in wet areas like swamps, marshes, and other moist-soil areas. Its leaves grow in pairs along a reddish stem with a final leaf at the end of the stem. The leaves are oblong in shape, have smooth edges, and have a point at the tip. In the fall, the leaves of this plant will turn to beautiful shades of red and orange. Wild parsnip is a weed that has recently invaded midwestern prairies. It looks like a yellow wildflower, but skin contact can produce severe allergic burn reactions. Wild parsnip has become very common near campsites in Wisconsin and Minnesota. It is especially plentiful in Governor Dodge State Park near Dodgeville, Wisconsin. Giant hogweed is another poisonous plant that can be found near campgrounds in northern Indiana.

When you first arrive at a campsite and begin to plan the setup, look for these plants and plan accordingly. Try to set up the camp to avoid accidental contact with these plants. Carelessly tying guy lines to trees, tying hammocks to trees, and driving stakes into the ground can cause several days of misery. When walking in the woods or brush, wear boots rather than shower shoes and stay on marked trails.

If someone accidentally contacts one of these plants, he or she should remove any clothing that may have contacted the plant, wash the affected area with Zanfel soap or another poison ivy soap, and perhaps apply an antipruritic cream or lotion, such as calamine lotion. If a moderately severe reaction occurs, he or she may want to take a

Benadryl tablet from the first aid kit. If the camper experiences difficult breathing, he or she should be transported to the nearest medical facility.

Several other plants are poisonous to eat. Since basic tent campers have ready access to grocery stores, there is little reason to eat wild plants and berries. In particular, campers should not be tempted to eat wild mushrooms. The best advice is to refrain from eating wild plants unless you have extensive training in edible foods and are able to positively identify edible and inedible species.

Insects and Arachnids

On many trips, campers can encounter a variety of insects and arachnids. Insects are small arthropods with six legs and usually wings. They include mosquitoes, bees, chiggers, ants, caterpillars, and other biting or stinging insects. Arachnids are arthropods or insect-looking creatures with an exoskeleton that have four pair of legs and a body that is divided into two regions. They include ticks, spiders, and scorpions.

Mosquitoes. Mosquitoes are commonly found in many campgrounds across the country. They breed in standing water and are likely to be plentiful in campgrounds located near swamps, marshes, backwaters, and other places where water stands still. They are more active during the early-morning hours and the evening hours. In the southern United States and in other parts of the country, they present only a minor annoyance, but in some parts of the country, such as the upper-midwestern states (Minnesota, North Dakota, South Dakota, and Wisconsin), they can make camping trips miserable for people who are unprepared to deal with them. Campers who are unprepared for them will have difficulty staying out during certain parts of the day. In addition to the immediate discomfort they cause, mosquitoes can carry several serious diseases, including chikungunya, dengue, malaria, yellow fever, West Nile virus, and several different types of encephalitis. Therefore, campers should have appropriate repellent, candles, and clothing to minimize discomfort and illness. Ideally, campgrounds with serious mosquito problems should eliminate pools of standing water, periodically spray insecticide, and use other means to control the population.

The most frequently used method to prevent mosquito bites is to apply mosquito repellent. As previously discussed, most experts recommend products with DEET, such as Off! Deep Woods or Repel, because these products provide longer protection and repel more mosquitoes. But DEET-based products have some limitations that encourage some families to use other products. For more information about insect repellants, see chapter 8 "Protection and First Aid."

Biting flies. Campers may encounter biting flies in several regions of the country. For example, biting flies are typically present on the Florida Gulf Coast during September and make it difficult to sunbathe on the beach. Biting black flies can also be found during certain parts of the year in Michigan's Upper Peninsula, Minnesota's Boundary Waters Canoe Area Wilderness, and Wisconsin's Door Peninsula. Deerflies and horseflies can be encountered in other parts of the country, including Wisconsin's prairie areas. These flies bite legs, backs, and faces and can make outdoor activities unbearable. When campers encounter swarms of biting flies, they can apply a DEET- or Picaridin-based product, but it may not repel the flies. In this case, head nets and insect-repellent clothing may be necessary.

Yellow jackets and other stinging insects. Campers may occasionally encounter stinging insects, such as yellow jackets, bees, wasps, and hornets. Reportedly, more people are hospitalized because of allergic reactions to insect stings than because of any other type of animal attack. Stinging insects can pose a potential problem all summer, but they seem to be most aggressive on hot days at the end of the summer. To prevent insect stings, campers should look where they are walking and where they put their hands. Yellow jackets make their nests in the ground. If a person steps on their nest, the yellow jackets are likely to attack in a mass, inflicting several stings. During their attack, they will get inside clothing to sting the victim. Hornets build large nests in trees and usually swarm around these nests. If you see a nest, move away as quickly as possible, and not disturb it. Bees, especially Africanized bees, have also caused occasional problems.

When a person is stung by any of these insects, he or she should first wash the skin around the sting. The person may want to take a Benadryl tablet and dab Itch Eraser on the bite to relieve initial discomfort. Sometimes ice packs or cold water will relieve the pain for a short time. Some experts recommend scraping a honeybee sting with a credit card to remove the stinger. Other authorities recommend applying meat tenderizer, if it is available, to the sting. Anyone who receives several stings or has difficulty breathing should seek immediate medical attention.

Chiggers. Chiggers or red bugs can also cause problems in certain parts of the country. Chiggers are plentiful in Gulf State Park in Gulf Shores, Alabama, in particular. Although the grass is neatly groomed and the ground is mostly sandy, anyone who allows their bare skin to touch the ground will likely incur dozens of bites. Typically, the person does not feel the bites when they occur but will notice dozens of bright-red spots about fifteen minutes later. After a little time these bites will produce a mild itch that can be controlled with Itch Eraser. But the red spots will continue to be visible and itch for about a week after the trip. To avoid chigger bites, avoid kneeling or lying on the ground when setting up tents and kitchen canopies.

Ants. Ants, especially fire ants found throughout the South, can cause occasional problems for campers. People should look for ant mounds as soon as they arrive in a campsite. Ants may be drawn to a particular campsite by food or sweetened beverages that were spilled on the ground by previous site occupants. If any food has been spilled on the ground, campers should remove as much as possible and rinse the ground with water. If ant mounds are present, tents and kitchen canopies should be set up as far away from them as possible. Campers do not want to accidentally step in a mound after dark. If a person stepped into a mound, he or she would likely receive numerous bites before getting the ants off his or her feet and legs. When bitten by ants, apply Itch Eraser.

Stinging caterpillars. Although other camping books do not discuss stinging caterpillars, I decided to include these insects because I had an unpleasant experience with them on a camping trip a few years back. My companion and I arrived at the Deep Creek campground in Great Smoky Mountains National Park early one morning and secured what seemed to be a choice site under some trees near the creek. As we began to unpack and set up our site, we noticed numerous white, fuzzy caterpillars around our campsite. We saw them on the picnic table, the landscaping timbers that defined the tent pad, and on the tent as we were setting it up. After setting up our sleeping quarters, we even found a few that we had inadvertently brought inside our tent. We generally tried to avoid contact with them but did not yet realize that they could cause considerable discomfort.

During the first night, one of my legs felt as if small needles were sticking it inside my sleeping bag. At first I thought it might be a stiff nylon thread or a twig, and so I rubbed my legs and moved about several times to adjust my sleeping position. But the stinging continued. The next day my legs were red and still stinging. My companion also complained that her neck was stinging. Initially, we had no idea what could have caused our problems, but a few days later, when packing up, we found four of these caterpillars in our bedding. A few days later, when our symptoms seemed to worsen, I began to suspect that the caterpillars had caused our problems. To confirm my hypothesis, I searched the web and found several sites that described skin irritation caused by the fine hairs of caterpillars.

Most caterpillars do not cause skin irritation, but a few stinging (or urticating) caterpillars do exist. While they do not attack people, they will release toxins if people accidentally contact them. Some of the well-known stinging varieties are saddleback caterpillars, flannel moth caterpillars, and puss caterpillars. When people contact stinging caterpillars, they may experience the sensation that needles are sticking them followed by a rash, stinging or burning sensation, numbness, and nausea. The irritation varies in severity from person to person. Untreated, it subsides in about seven days.

If you believe that you have contacted stinging caterpillars, change clothes, and wash the contacted area with soap and water. If a stinging sensation or rash develops, stick duct tape on the skin area and pull it off quickly. Hopefully this procedure will remove many of the stinging hairs. After using tape to remove the hairs, apply a cortisone cream from the first aid kit.

Ticks. Ticks are a common arachnid found around many campgrounds. There are at least fifteen varieties, but the most common are small deer ticks, dog ticks, and lone star ticks. They are found in tall grass and weeds almost anywhere in the country. They typically rest on the grass and wait until a warm-blooded animal brushes against the grass. Then they jump or climb onto the host animal. Once on the host, they will walk around for a while until they attach to the skin and begin to suck the blood. They seem to like areas that are covered with tight-fitting clothing like socks and underwear.

Ticks present a major health concern because they can carry several diseases, including Rocky Mountain spotted fever and Lyme disease. Lyme disease may be transmitted by small deer ticks in all parts of the country, but, according to the Center for Disease Control, almost all the reported cases are concentrated in upper-midwestern and northeastern states. Most of the cases were caused by tick exposure in the person's own yard rather than in a campground.

To prevent problems caused by ticks, stay on paved or hard-packed pathways and avoid walking in tall grass as much as possible. When you must walk in tall grass, wear long pants tucked into your socks. Also apply insect repellent such as Off! Deep Woods. Each evening inspect your body when you bathe. In particular, examine your scalp, armpits, groin, lower legs, waist, and the backs of your knees.

Several methods have been recommended for removing embedded ticks. The method that seems to be most accepted is to grasp the tick as near to the skin as possible with a pair of tweezers and slowly pull until the tick releases. Do not jerk a tick out or pull it out with fingers. If some parts of a tick remain in the skin, remove them with the tweezers. Once the tick has been removed, kill it by cutting it with a knife or stepping on it with a boot. Then wash the wound with soap and water.

Spiders. In most campsites, campers will see a few different types of spiders. The daddy longlegs is the most common spider in many parks. It is harmless, and experts claim that it controls the populations of other spiders. When a daddy longlegs gets in the tent, just grab one of its legs and throw it outside the tent. Most other spiders are harmless, but you should take a few precautions to avoid annoying spider bites. In particular, look where you will be sitting or lying down (especially in hammocks and chairs that have been up all night), and shake out socks and shoes.

Two spiders deserve a little more attention. One is the black widow, a glossy black spider with a red spot (frequently described as an hourglass) on its abdomen. Black widows have potent neurotoxin venom, but their bite usually is not fatal to most healthy adults. They are very easy to spot during daylight hours. They like moisture and seem to have an affinity for pit toilets, woodpiles, and objects that have been lying on the ground for a few days. They are not very common, but campers should be watchful. Whenever visiting an outhouse, lift the seat, look into the toilet, and run a stick around the base before sitting down. When picking up firewood or other objects lying on the ground, use gloves and move the object first so you can look under it before picking it up. Recently, red and brown widow spiders have been reported in Florida and other parts of the country.

The second poisonous spider to know is the brown recluse. This tan-brown spider has a small dark violin- or fiddle-shaped mark on the back of its head and upper body. It is primarily found in the southern states ranging from Texas to Georgia and from the Gulf Coast up to central Iowa, Illinois, and Indiana. It likes dark, dry places such as attics and storage sheds, but it may also be found underneath logs, rock piles, and stacks of lumber. Typically these spiders do not attack humans but may bite when touched or crushed.

To avoid spider bites, wear gloves, and look before picking up wood and stones from the ground. If a person is bitten by a black widow or brown recluse, the bite is unlikely to be fatal but can cause serious reactions in some people. The bitten person should apply ice packs and seek medical attention.

Scorpions. Scorpions are nocturnal creatures that avoid human contact. They are found in many warmer parts of the country. Most are not dangerous to healthy adults. In fact, small scorpions found in Henderson Beach State Park Florida produce a very mild sting. However, one very dangerous type is the Arizona bark scorpion, which lives in the desert Southwest, especially in Arizona. Most of the time, its sting is not fatal to healthy adults, but it can kill people who are allergic to it or who have been weakened by other medical problems. To avoid scorpion stings, shake out your sleeping bag before entering it at night, and shake out clothing and boots in the morning before putting them on.

Reptiles

Three major types of reptiles are snakes, lizards, and alligators. All three could cause problems for campers but rarely do.

Snakes. Many noncampers cite possible snakebites as a primary reason for not camping, but their fears are generally unfounded. According to several sources, such as *American Family Physician* (April 1, 2002), only five to ten deaths a year in the United States are caused by venomous snakebites, and the majority of these bites occur when people try to capture snakes for recreational or religious activities. Over my past forty-plus years of camping, I have seen a few snakes but never been attacked by one. In fact, none of the few snakes I have seen were venomous. I have seen many more snakes in my backyard at home and on hiking trails than in public campgrounds.

Despite the low risk of snake-related problems, basic tent campers should learn how to identify various species of snakes in case they encounter one. Most venomous snakes are pit vipers with wide heads. They are most active on dry, hot, late-summer days, especially after the sun goes down. The most common venomous snake is the copperhead.

This particular species is more likely to live near humans and is known to hang around houses in flowerbeds here in the South. Of the four venomous snakes, the copperhead is the one that campers would most likely encounter near a campground. Its bite is painful but not deadly for most healthy adults. Bite victims should be taken to a hospital for observation, but most of the time antivenin and other aggressive medical treatments will not be necessary.

The cottonmouth, or water moccasin, is the second venomous snake and is also found in southern states. This snake lives near water and has been known to strike people who walk too close. To avoid this snake, set up camp at least two hundred feet (seventy paces) away from rivers, lakes, ponds, ditches, and other bodies of water, and be very cautious when walking near water.

The rattlesnake is perhaps the best known of the venomous snakes. There are over thirty different species of rattlesnakes, but the eastern diamondback, found in the southern Gulf Coast states, and the western diamondback, found in southern Texas, New Mexico, and Arizona, are considered to be the most dangerous of all the venomous snakes in the United States. Other species can be found in most other states, but rattlesnakes are more plentiful in warmer southern states.

The coral snake is the fourth venomous snake found in the United States. This snake is different from the first three in that it is not a pit viper, and, thus, its head is much smaller than the heads of the other three venomous snakes. Most coral snakes live in remote, heavily forested areas and in rotting wood. They are very unlikely to be found in developed campgrounds. Coral snakes have bright red, yellow, and black bands. Other colorful snakes, such as king snakes, have similar coloring, but the coral snake is the only one that has yellow bands adjacent to red bands. To help remember this specific combination, many people memorize the saying "Red touch yellow, kill a fellow."

The primary way campers might encounter venomous snakes is by hiking in an isolated area or picking up logs or flat pieces of wood, metal, or plastic lying on the ground. So be watchful for snakes when in the woods and when around logs, firewood stacks, and rock piles. When walking about the campground after dark, use a headlamp or flashlight since a few bites occur when people accidentally step on snakes after dark. When walking near lakes, slow-moving rivers, and other bodies of water in the South, watch for water moccasins.

The best way to prevent snakebites is to keep your distance from the reptiles. Use a stick to move objects on the ground. Look where you put your hands and where you step, especially in tall grass or near water, fallen logs, and rocks. If you see a snake, give it room. Do not try to kill it or capture it. In the highly unlikely event that a person is bitten by a venomous snake, get a good description of the snake (head shape, color, body markings, length, and diameter); wash the bite with soap and water; remove rings, watches, and other jewelry; immobilize the bitten area, keeping it lower than the heart; and get medical attention. Some experts recommend applying ice to slow the blood flow, but other experts debate the value of this treatment. All experts agree that cutting the skin and applying tourniquets can cause more harm to the victim and consider these methods to be ineffective. The most important thing to do is to get the person to a medical facility as quickly as possible.

Lizards. Campers may see a variety of lizards, but most of them are harmless. Only one venomous lizard lives in the United States: the Gila monster, which is found in Arizona and adjacent parts of California, Nevada, Utah, and New Mexico. These lizards are much larger than most others. Generally they live underground and ordinarily pose little threat to most campers. Use the same precautions as for snakes and scorpions. If a person is bitten, take him or her to a medical facility.

Alligators. One last reptile to mention is the alligator. These reptiles are common in Florida and several southern states and frequently eat dogs and other small animals but rarely attack humans. However, during the 1980s, a man swimming in the small lake at Open Pond campground in the Conecuh National Forest in south Alabama was attacked. The alligator grabbed his arm and tried to pull him out to deep water. The man fought against the alligator's pull and lost his arm in the struggle. Avoid alligators by camping several feet away from the water's edge, and exercise caution when swimming or walking near water. Never feed or tease alligators.

As Holding observed over a hundred years ago, the risk of being injured while camping in developed state and federal campgrounds is very low, but basic tent campers should become familiar with things that could cause injury and be prepared to treat or stabilize these injuries if they do ever occur.

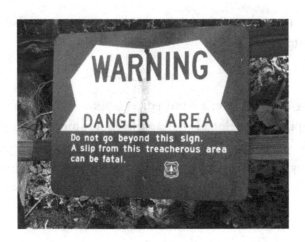

Falling from high cliffs and bluffs is the primary
cause of injury in state and national parks.

Despite warning signs and documented deaths, many
people climb on slippery waterfall rocks and encourage
their children to do the same. Photo of Abrams Falls in
Great Smoky Mountains National Park in Tennessee.

Poison ivy and poison oak have three leaves. This is poison oak.

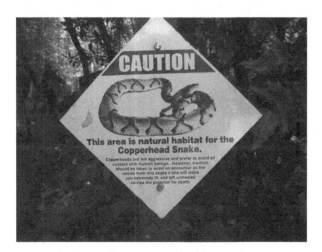

Campers should become familiar with the four venomous snakes in North America. Copperheads are more likely to be encountered in the Southeast than other species.

17

ETHICS

Camping in the woods several miles away from supervisors, coworkers, neighbors, and family members creates a profound sense of anonymity and personal freedom that cannot be experienced anywhere else. Campers can set up their campsites any way they want, prepare any food they want, engage in any recreational or leisure activities they want, say what they want, wear any clothes they want, and go to bed anytime they want. They can read books when they want, relax in their hammocks, or spend hours gazing into a campfire. They do not have pressing demands and do not have to seek approval from anyone. This sense of personal freedom is further reinforced by the fact that park rangers have traditionally maintained a low profile and campground neighbors do not care to know about other people's business in the campground. After a few days, these neighbors will leave the campground and probably never be seen again. Even if a person does something embarrassing, the odds are that no one at home will ever know about it. Like in Las Vegas, things that happen in distant campgrounds usually stay in those campgrounds.

Unfortunately, a significant number of park visitors have abused this freedom in past years and engaged in various inappropriate and destructive behaviors. For example, many people have used unsupervised public campgrounds for all-night drinking parties and have engaged in a litany of obnoxious behaviors that would offend the sensibilities of most decent people. During these parties, people play loud music, argue, break glass bottles, curse, fight, urinate in public, engage in inappropriate sexual behavior, and drive recklessly. Anyone else in the campground is forced to endure this obnoxious noise all night long or pack up their campsites in the middle of the night. If another camper asks the partiers to settle down, someone in the party often becomes belligerent and wants to fight. During the 1980s and '90s, these parties were especially plentiful because many public parks had limited overnight supervision.

Other park visitors have engaged in deliberate acts of vandalism. Over the past forty years, park visitors have intentionally damaged picnic tables, driven cars or trucks on the grass, cut trees for various reasons, defaced buildings, killed wildlife, moved stones, pulled plants, collected souvenirs, and painted graffiti on beautiful rock formations. In Mammoth Cave, for example, hundreds of past visitors have written their names with lantern soot on the ceiling and walls of the cave. In Great Smoky Mountains National Park, dozens of past park visitors have carved or spray-painted their names on the walls of historic buildings and other surfaces throughout the park. In other parks, visitors have stolen historically or archeologically important rocks, stalactites, pieces of driftwood, flowers, plants such as sea oats, and more. Campers have cut trees for whimsical reasons, such as making fires, shelters, and beds. They have killed or injured wildlife and trampled fragile vegetation to make paths and campsites. In general, many park visitors have apparently believed they have the freedom to do whatever they want in public parks, to leave their mark, and to take whatever souvenirs they can find.

After considerable damage had been done in many parks, conservationists realized that park visitors were slowly and systematically destroying the parks and their natural resources. While one destructive act may not produce a significant impact, thousands of repetitive, thoughtless destructive acts could eventually destroy animal habitat and historic buildings and prevent future generations from being able to experience the beautiful and historic areas that parks were created to protect. Consequently, park officials began implementing procedures designed to control these destructive acts.

Rules and Regulations

Within the past thirty years, state and federal parks have begun publishing, distributing, and posting several park rules and regulations designed to protect park property, wildlife, and other users from careless and intentionally destructive acts committed by park visitors. Ethical campers should become familiar with these rules and obey them even when park rangers are not present to enforce them. Common campground rules are summarized below.

Firewood. In past years, campers could bring firewood from their homes and save the expense of buying it near the park. But today, most parks require that all firewood be purchased locally to help reduce the spread of harmful pests. The primary reason for this firewood ban is to control the spread of the emerald ash borer, which lays its eggs in ash trees and has killed thousands of these trees in the Upper Midwest. When an egg-infested tree is cut for firewood and moved to a new location, the eggs hatch, and new insects are released into a previously uninfected area. Today, biologists are concerned that other pests can also be spread by moving firewood. Therefore, ethical tent campers should plan to purchase their firewood from vendors located within twenty-five miles of their campground.

Speed limits. Most campgrounds post speed limits of about ten miles per hour to prevent injury to children, bicyclists, and other campground occupants who may not be paying attention to cars and trucks traveling along the campground roads. Popular campgrounds are especially congested places where children may play in the road and adults walk or run into the road without looking. Children are frequently unaware of potential dangers and run about impulsively. Furthermore, many children learn to ride bicycles on campground roads and so may not have full control of their bicycles. Even when they see a car, they may not have the physical skills needed to avoid it. Pet dogs might run into the road to greet people or meet other dogs. And adults frequently stroll and ride bicycles through campgrounds looking at neighbors' campsites and speaking with anyone who happens to be present. Therefore, anyone driving through a campground should stop for children and slow down for adults. Obeying posted speed limits protects others from injury and shows respect for fellow campers.

Registration and occupancy. Many campgrounds require campers to register before (or soon after) setting up their campsites, and many campgrounds require campers to place a copy of their registration slip with occupancy dates on a post near the road so that park rangers can verify that site occupants have properly registered. The overall purpose of these rules is to clearly demonstrate that the site is unavailable for any other party and the camping fee has been paid. If a person failed to set up camp on a site after registering for it, the site would look unoccupied. Other people riding through the campground looking for unoccupied sites could easily assume that this site was available and begin setting up camp on it. Logically, they might assume that the previous occupant had decided to depart early. When one party sets up their camp on an empty site that has been reserved by another party, arguments can get very heated.

After a site has been set up, many popular campgrounds require that occupants must be physically present in their sites a few hours every day for the duration of their stay. The purpose of this regulation is to prevent people from setting up RVs or camping units and using them as occasional weekend getaways when other people would like to camp in the park.

Parking. Many campgrounds restrict the number of vehicles per campsite to two and require that these vehicles be parked on paved or gravel parking areas. Additional vehicles, including those of visitors, must be parked in an overflow parking lot. These rules protect vegetation and soft ground and prevent congested areas that could block traffic flow. Repeatedly parking heavy vehicles on the grass or in the bushes will eventually kill fragile vegetation and thereby eliminate habitat for small plant and animal species. Parking on the grass after heavy rain leaves unsightly tire tracks and muddy ruts that detract from the beauty of the park for future visitors. Limiting the number of vehicles parked at a site can also help to prevent large crowds and parties from forming. Finally, parking on the grass could lead to driving on the grass, and driving on the grass could lead to injuring other campers or damaging their tents and property.

Number of occupants. As a part of the registration procedure, campers usually must indicate the number of children and adults that will be occupying the site. Most parks will allow only six to eight people per site. Sometimes campgrounds will allow only one family to occupy the site. One reason for limiting site occupancy is to avoid overcrowding the site and the campground. Another reason is to avoid overtaxing the water supply and bathroom facilities. A third reason is to prevent large groups of people from using campsites for parties and disturbing other campers during quiet hours.

Set up within defined campsite limits. Most campsites have obvious limits defined by landscape timbers or understory vegetation. Michigan campsite limits are frequently defined by white lines painted on the campground roads. When campers begin to set up their campsites, they should position their tents on the designated tent pads, if present, and keep all hammocks, chairs, and kitchen canopies within the defined site limits. In gravel sites defined by landscape timbers, campers should set up their tents and kitchen shelters on the gravel rather than adjacent grass or bare ground. They should not place tents back in the trees away from their designated sites. Keeping tents on durable surfaces within the designated sites helps prevent additional damage to the vegetation of the park. Exceptions to this rule can be found in a few parks, such as Gulf State Park in Gulf Shores, Alabama, where campers are not permitted to set up their tents and kitchen canopies on paved parking areas and must set them up on adjacent grassy areas.

Quiet hours. Most parks define quiet hours from about ten at night to seven in the morning. During these quiet hours, campers are expected to be quiet so that other people can sleep peacefully. Ideally, campers should go to bed during these times, but those who choose to stay up late should talk in whispers. Campers should not play radios, strum guitars, sing, or talk loudly during this time. Cars and motorcycles should be parked, dogs should be quiet, and children should be in bed. New campers should not arrive late and set up their campsites after quiet hours, and old campers should not take down their campsites in the morning until the end of quiet hours.

Wildlife. Many parks provide a sanctuary for a variety of wildlife species, including squirrels, raccoons, skunks, bears, foxes, coyotes, bobcats, birds, toads, lizards, and snakes. These animals lived in the area before the park was established and should be allowed to continue living there after campers come and go. To protect these animals, many parks have rules that forbid molesting or feeding them. Campers should enjoy their presence from a distance but not approach them, tease them, throw rocks at them, try to catch them, or attempt to injure or kill them. Instead, campers should learn to respect the animals' right to exist in the park and leave them alone. If an animal presents a problem, campers should inform a park ranger.

Most parks prohibit feeding park animals or allowing them to access food or garbage. If wild animals consistently get food from humans, they will lose their ability to forage for food, become dependent upon easy food, lose their fear of humans, persistently beg food from people, and could injure people by aggressively taking food from them. When animals become too aggressive toward humans, they may have to be destroyed. In cooler months when humans are no longer camping in an area, frequently fed animals may not be able to find food and could starve to death. As a result of these problems, many parks have signs stating, "A fed animal is a dead animal."

While this rule makes perfect sense, many people feed animals in public campgrounds. When camping in different parts of the country, campers will see their neighbors feeding birds, squirrels, and other animals in their campsites. For example, some campers and day users in Great Smoky Mountains National Park feed bears to get close-up photographs. In other parks, campers have obviously fed raccoons, skunks and other animals because these animals fearlessly approach new campers in the campgrounds. Once these animals learn that some people will feed them, they lose their fear of people and can become dangerous.

Plants. Most public parks forbid the cutting, picking, or defacing of plants in the park. More specifically, parks forbid cutting live trees for firewood, tent poles, bedding or other reasons, and many parks are now forbidding picking up dead wood in the forest because it provides food and habitat for microorganisms at the bottom of the food chain. Parks on the Alabama and Florida Gulf Coast have forbidden picking sea oats for over twenty years because the sea oats provide root structure that holds the sand and allows sand dunes to grow and protect the inland from high tidal surges. The oats also provide habitat for wildlife. But some people pick them despite the prohibitions. Henderson Beach State Park in Destin, Florida, and other parks prohibit walking through the undergrowth from one campsite to another site and tying clotheslines, hammocks, and other objects to any vegetation. This general rule also forbids driving nails into trees, but a few thoughtless people do it anyway. On a few occasions, I have observed neighbors trying to stick knives and axes into trees and other neighbors hanging hot lanterns on the sides of trees. Ethical campers should not engage in any of these destructive practices and should report them if observed in other campsites.

Fires. Most parks provide fire rings and have rules regarding campfires. Parks with fire rings usually allow small fires most of the time but may not allow them during prolonged dry weather. If a fire ring is provided and campfires are permitted, campers should build their fires in the fire ring, wherever it is located. Campers should not try to move a fire ring to a new location. Campers should also keep their fires small and have water handy in case a fire gets out of control. Fires should be completely extinguished before going to bed at night and whenever campers leave the campsite.

Alcoholic beverages. Many state parks, including those in Tennessee, Kentucky, Illinois, and Michigan now restrict the possession and consumption of alcoholic beverages. Some parks restrict alcohol use to designated areas, such as individual campsites, while other parks completely forbid it. When planning a trip, campers should read the alcohol policy and be prepared to comply with it. The purpose of these rules is to prevent obnoxious drunken behavior, destruction of park resources, and litter (beer cans, bottles, and cardboard cartons). In past years, many parks were lenient in their enforcement of rules regarding alcohol possession, but because of repeated problems with disorderly behavior and littering, many parks have begun to strictly enforce these alcohol rules.

Pets. Most parks require pet owners to keep their pets on relatively short leashes and under control at all times. Pet owners are also expected to clean up their pets' fecal material. If pets are aggressive or make noise, many park rangers will usually demand that the animals be boarded or that the owners leave the park.

Checkout time. Most parks require that campers vacate their sites by noon or one in the afternoon on the day of departure. This rule is especially important in popular campgrounds, such as Peninsula State Park in Wisconsin, where most campsites are immediately occupied by a new party soon after the previous party leaves. The purpose for this rule is to give the departing occupants plenty of time to eat breakfast and pack up but also give the next occupants plenty of time to set up their camp before dark.

Maximum length of stay. Many state and federal campgrounds impose a maximum length of stay of fourteen days to prevent public campgrounds from becoming permanent trailer parks and tent cities. Every camper, other than campground hosts, must physically pack up their campsite and possessions and vacate the site after the maximum length of stay so that other people have an opportunity to enjoy the campground and any particular campsite. A few parks do not have this rule and allow seasonal campers to stay in one site all summer.

Leave No Trace Principles

In 1994, the Center for Outdoor Ethics officially assumed responsibility for the Leave No Trace (LNT) program. This LNT program promotes seven guidelines for visitors to wilderness areas where law-enforcement officers may be scarce. Hikers are expected to become familiar with these guidelines, follow them as much as possible, and encourage children and other park users to follow them. While these guidelines were specifically formulated for wilderness areas, they also apply in any public park or campground. Basic tent campers should become familiar with these guidelines and try to follow them at all times.

Plan ahead and prepare. Backpackers and backcountry hikers should plan their trips several weeks before their departure date so that they will have the appropriate equipment (especially maps and navigation equipment) and permits. Being prepared prevents having to improvise by cutting bushes and trees and also prevents having to mobilize search and rescue missions when hikers get lost. Backcountry campers should familiarize themselves with the rules of their destination so that they will be prepared to comply with them and can secure all necessary permits. Backpackers should pack necessary supplies and equipment to comply with all regulations. Backcountry hikers should also know the location of their trailheads so that they do not have to waste time and gas driving from one location to another.

Basic tent campers should read books and websites describing their campground destinations and the rules and procedures for securing campsites there. Frequently, campers must make advance reservations to ensure that a site will be available on the date of arrival. Other campgrounds only offer sites on a first-come basis, and visitors should have backup plans in case all sites are taken. When campers arrive at a campground, they should have proper shelter, clothing, and equipment so that they will be able to stay warm, dry, and comfortable during their stay and not have to cut vegetation for emergency shelter. If alcoholic beverages are prohibited, campers should be prepared to comply with this rule.

Travel and camp on durable surfaces. In most wilderness areas, backcountry campers are encouraged to stay on established paths rather than tramping through virgin fields and undergrowth. They should set up their camps in places that have been previously used for camping or on rocky ground that has little vegetation. Basic tent campers should set up their tents in established campsites and on tent pads, if provided. They should also keep the rest of their campsites within the defined campsite limits. When walking or biking around the campground and park, campers should stay on paved or gravel paths or designated trails rather than traipsing across the grass or through understory plant growth.

Dispose of waste properly. Backpackers and backcountry campers should bag all their empty food containers, paper, plastic, and metal. They should pack this trash in their backpacks and bring it back out with them and dispose it into proper recycling or trash receptacles. They should also learn and follow rules regarding the disposal of human feces. Sometimes they can bury it, but some parks require backpackers to bag it and bring it out also. Backpackers should also use biodegradable soap and learn proper ways to dispose of soapy bathwater and dishwater. Basic tent campers should keep their campsites clean and frequently take their garbage and recyclables to the proper disposal locations. They should also determine the proper procedures regarding the disposal of soapy dishwater. Some campgrounds require campers to dispose their soapy water into gray water disposal stations, while other campgrounds suggest pouring it into flush toilets.

Leave what you find. This rule seems to apply equally to both backpackers and basic tent campers. Hikers and campers should not pick up rocks, wood, flowers, or other objects for souvenirs. Furthermore, they should not move large stones or landscape timbers. Campers should enjoy the park but understand that they are not free to make changes to it. They should not carve their names or initials onto trees, write their names on walls with markers or spray paint, rearrange landscaping rocks or timbers, or take souvenirs such as rocks or pieces of wood. A well-known directive for park preservation is "Take only pictures, leave only footprints, and bring home only memories." If possible, ethical basic tent campers should go another step further and try to have a positive environmental impact. They should clean up trash and waste left by previous campers and, if possible, repair things that were damaged by previous campers, like removing nails from trees.

This guideline has also been used to discourage digging unnecessary trenches around tents and kitchen shelters. Unnecessary trenching by many campers could increase soil erosion and damage soil and plants that serve as food and habitat for small organisms in the food chain. Although basic tent campers staying in developed campsites may occasionally have to fill depressions or rechannel running water, most of the time they can set up their campsites on high ground and never have to dig a trench.

Minimize campfire impacts. Backpackers and backcountry hikers should be aware of wildfire hazards and keep their fires under control at all times. They must take every precaution to prevent forest fires that could kill local plants and animals. When building a fire, hikers should make mound fires or use previously used campfire sites to avoid burning fresh ground. Hot fires kill microorganisms that constitute the first level of the food chain. In fact, some backpacking books recommend avoiding campfires altogether and using small stoves to cook meals.

Basic tent campers staying in developed public campgrounds will usually have fire rings in their campsites. These rings should not be moved, and fires should be kept small and under control at all times. As already mentioned, basic tent campers should purchase firewood from local vendors to prevent the spread of destructive pests. Living, or green, trees or bushes should never be cut, because they are difficult to burn and provide food and habitat for various animal species living in the park.

To keep campfires under control, campers should have water nearby and never leave their fire unattended, even to go to the bathroom. When campers must leave the campsite or go to bed, they should extinguish the fire completely. To extinguish a fire, douse it with water, stir the ashes with a crowbar or long stick, douse it again. Repeat this sequence until the fire is completely out. Some outdoor ethicists recommend scattering the ashes before leaving the site.

Respect wildlife. Both backpackers and basic tent campers should observe wild animals from a distance and never approach, feed, or touch them. This guideline includes snakes. Ethical campers should leave them alone. Do not try to catch or kill a snake in a public park. If a potentially dangerous snake ventures into a campground, campers should tell park employees, and those employees will then probably notify park officials who can safely catch the snake and relocate it to another part of the park. Similarly, campers should not feed birds, squirrels, raccoons, alligators, and other animals.

Be considerate of other visitors. This principle seems to apply equally to backpackers and basic tent campers and covers a lot of territory. Hikers walking downhill on a narrow path should stand to the side to allow room for uphill hikers to pass. If other campers have selected a campsite, move on and find another site. If you have stopped to view a wild animal, take your photos, and move to the side to allow others to take their photos. After enjoying a panoramic view from an observation area, move aside to let others enjoy the view. If lines have formed, at the bathroom, for example, take your place at the end of the line and wait your turn. Drive carefully in the campground, keep radio volume low, speak softly, keep noise level down, and avoid reckless behavior. If other campers or park visitors need help, stop and lend assistance.

Basic Courtesies

In addition to written rules and LNT guidelines, several basic courtesies should be observed whenever camping in public campgrounds. This list of common courtesies is based upon my experiences on past camping trips and conversations with other campers. Hopefully basic tent campers can also embrace these courtesies and encourage other campers to do the same.

Arrive early. Basic tent campers staying in developed campgrounds should plan their day so that they can arrive in the afternoon and set up their campsite before six o'clock. Campers will need time to register, set up camp, go for food and supplies, prepare the evening meal, clean up the campsite, and take a shower before ten o'clock, when most campgrounds insist that campers observe quiet hours. Campers who arrive late may disturb their neighbors while completing their tasks before bedtime. When campers arrive after dark, their headlamps, noise, and other activities during camp setup may disturb other campground occupants who are trying to relax and enjoy the quiet, peaceful evening. When campers cannot get to a campsite early, they should consider staying at a motel for the night.

Be quiet. As previously discussed, most campgrounds impose quiet hours after ten at night, but courteous campground neighbors should be quiet all the time. Campers should not yell, curse, or play loud radios—even during the day. Although families can yell at each other, play radios loudly, and make excessive noise in their homes and not disturb their neighbors, engaging in these behaviors in a campground can disturb many other visitors. Sound seems to carry more in campgrounds.

Unfortunately, a few families seem to be unable to talk with each other at normal volume levels or with inside voices. When they arrive at a campsite, they immediately begin yelling and shouting at each other as they unpack and set up their site. After the site has been set up, they continue shouting at each other as they make simple requests and demands. Sometimes simple questions like "Where is my towel?" may be shouted at such volume levels that the speaker can be heard several campsites away.

Some campers like to stay up late, sit around the campfire, play musical instruments, sing, and talk until the wee hours of the morning.

Unfortunately, when everyone else goes to bed, what may seem like normal conversation will sound very loud to neighbors who are trying to sleep. Most of the time, other campers can ignore the noise, but sometimes the noise is so loud and constant that other campers cannot sleep. Another common noise problem occurs when campers try to set up their sites late at night or break camp early in the morning. As they set up their camp or pack their gear, they will hit aluminum tent poles together, slam car doors, and rev car engines. They also will shout to each other in loud voices and make other noise that can disturb people trying to sleep or relax in neighboring sites.

Ethical campers who want to listen to music should have personal music players, such as iPods, with headphones. Campers with dogs should make sure that their dogs are quiet. Motorcycle riders should park their motorcycles and turn off the motor as soon as they arrive at their campsite. Parents with children should encourage them to play quietly. Courteous campers should respect their neighbors who want to enjoy the peace and quiet associated with the outdoor experience.

Be polite and respectful. When campers first arrive at a campsite, they should smile and speak to their neighbors. This simple gesture will help to establish cordial relations with others. If neighbors show a willingness to talk, newly arriving campers should take a few minutes to visit, asking about the neighbors' hometowns or camping rigs. Most people are more than willing to talk and will likely ask similar questions. Many times this brief conversation establishes a foundation for future social interactions and offers of assistance. When campers establish a connection with their neighbors, these neighbors may invite the new arrivals to visit with them, offer food or drink, and assist them with difficult chores, such as setting up a tarp or moving a picnic table.

Keep campsites clean. Basic tent campers should keep their campsites clean for several reasons. First, picking up trash and disposing it in trash cans will prevent mice and other animal scavengers from causing overnight problems. Second, clean campsites prevent the wind from blowing trash into the bushes or other campsites. Third, clean campsites will keep wild animals from becoming dependent upon human food and becoming a nuisance to future site occupants. Finally, clean campsites will reduce chances of tripping or stumbling and subsequent injury. Campers should keep trash bags handy and put their trash in it as soon as possible. When they must leave the campsite or go to bed, campers should take their garbage and recyclables to the proper receptacles and dispose of them properly. Campers should also arrange their tables and chairs so that they do not block logical corridors through the campsite and should stack firewood away from high-traffic areas.

Campers should also keep their sites clean so they have less work on the day of departure. Glass, plastic, and aluminum cans should be separated and placed in recycle containers. They should never be thrown into the fire, because they will not burn completely, they give off unpleasant fumes, and they will be an unsightly mess that the next campsite occupant will have to clean up. Cigarette smokers should put their butts in the garbage rather than throwing them on the ground or in the fire. These butts are unsightly and will take years to decompose. Occasionally, children who later occupy the site will pick up these butts and put them into their mouths. Before packing up and leaving a campsite, campers should police the entire area and pick up all trash, especially cigarette butts.

Do not walk through other campsites. One of my biggest peeves is adults, teens, and children who take shortcuts to the bathhouse, water pump, playground, or other park areas by walking through my campsite. All people should understand that when another person rents a campsite, he or she is renting a temporary residential property similar to a motel room or house. When a neighbor takes a shortcut through the property to another park location, he or she is invading the renter's private room without permission. Therefore, all campers must learn to stay on established roads and pathways rather than walking through other campers' sites. Ethical campers will resist the temptation to take shortcuts and teach children to do the same.

Do not wash dishes in bathroom sinks. A few campers in every campground will wash their dishes in bathroom sinks, water fountains, and pumps. These campers will take all their dirty cookware and dinnerware to a potable water station or bathroom sink and spend thirty minutes or more washing these dishes. Other campers who just want to get a little water may have to wait several minutes while the thoughtless campers waste time washing and rinsing a sink full of dishes from their last meal. In addition to making other campers wait for water, this practice could increase the presence of bacteria and food pathogens at the water station that could attract mice and other animals and cause illness for other campers. A better practice would be to wash dishes in the campsite, catch soapy gray water in a bucket, and then dump the gray water in the appropriate disposal area after the dishes have been washed and rinsed.

Keep bathrooms clean. Another basic courtesy is to help keep bathrooms clean. Many people sharing a public bathroom can mess it up in a hurry. Although park employees typically clean bathrooms once or twice a day, bathrooms may not stay clean for long—especially if the campground is full. Bathrooms in popular campgrounds will quickly get nasty unless everyone helps to keep them clean. Each user should dispose of all their trash. If another camper has left paper or trash in the bathroom, the next campers should put it in the trash receptacle. After using the sink area, campers should get a paper towel or some toilet paper and wipe up before leaving. They should also flush the toilet and be sure it is ready for the next person. If the toilet gets stopped up, campers should notify park personnel immediately. After using showers, campers should leave them as clean as possible for the next users.

Help neighbors in need. By paying attention to what is going on in the campground, campers will frequently notice neighbors who need assistance. Perhaps a neighbor does not have enough firewood, charcoal, or ice. Maybe another neighbor forgot to pack an important food item, such as pancake syrup, before leaving home. Possibly a child will get injured. Or perhaps someone's car battery will die. Simple difficulties such as these could ruin a camping trip. Therefore, when another person has a problem, campers should be willing to lend a hand. If someone needs some firewood, campers can give them a few logs from their own stacks. If someone's car battery is dead, an ethical camper can offer to give him or her a jump. Small acts of kindness like these will make the camping trip more enjoyable for both parties.

Return lost property. Occasionally, campers may find property that belongs to another person. For example, a water container may have been left near the water spigot or a towel may have been left in the bathhouse. When campers find these relatively inexpensive items, they should leave them where they are and assume that the owner will return to retrieve them. On a trip to Wind Creek State Park in Alabama, Eva left one of her favorite pairs of shorts in the bathroom after her evening shower. Upon returning to our campsite, she realized that she had left the shorts and returned to the bathroom to retrieve them. Unfortunately, they were gone. Someone had already taken them.

Sometimes, campers may find valuable property, such as jewelry, eyeglasses, cell phones, purses, or wallets. When they find these more-valuable items, campers should take them to the park office and turn them into the lost-and-found department. Campers should wait to open wallets and purses until they are in the presence of a park employee. Then together the finder and park employee can open the wallet or purse to determine the owner's name and contact information and inventory the contents. Then they can call the owner to report that the item was turned in to the park office. Hopefully the owner will be relieved to know that all his or her cash, credit cards, and other contents are still intact.

Clean site when leaving. When the time comes to leave a campsite, basic tent campers should police the site after packing their equipment into the car. In other words, they should systematically walk around the site and pick up all trash, whether it is theirs or a previous occupant's. They should clean out the fire ring and neatly stack remaining firewood near the ring for the next occupant or a neighbor. When policing a campsite, campers will occasionally find some of their own gear, such as rope or a tent stake, that was accidentally overlooked. More importantly, campers will be leaving their site ready for the next occupant.

Leave firearms at home. For many years, pistols and other firearms were prohibited in most state and national parks. In 2010, a new federal law modified these regulations, but firearms are still prohibited in many developed campgrounds, registration stations, and public buildings. Campers staying in developed campground with good security will not need them.

Ecological Concerns

Early concerns about environmental pollution began to emerge in the mid-1800s when large factories began emitting noxious smoke into the air and dumping toxic chemicals into rivers, but concerns about environmental pollution and global warming really exploded in the 1960s. Environmentalists began to educate the public that our daily habits plus the clothing and equipment we purchase for recreational activities such as camping can have a negative impact upon our environment. Driving long distances, leaving lights on for extended lengths of time, and wasting clean drinking water are common habits that deplete valuable resources that could be exhausted in a generation or two if strict conservation practices are not implemented. Increased demands for clothing and equipment made from polyester and nylon will increase the depletion of coal and oil reserves and increase greenhouse gases and global warming. And increased demands for clothing and gear made from cotton and other plants require increased usage of potentially deadly pesticides and herbicides. Today, most scientists believe that global warming due to thoughtless consumerism has reached an environmental crisis point. Extreme climate and weather changes are beginning to cause the extinction of fragile species. If nothing is done to correct the problem, future human existence may be threatened.

Fossil fuel depletion. Many eco concerns are related to the manufacture of consumer goods, including camping gear and clothing. The first general concern relates to the overall amount of fossil fuel required to manufacture, transport, warehouse, and sell each particular product. Environmentalists have pointed out that standard manufacturing processes rely heavily upon nonreplenishable fossil fuel energy sources. In addition to the fact that many products are now being made from coal and petroleum, factories typically burn oil or coal to heat their buildings, to power their lights, and to run their machinery. After products have been produced, trucks burn gas or diesel fuel to transport goods to wholesalers and to retail outlets. Wholesale and retail outlets require energy for light and heat or air conditioning, and this energy is typically derived from burning fossil fuels. Overall, a considerable amount of fuel is burned to manufacture, transport, and store any particular product sold to consumers. Once all fossil fuels have been depleted, people may struggle to satisfy their daily needs for food, clothing, and heat.

Environmentalists have coined the phrases *carbon footprint* and *ecological rucksack* to quantify the amount of energy that is expended each year by each person. The concept can also be applied to quantify the amount of energy that is expended to produce a particular consumer product. On the web, readers can find several sites that offer formulas for estimating the carbon footprint of various activities. The calculation methods and statistics vary from one site to another, but all the sites agree that most Americans are expending two to three times the amount of energy and carbon than is environmentally desirable. These sites urge Americans to become more environmentally conscious and to reduce their carbon footprint. Many sites also urge Americans to drive fewer miles, drive fuel-efficient vehicles, use public transportation, and voluntarily pay carbon offsets (fees) to select organizations that support environmentally friendly projects, such as planting trees and using solar or wind energy to generate electricity.

Carbon dioxide. When fossil fuels are burned, they release tons of carbon dioxide into our atmosphere, which presumably accelerates the process of global warming and the consequent extinction of plant and animal species. Many environmentalists believe that global warming will have a catastrophic effect upon our planet in a relatively short time unless we quickly change our energy consumption patterns.

Toxic chemicals. A third environmental concern focuses upon chemicals used to manufacture camping gear. A lot of camping gear is made with chemicals that can harm our environment and health. For example, people working in fields and factories may be exposed to harmful and sometimes deadly levels of herbicides and pesticides. Because these chemicals become embedded in their clothing, these workers may take them home after work and expose their spouses, children, and other family members. After the manufacturing process has been completed, consumers, users, and anyone else who comes into direct contact with some of these products can be exposed to potentially harmful chemicals. Waste chemicals from the manufacturing process are frequently released into the air or into rivers where they can be inhaled, absorbed through the skin, or ingested either directly from the water supply or indirectly by eating fish, fowl, or animals that were exposed to the chemicals. Finally, many products thrown into landfills will not degrade and may release small amounts of chemicals into the soil for years to come. Different types of materials have different potentially toxic chemicals involved in their production.

Cotton, used to make clothing for recreational campers and for the general population, traditionally requires the application of considerable amounts of potentially harmful fertilizers, pesticides, and herbicides. Pesticides, in particular, have been the focus of considerable concern. Pesticides are liberally applied to prevent boll weevil and other insect infestations. Unfortunately, field workers in many countries are exposed to extremely high doses of these dangerous pesticides by physical contact and by inhalation. According to the World Health Organization, approximately three million cases of pesticide poisoning and twenty thousand deaths have been reported each of the past ten years (mostly in third world countries). Herbicides are another concern. They are applied early in the growing cycle to control weeds and then again at the end of the growing cycle to kill the leaves of the plants to facilitate picking. Unfortunately, these herbicides can be inhaled by anyone working in the fields or living nearby and can be ingested due to runoff into local water supplies.

After cotton has been converted into cloth, chromium and heavy metals such as copper and zinc are used to make dyes to color the fabric. These metals can be especially hazardous to textile workers and also pose an environmental problem to nearby residents because they are typically released into the air or dumped into nearby rivers, where they can be ingested by other people through foods and drinking water. Prolonged exposure can cause skin ulcerations, breathing problems, and possibly cancer.

Wool made from sheep is associated with increased levels of methane gas and toxic chemicals. Methane gas, produced from the digestive process in sheep (as well as cows) and belched into the air, is a powerful greenhouse gas that presumably contributes to global warming. Pesticide dips and antibiotics are used to maintain high wool production, and food mixed with formaldehyde is fed to sheep to increase wool production. After the wool has been harvested, chlorine (which is also used to make household cleaners and to sanitize water) is applied to the fabric to reduce shrinkage. Excessive exposure to chlorine can cause pneumonia, emphysema, hypoxia, pulmonary edema, asphyxia, cardiac arrest, and death. Later in the manufacturing process, heavy metals are used to make dyes to color the fabric.

Soft plastic products used to make water containers and other camping gear are frequently made with polyvinyl chloride (PVC or vinyl). PVC contains large amounts of chlorine and, when burned in the trash, produces dioxins that are powerful carcinogens. Soft plastics also contain traces of mercury and phthalates such as DEHP that can leech out and possibly poison anyone who comes into contact with the product by inhalation, skin absorption, or ingestion. Excessive exposure to these chemicals can cause lung cancer, lymphomas, leukemia, brain cancer, and liver cirrhosis. PVC products may be identified by the number 3 inside the universal recycling symbol or by the letter *v* under the symbol.

Hard plastic used to make buckles, water bottles, and cups may contain bisphenol A (BPA). When this type of bottle is heated (e.g., in a dishwasher, by hot drinks, or by direct sunlight), BPA could leech out of the plastic into liquids inside the bottle and perhaps cause health problems to anyone who drinks the liquids. BPA is a synthetic variation of estrogen and may cause reproductive problems, cancer, and other health problems. It may be found in bottles that have either the number 3 or the number 7 inside the universal recycling symbol.

Leather, used to make boots and various articles of motorcycle riding apparel, is associated with increased levels of methane gas from cow belching and chromium used to tan leather products.

In sum, basic tent camping offers considerable personal freedom that can be enjoyed many ways. Campers can piddle in the campsite all day, stroll around the campground, talk with neighbors, or enjoy various recreational and educational activities. Many campers like to read books, listen to their favorite music, or chat with neighbors. Campground chefs like to cook great-tasting meals, while other campers prefer to find good local restaurants. The fact is—campers are free to do almost anything they want on a camping vacation. But with this freedom, campers should also accept five general responsibilities:

- Be considerate and respectful toward other people.
- When possible, buy products made with recycled materials.
- Help to preserve the park's beauty, animal habitat, and natural resources.
- Repair, restore, and recycle clothing and equipment as much as possible.
- Be careful.

These five principles should guide everyone's behavior when camping and when engaging in other life activities. If everyone followed these basic principles, this would be a near-perfect world with few, if any, problems. Readers who want to learn more about ecological concerns can visit the Leave No Trace website as well as websites like www.ClimateCrisis.com, www.Nature.org, www.WeCanSolveIt.livejournal.com/, www.ClimateProtection.org, and www.BlueSign.com/.

Everyone should drive slowly in campgrounds because children, adults, and other vehicles may be encountered in the roads.

Tims Ford State Park in Tennessee and many other state and national parks prohibit alcoholic beverages.

Hikers and campers should stay on paved roads and designated pathways to preserve vegetation and prevent soil erosion. This photo was taken in the Chattahoochee National Forest in North Georgia.

18

EQUIPMENT MAINTENANCE

Although early camping books usually mentioned the importance of drying tents after each camping trip, they rarely offered additional advice about long-term maintenance of other equipment items. But in the 1960s, environmentalists began to focus upon the negative environmental impact of mass manufacturing and increased use of disposable products. This focus encouraged campers and other outdoor enthusiasts to consider innovative ways to extend the life span of their camping equipment in order to reduce their carbon footprints. In particular, conservation leaders emphasized the importance of recycling, repairing, and reusing camping equipment to reduce the depletion of nonrenewable fuels, exposure to toxic chemicals, and emissions of carbon dioxide. Over the next fifty years, camping books and articles began mentioning ways to repair equipment to extend its life span but never stated how long equipment should last. Even today, camping books and articles frequently report ways to repair specific types of equipment but still do not state the expected life span of camping gear. So the first question to consider is, How long should camping equipment last?

After buying and using camping equipment for over forty-five years and talking with hundreds of other campers and dozens of sales associates, I have concluded that most good camping equipment should last at least twenty years with proper care. To support this position, let me cite a few examples. In 1976, my wife at the time bought a canvas cabin tent at a yard sale for about ten dollars. It was about ten years old but was still in good condition. It had a sewn-in floor and nine heavy steel poles—one for each end, one ridge pole, and six side poles. Although the tent and poles weighed over fifty pounds and required considerable packing space, my family and I used this tent for dozens of summer camping vacations around the southeastern and midwestern United States over the next fifteen years. In 1992, I gave this tent to my son, and he continued to use it for camping trips over the next five years. I think the tent was eventually lost during a move, but we certainly got our money's worth out of that used ten-dollar tent. Other examples of camping equipment lasting over twenty years can be found in many places. For example, the Eureka Tent & Awning Company has a one-hundred-year-old tent on display in their corporate office. Several websites offer parts to restore fifty-year-old Coleman stoves. And many veteran campers report that major equipment items like sleeping bags, hatchets, mattresses, and cook sets have lasted at least twenty years. Procedures for maintaining various pieces of camping equipment are summarized in the following sections.

Open and Dry

After every camping trip, basic tent campers must unpack their equipment, open duffel bags, and spread all items out so that they can dry. Tents, ground cloths, hammocks, and sleeping bags (inside out) should be hung up to dry; bundles of cord, kitchen tarps, and poles should be opened up and spread out on tables and chairs; mattresses should be opened and stored under beds; folding chairs and tables should be opened; coolers should be emptied and dried; kitchenware should be washed and dried; gloves should be laid out; and clothing should be washed and dried. Once all items have been opened to dry and a load of clothes has been started in the washer, campers can relax for the rest of the evening. After drying one or two days, most equipment can be cleaned and repacked for the next trip. To prevent mold and mildew, tents should be dried for at least three days.

Clean and Repack

A day or two after spreading equipment out, inspect each item to determine if it needs to be cleaned before repacking. Some cleaning and repacking tips are offered below.

Tents. After allowing tents and tarps to dry for a day, brush dried sand and dirt away with a whisk broom, and then look for dried mud or bird poop. To clean these items, use mild unscented soap and a wet shop rag or toothbrush. Tent makers advise owners to avoid stronger detergent soap because stronger soap may have perfumes that could attract animal scavengers on future trips or detergents could can damage the waterproof coatings. If the damp rag or toothbrush does not clean the area, refer to the tent manufacturer's recommendations. Tent makers also recommend cleaning zippers, when necessary, with a quick dip in water and a toothbrush.

If tents are badly soiled, call the manufacturer's technical support department to get further advice before trying to remove persistent stains. Several years ago, REI recommended using small amounts of kerosene to remove tree sap from my Camp Dome 4 tent. More recently, *Backpacker Magazine* recommended mineral oil, rubbing alcohol, nail polish remover, or Goo Gone to remove tree sap. To remove mildew, REI recommends a solution of MiraZyme and water. Once the tent has been cleaned, rehang it for at least three days before packing.

The best way to repack a tent has been the subject of considerable professional debate. While Holding and many other authorities have recommended folding and rolling for long-term storage, several recent books and manufacturers have recommend stuffing tents into their stuff sacks, arguing that stuffing avoids damage to the fabric and waterproof coatings caused by repeatedly folding tents in the same place.

After trying both methods over the past forty-five years, I use the fold and roll method for several reasons. For example, most new tents are folded and rolled into their stuff sacks and may remain in this condition months before they are sold. Folding and rolling allows users to quickly squeeze air out of the tent and pack the tent along with its poles in a small stuff sack. Furthermore, I have used the fold and roll method for over forty years and have never noticed any damage to any of my tents, including my old REI Family Dome 4, which I used for eleven years. When I tried stuffing tents, the procedure required much more time to squeeze air pockets out and made it difficult to include the poles in the stuff sack. Follow this procedure to fold and roll a tent:

- Spread the ground cloth flat on a clean concrete or asphalt surface, such as a garage floor.
- Fold the long side in half, and then fold it in half again. For example, an eight-foot-long ground cloth would be four feet wide after the first fold and two feet wide after the second fold.
- Roll the folded tent poles inside the ground cloth, and set aside.
- Lay the tent canopy flat on the clean floor, and spread it as flat as possible.
- Spread the rain fly on top of the canopy, pull flat, and fold over so that the edges of the fly are all within the boundary of the canopy edges.
- Fold the long side of the tent in half and then in half again. The width of the tent should now be the same as the length of its stuff sack.
- Place the rolled ground cloth with the tent poles at one end of the folded tent and loosely roll all parts together.
- Slide rolled tent into stuff sack.
- Store tent stakes in the tool bag.

Tools. Lay all tools from the tool bag on a clean table to dry. Brush dried mud and sand away from tent stakes. Then shake dirt and sand out of the bag, and lay it on its side to dry. Clean small rust spots on the hatchet head by spraying a little WD-40 on it and cleaning it with a pot scouring pad. If other tools are wet, dry them with a shop rag and apply a thin coat of WD-40 or machine oil to prevent rust. Wash the microfiber towel from the tool bag with other dirty clothes.

Furniture. Most of the time, furniture does not require special cleaning, but occasionally tree sap or bird poop must be removed from chairs, hammocks, and tables. In these cases, try liquid detergent and a toothbrush. If this does not clean the area, try Goo Gone or isopropyl alcohol.

Kitchenware. After longer trips and especially after damp trips, run all kitchenware through the dishwasher to thoroughly clean it. After cleaning, place a light coat of vegetable oil on the springs, pivot pins, and locks of folding knives. Also clean the camp stove and cooking grate with a scrubbing pad and soap to remove burnt food and grease. Discolored coolers can be cleaned with a mild bleach-and-water solution and exposed to direct sunlight. When repacking the kitchen items, make a point to refill the travel-size dish detergent and laundry detergent bottles.

Bedding. All clothing, towels, sheets, and pillowcases should be washed and dried after each trip. After sleeping bags have dried for a day, inspect them to determine if any places need to be cleaned. If campers bathe before bed and sleep in clean clothes while camping, they will not need to wash the bags often but may need to clean a spot of dirt or oil or two. To clean small spots, pull the cover or liner away from the insulation and clean it with a little mild soap (such as Woolite), water, and a toothbrush. Most camping experts recommend washing sleeping bags as rarely as possible to avoid damaging their insulation and coverings. But eventually bags must be completely washed. Procedures for washing sleeping bags will be discussed in the "Repair and Restore" section of this chapter. After cleaning any spots, allow bags to dry on a carpeted floor for at least one day. Then flip them over and allow them to dry for two more days. After drying at least three days, loosely stuff them into large mesh laundry bags or pillowcases, and store them on a shelf in a closet.

Clothing. After most trips, campers will have a large bag of dirty clothes for each camper plus towels, washrags, dishcloths, dish towels, and a tool towel. Cleaning everything will take several loads of laundry, but everything does not have to be washed on the first day home. Just open bags so that garments can dry, and wash one or two loads a day for the next two or three days.

Some garments and towels may have a strong smoke smell after camping trips, but this smell can usually be removed by ordinary washing with laundry detergent and Suavitel fabric softener. Hard rain shells, however, should be washed with Nikwax Tech Wash, which can be purchased in most camping outfitters. In addition to removing the smoke smell, the product will help to restore water repellency.

Fortunately, I have never had to clean garments saturated with skunk musk, but occasionally campers must deal with this problem—especially campers that bring their dogs on camping trips or bring food into their tents. Several suggestions have been offered in other books, but the best way to clean skunked clothing appears to be with McNett MiraZyme, which is sold in most camping outfitters. Mix half an ounce with twenty gallons of water, and soak garments for thirty minutes. Other suggestions presented in books and on the web have notable limitations. For example, some books recommend applying beer or tomato juice, but these items leave a food smell that could attract more animal scavengers. Yet other books and articles recommend mixing hydrogen peroxide, baking soda, and mild liquid soap, but this recipe can be explosive and can damage delicate fabrics. Nature's Miracle and Brampton sell skunk-odor removers, but these products are intended for dogs and human skin and may not be safe for clothing.

Dirty hiking boots will occasionally have to be cleaned after a camping trip. To clean them, first remove the laces and insoles. Then wash the laces with other clothes. Use a stiff brush to brush away as much mud as possible from each boot, and wipe the boots with a damp cloth. You may have to brush and wipe small cracks and crevices several times to remove mud and dirt. Once the boots are clean, rinse thoroughly, insert crumpled newspapers, allow to air-dry, and then apply appropriate conditioner to keep the materials pliable. For example, mink oil or some other leather conditioner should be applied to leather boots. Nikwax makes conditioners and waterproofing products for both leather and fabric boots.

Personal items. Personal items such as medicine, electronics, books, grooming kits, and bath supplies usually do not require special cleaning, but supplies should be restocked. Replace empty toothpaste tubes, razors, soap, and batteries, and then pack these items in their designated day pack.

Protection and first aid. These items do not require cleaning, but items that were used on the trip, such as sunscreen, insect repellent, adhesive bandages and ibuprofen, should be restocked.

Repair and Restore

To preserve good-quality equipment, campers must learn how to repair and restore it to maximize its life span.

Tents. To save money, many inexperienced campers purchase inexpensive summer tents from local department or sporting good retail stores. Unfortunately, these inexpensive tents will soon begin to leak. To solve this problem, apply liquid seam sealer to the seams. A small tube of McNett's Seam Grip costs less than ten dollars and can quickly stop the leaky seams. Coghlan's and Gear Aid also make good seam sealing products. Procedures for sealing tent seams are summarized below.

- If the tent maker provides a technical support office, call and ask for specific recommendations.
- Determine the type of sealer to be used. Economy-priced tents can be sealed with any sealer, but a few tents made with ultralight materials may require special products.
- Determine the seams that need sealing. Only a few seams on rain flies require sealing.

- Determine the side of the seam to be sealed. Some makers recommend only sealing the inside seam, while other experts recommend sealing both sides.
- Set up the tent.
- Clean the seam. Several experts recommend using isopropyl alcohol, but consult tent maker's recommendations before applying.
- Apply enough liquid seam sealer with a small foam pad or brush to soak all the crevices and stitch holes on the seam.
- Allow the sealer to dry for eight to ten hours.
- If the seam is tacky, apply talcum powder before packing.

In addition to sealing the seams, most tents will require occasional repair during their lifetimes. Several recent books and magazine articles have offered tips for making common repairs, but a tent owner should call the maker's technical support department before attempting any repair. Technicians will sometimes recommend specific products that work especially well or identify unforeseen problems that could cause further damage to the tent. Sometimes technicians will recommend sending the damaged tent back to the factory to be professionally repaired rather than risk further damage to the tent. In fact, some companies, including Eureka, will repair their tents for many years after purchase. Some common home-repair and restoration procedures are summarized below.

- Bent or broken aluminum poles—Call the tent maker's technical support department or call Tent Pole Technologies in Vancouver, Washington (360-260-9527). This company makes replacement poles for most tents, and from personal experience I can say that their service is outstanding!
- Broken fiberglass poles—If the maker does not provide a technical support department, call Campmor (888-226-7667) or REI (800-426-4840) technical support and ask for advice. A few companies, including Coghlan's and Coleman, sell tent-pole repair kits. Although it is an expensive option, campers

could call Tent Pole Technologies and replace broken fiberglass poles with aluminum poles.

- Stretched or broken shock cord—Replace with Coghlan's shock cord, which is sold in local department or sporting goods stores. Sew one end of the new cord to one end of the old cord end and use the old cord to pull the new cord through the pole sections. Do not tie the two ends together, because the knot may be too large to pass through the pole channels. If the old shock cord is no longer in the channel, use a small-gauge wire such as bailing wire to guide the shock cord through the pole sections.
- Small fabric holes or tears—Apply Tear-Aid patches to both sides of the damaged area.
- Mold and mildew—Scrub with a wet shop rag and mild soap. Soak in MiraZyme if necessary.
- Bad smell—Soak tent in MiraZyme solution.
- Leaking rain fly—Spray with Nikwax Tent & Gear SolarProof.

Tarps. Although tarps used for ground cloths and kitchen canopies require very little maintenance, campers may want to modify their tarps by inserting new grommets. For example, grommets can be used to add webbing to ground cloth corners with seats for tent-pole tips. Brass grommets are best for basic tent camping because they will not rust. Smaller grommets about one-quarter inch in diameter are best for ground cloths, while larger grommets about one-half inch in diameter are best for kitchen canopies. Coghlan's kit with three-eighth-inch grommets, which is sold in many department stores, could be used for most repairs. Follow these steps to insert a grommet:

- Mark the spot on the tarp for the new grommet with a felt-tip pen.
- Place a piece of scrap wood on a solid surface such as a concrete floor, and place the marked spot on top of the wood.
- Put the hole punch from the kit on top of the marked spot, and strike firmly with a hammer.

- Gently remove the punch from the wood, and inspect to be sure the center hole piece of tarp has been completely severed.
- Place the male side of a grommet (with the extended collar) onto the grommet anvil from the kit, and insert the extended collar through the newly cut hole.
- Place the female side of a grommet over the collar with cupped side up.
- Place the grommet setting tool on top of the collar, and strike firmly two or three times with a hammer.

Sleeping bags. The primary maintenance for sleeping bags is occasional washing when dirty or smelly. Campers who take several trips a year should wash their sleeping bags every winter. Cleaning a sleeping bag is a relatively easy process, but before proceeding, campers should refamiliarize themselves with their particular makers' recommendations. Procedures for each bag may vary somewhat, and procedures for down-filled bags differ from those for synthetic-filled bags. In general, bag owners can hand-wash their bags in bathtubs with nondetergent soap or sometimes wash them in front-loading commercial washing machines. Sleeping bags should never be dry-cleaned! The basic procedure for washing sleeping bags in a bathtub is summarized below:

- Draw lukewarm water in the bathtub, and gently wash the bag with Woolite, or Nikwax Down Wash 2.0 for down-filled bags.
- Spread the bag flat in the tub, and rinse it several times.
- After rinsing, allow water to drain from the bag for thirty minutes.
- Carefully pick up the entire bag. Do not pick up just one end because the weight of the water in the hanging material could tear the insulation or coverings.
- Lay the bag flat on a sunny surface, such as the back porch or driveway, to begin air-drying.
- After about one hour, gently flip it over to allow the other side dry.

- After another hour, hang it from a clothesline or similar safe spot to completely dry.

People who do not want to fuss with washing their bags can ship them to Rainy Pass Repairs (206-523-8135) for commercial washing. This company also repairs sleeping bags and other outdoor gear. For additional suggestions for equipment cleaning and repair, contact REI.

Sometimes, sleeping bag covers, blankets, and other fabrics tear. Before attempting a repair, call the item's technical support staff, and determine the best way to repair it. Sometimes a Tear-Aid patch will solve the problem, while other times a patch must be sewn with needle and thread. Occasionally zippers on sleeping bags become damaged. Other books have suggested that these problems can be fixed with a pair of needle-nose pliers, but I have not had much luck fixing them. Whatever the problem, campers should call the appropriate manufacturer's technical support department to determine the best way to repair the product. Many times, support staff will recommend that the owners return the product to their company for professional repair.

Air mattresses. Although I have never had to repair an air mattress, other campers have reported a few common problems. The most frequently reported problem is a punctured air mattress. See chapter 13, "Base-Camp Chores," for instructions on the best way to fix this issue. A mattress with a leaky valve may have to be returned to the manufacturer for professional repair or replacement.

Hammocks. Hammocks can develop a smoky or sweaty smell after several camping trips. To remove this smell, wash the hammock in a bucket of water with a little Woolite and rinse. If this wash does not solve the problem, soak it in a bucket of water with MiraZyme. Perhaps a more serious problem for hammocks is excessive exposure to ultraviolet light that will gradually degrade nylon and polyester fibers. To avoid this problem, campers should take their hammocks down when not in use and store them in cool, shady places. With proper care, hammocks should last twenty years or longer.

Tools. Most tools require very little maintenance and will last twenty years or longer. I bought an inexpensive Wenzel hatchet from a discount department store twenty years ago, and despite a little rust and a few dings, it still drives tent stakes and splits firewood as well as it did new. The only maintenance it has needed has been occasional resharpening. To sharpen a hatchet, clamp it to a worktable with a small wood wedge under the bit and use a metal file to shape each edge. The file must be pushed hard enough to shave away small amounts of metal. Then sharpen the edge with a Smith's JIFF-S sharpening tool or a stone. Some people use grinding wheels, but the heat from the grinder can damage the steel's hardness. After sharpening the axe, cover the bit with a sheath so that it does not get nicked by other tools in the bag and so that it does not accidentally injure someone or damage other equipment. If a sheath is unavailable, make one or cover the bit with a towel secured with a hair tie. Knives should also be sharpened occasionally. Other camping books recommend sharpening knives with stones, but considerable skill and time is required to get a sharp edge. A much easier way to sharpen knives is to use Smith's JIFF-S. Just lay the knife on a bench with the sharp edge up, and pull the sharpener over it three or four times. Other tools, such as the pliers, multi-tools, screwdriver, and crowbar, require very little off-season maintenance other than applying a light coat of machine oil.

Rolltop tables. The primary problem to expect for rolltop tables is the gradual deterioration of the elastic shock cord that holds the table slats together. When a shock cord breaks, call the table maker to seek advice before attempting a repair. Typically replacement is a simple task, and service department technicians will explain how to do it, but some tables may be more difficult to repair, and the technicians may recommend that the table be returned to the company for professional repair.

Camp stoves. Camp stoves require a little maintenance but with care should last for well over twenty years. In fact, YouTube videos show how to restore forty-year-old Primus and Coleman stoves so that they work as well as they did when new. After the season is over, campers should thoroughly clean camp stoves with a toothbrush, dish detergent, and hot water. After cleaning, turn them upside down to drain water, and dry them completely to prevent the development of rust.

Liquid-gas stoves, such as Coleman gas stoves, require additional off-season maintenance. At the end of each season, campers should pour leftover fuel from the stove tank into another container, allow the tank to air-dry, and oil the pump cup on the plunger. After about ten years of use, the generator assembly may need to be cleaned or replaced. Before proceeding, call the stove maker's technical service department and seek advice. Cleaning and replacing individual parts such as the needle and spring is relatively easy and economical, but replacing the entire assembly will ensure that the stove will not need additional maintenance for ten more years. Replacement parts for old Coleman stoves can be found on www.oldcolemanstoves.com.

Clothing. Polyester, nylon, and wool garments require no off-season maintenance and last many more years than cotton garments. One desirable quality of polyester shirts is they do not hold stains as do cotton garments. When someone spills spaghetti sauce on a white polyester shirt, it can be completely removed with a little cold water and gentle liquid soap. The primary limitations of these garments are they burn and snag easily. To avoid burning, campers must be careful around campfires and cooking equipment. To repair large snags, owners can insert a loop of thread through the eye of a large needle, push the needle partly through the material at the point of the snag, put the loop of thread around the snag, and gently pull the needle and loop all the way through the material—this method pulls the snag inside the garment where it cannot be seen.

Hard-shell jackets. Old hard-shell jackets occasionally need to be washed and rewaterproofed. To wash them, fill the washing machine with water, add five ounces of Nikwax Tech Wash, place up to two jackets in the washing machine, and wash them on the gentle cycle. Then refill the washing machine, add ten ounces of Nikwax TX.Direct

Wash-In, and put the jackets through again on the gentle cycle. Once done, hang the jackets in the garage to dry overnight.

Drawstrings. Sometimes drawstrings in jackets and stuff sacks must be replaced. If the old drawstring is still in place, sew a new one onto the end of the old one, and pull the new one through the channel. If the old string is no longer in the channel, tape a one-foot-long clothes hanger wire to the string and work the wire through the channel.

Boots. Boots and hiking shoes also need occasional attention. Leather boots should be washed and reconditioned at least once a year, and fabric shoes can be washed in washing machines. Before washing boots or shoes, remove the insoles and shoestrings. Sometimes these insoles and shoestrings can be cleaned, but after a while they need to be replaced. When boots develop small tears and separations, owners can clean the crevices, fill the crevices with Seam Grip, Freesole, or Shoe Goo, and then apply pressure with duct tape or shop clamps. If the shoes need resoling or another major repair, take them to a cobbler. If a good local cobbler is not available, call the REI technical support department and ask for a recommendation. Several cobblers around the country accept work from long-distance customers.

Personal items. Several personal items need occasional maintenance to extend their life spans. For example, nylon straps on backpacks, waist packs, and duffel bags occasionally need to be repaired or replaced. To make these repairs, cut the original strap, cut the new splice, burn all ends to prevent them from unraveling, and then sew the splice in place with an upholstery needle and thread. Use the pliers of a multi-tool to push the needle through thick materials. Tears in duffel bags occasionally need to be repaired as well. To make these repairs, sew a patch over the tear with a sewing machine. Bags with large tears may have to be taken to a professional seamstress. Although basic tent campers typically do not need large backpacks, backpackers frequently break plastic buckles. When they do, they must buy replacement buckles and replace them with a patch, needle, and thread.

Upgrade

Entry-level campers frequently buy economical camping equipment that will have to be replaced at some point in time. Those that come to enjoy camping will typically want to upgrade their equipment over the next five or so years. The first year, for example, they may want to buy better sleeping pads. The second year they may want to buy better clothing. In subsequent years, they may want to upgrade their kitchen gear, furniture, and tents. The winter months are best for upgrading camping equipment because many campers have more time to shop for equipment, Christmas allows people to distribute wish lists to their family and friends, and many companies sell last year's inventory at reduced prices to make room for newer models coming out in the spring. Furthermore, members of the REI cooperative receive their annual dividend checks at the end of March plus substantial discounts on new items.

When buying new equipment, campers should look for good-quality gear made by reputable companies that will last at least twenty years. In addition, campers should consider ecological issues and purchase green equipment when possible. In particular, campers should look for good-quality products that are made from organic cotton, renewable resources such as bamboo, recycled materials, chemical-free dyes, and acid-free tent-manufacturing processes. Patagonia was one of the first companies to invest in green technologies, but many other manufacturers have now joined the movement.

When thinking about upgrading a piece of equipment, first decide what to do with the old piece of equipment. If an item is still serviceable, it should be recycled rather than thrown into a landfill. In the past, I have sold a few tents and other camping items on Craigslist but have given most of my older camping items to family members. Over the past twenty years, I have given several old tents, sleeping bags, and tools to my sons, my sister, and my brother-in-law. A few years back, I gave an older tent to a family in my community who wanted to take their children camping but couldn't afford the equipment. Other campers could donate their camping equipment to local Boys & Girls Clubs and to Scouts whose families are unable to afford good camping gear. In larger cities, camping clubs organize annual gear exchanges.

After cleaning and repacking all your camping equipment, store each equipment group in a specific place so that it is ready for the next trip. Eva and I store our shelter, furniture, tools, and kitchen equipment in the garage near the door so it is ready to load into the car at moment's notice. We store our air mattresses under our bed and our sleeping bags and personal items in a hall closet. A few days before each trip, we pack our clothing and food and are ready to load the car.

We purchased this old canvas tent in 1976 for about
ten dollars from a yard sale. It was about ten years old
at the time and lasted for another twenty years.

Upon returning home from a camping trip, I typically hang
our tent from two hooks inserted into our garage ceiling.

After hanging the tent, I open and spread all tents, tarps, furniture, tablecloths, hammocks, and tools in the garage so they can dry. On this particular trip, we had to dry an extra tent and other items used by our grandsons on the trip.

After drying all items, repack each equipment group into its respective duffel bag or milk crate, and organize these containers near the garage door so that they are ready for the next trip.

Here are a few products that I use to restore
my old camping equipment.

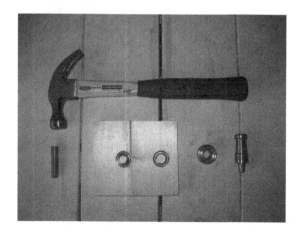

Grommet kits come with a hole puncher (*left*), brass grommets
(*center-left*), anvil (*center-right*), and setting tool (*far right*).

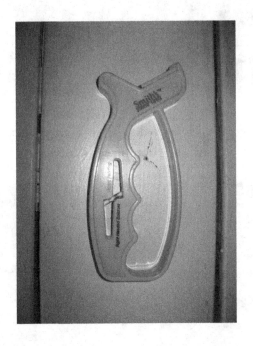

I use this Smith's JIFF-S to sharpen my knives.

CONCLUSION

Although summer tent-camping vacations have been an important American family tradition for dozens of years, these trips are in danger of extinction unless current economic and social trends can be reversed. Today, many states are converting their family campgrounds into trailer parks for large RVs, and many families are opting to forgo family camping vacations. Many people think they don't have time because of various pressures from work, school, youth sports programs, and more. Some people would rather stay in hotels and are drawn to effective marketing by vacation resorts. Plus many people don't want to be parted from their electronic devices. In addition, seductive RV sales pitches that gloss over the excessive expense required to buy, insure, repair, and operate these vehicles are seducing many families into making economic decisions that they cannot afford and that frequently compel them to give up camping altogether.

As a result of these modern pressures, many young parents are no longer taking their children on family tent-camping trips. Consequently, their adolescent children may never have the pleasures of sleeping overnight in a tent, playing with new friends from neighboring campsites, attending interesting naturalist programs, walking through a campground in pajamas at night, or cooking s'mores over a campfire. As these adolescents grow older and become parents themselves, they will not have the knowledge, experience, or motivation needed to take their own children on comfortable tent-camping trips, and, thus, family camping vacations could gradually disappear unless something is done to reverse this trend.

Although parks in several states, such as Wisconsin, Michigan, Colorado, Tennessee, and Georgia, still attract large numbers of tent-camping families every summer, other states obviously do not. In my home state of Alabama, for example, the number of families who take their children on family camping vacations has dropped dramatically over my lifetime. Every year, the number of tents in any campground decreases noticeably while the number of large motor homes and fifth wheels increases. To generate income, many Alabama state park campgrounds are now being converted into trailer parks for retirees who drive from northern states in their RVs to enjoy the mild winter weather. Although many "campgrounds" may provide fifty-foot paved parking pads, 50-amp electrical service needed to run TVs and air conditioners, water connections, dump stations, and sometimes sewage connections, they do not provide the basic amenities needed by ordinary tent-camping families. In particular, they do not have large, level campsites needed to pitch tents and kitchen canopies, shade trees needed to block the hot summer sun, elevated tent pads that will stay dry during heavy rain, or children's programs. In fact, other than the paved parking pads, many Alabama state park campsites do not have decent places to set up tents, and some forbid setting them up on paved parking pads. To add insult to injury, they charge an extra fee for families who set up a second tent for their children but not for out-of state RV visitors who have unlimited access to electricity and water.

Other states are also drawing fewer and fewer tent-camping families each year to their campgrounds. Florida, for example, has several state parks, such as Topsail Hill Preserve, that cater to older retired couples living in RVs rather than younger tent-camping families with children. Illinois is another example. Other than a few premium campgrounds near Chicago, many parks and recreation areas throughout the state, including the beautiful Wolf Creek State Park, attract few camping families and have been proposed for closure because of budget problems. Indiana state parks are virtually deserted after the second week in August because public schools open early to begin their athletic programs. As the number of families visiting public parks drops, political leaders may first suggest that higher user fees will solve budget problems, but when these fees fail to generate sufficient income, these leaders frequently suggest that public parks be closed and either leased or sold to private profit-driven companies. And when a particular property is sold to a private concern, the park's unique resources that previous citizens fought to protect will be lost forever.

To reverse these alarming trends, basic-tent-camping advocates need to do a better job of recruiting other American couples and children and educating them about the benefits of basic tent camping. In particular, young couples need to be reminded about the joys of traveling economically, living independently, sleeping in tents, smelling fresh air, viewing wild animals, working together, eating home-cooked meals, enjoying simple family recreational activities, and savoring s'mores at the end of the day. Furthermore, basic-tent-camping advocates should lobby elected public officials to stress the importance of designing and managing state parks for tent-camping families who may not have the financial ability to buy expensive motor homes. To initiate this educational program, camping advocates could begin a new educational and promotional campaign: Take more trips, travel further, visit more attractions, and save money. Go tent camping!

PACKING GUIDE

Shelter—packed in large duffel bags
- essential: tent with ground cloth, poles, and doormats
- optional: kitchen shelter or tarp

Bedding—packed in large duffel bag
- essential: mattresses, sleeping bags, and warm clothes
- optional: ground blanket, sheet, small blankets, and pillowcases

Tools—packed in small tool bag
- essential: 200 feet of cord, knives or multi-tool, hatchet, tent stakes, channel lock pliers, duct tape, gloves, and microfiber towel
- optional: screwdriver, crowbar, carabineers (6), spring clips (6), small stones (6), pole repair tube, sewing kit, and whisk broom

Furniture—packed in large duffel bag
- essential: tablecloth with tie-down cords
- optional: folding chairs, table, hammocks, bath mats, and extension cord

Protection and First Aid—packed in small bags that remain in vehicle
- essential: hats, sunscreen, insect repellent, hand sanitizer, Band-Aids, sterile pads (3), elastic bandage, ibuprofen, aspirin,

Benadryl, antibiotic ointment, burn jell, Itch Eraser, and poison ivy cream
- optional: mosquito head nets and insect-repellent clothing

Clothing—packed in small duffel bags and day packs
- first day: underwear, shirts, pants/shorts/dresses, travel vests, socks, shoes or boots, and hats
- essential: shower shoes, knit caps, underwear (2 per person), socks (2 pairs per person), shirts (3 per person), pants/shorts/dresses, athletic pants, rain jackets, and liquid detergent
- essential for cold weather: base-layer pants, extra shirts, insulated jackets, and gloves
- optional: laundry bags and extra underwear, socks, shirts, pants/shorts/dresses, hats, and shoes

Personal Items—packed in pockets and day pack
- essential: highway map, pocketknives, sunglasses, cell phones with chargers, handkerchiefs or folded paper towels, cameras, medicine, headlamps (2 per person) with extra batteries, bath supplies, grooming kits, and extra car keys
- optional: GPS receiver, radio, portable media players, laptops, DVD player, books, games, movies, water shoes, fishing tackle, tennis racquets, hitch-mounted bike rack, bikes, roof-rack system, canoes, golf clubs, and solar charger

Kitchen—packed in milk crates
- essential: water bottles, cups, spoons, tongs, butane cigarette lighters (3), small GI can opener, paper towels (10), dishrag, dish detergent, water jug, and plastic garbage bags (2)
- motorcycle options: ultrasmall soft-sided cooler, backpacking stove, fuel canister, one-quart boiler, small bowls (2), aluminum foil, nylon stirring spoon, dish towel, and cooking grate
- small-car options: twenty-five-quart hard-side cooler, backpacking stove, fuel canister, small cook set, eight-inch

frying pan, small salad plates (2), bowls (2), aluminum foil, spatula, nylon stirring spoon, dish towel, and cooking grate
- large-car options: fifty-quart hard-side cooler, two-burner propane stove, fuel cylinders (2), large cook set, ten-inch frying pan, dinner plates and bowls, aluminum foil, nylon stirring spoon, spatula, cutting board, roll of paper towels, second water jug, bucket, charcoal, and cooking grate or folding grill

Nonperishable Foods—packed in milk crates
- essential: instant oatmeal packs, tea bags, hot chocolate, honey, salt, garlic salt, and onions
- optional: tortillas, vegetable oil, hamburger buns, pancake mix, bagels, dry cereal, breakfast bars, breakfast pastries, peanut butter, canned tuna or chicken, dehydrated rice or pasta meals, packaged seasonings for spaghetti, sloppy joes, fettuccine Alfredo, Hamburger Helper meals, ramen noodles, jalapeño peppers, canned vegetables, canned fruit, fresh vegetables, fresh fruit, chips, snacks, and cookies

Perishable Foods—packed in small containers and then in a cooler
- essential: milk, cheese, eggs, and butter
- optional: Italian salad dressing, mayonnaise, mustard, ketchup, pickles, maple syrup, bacon, kielbasas, steaks, cream cheese, sour cream, juice, and pop

BIBLIOGRAPHY

Abercrombie & Fitch. *Catalogue of Complete Outfits for Explorers, Campers, & Prospectors.* New York: Abercrombie & Fitch, 1903. Reprinted with introduction by Ross Bolton. Charleston, SC: CreateSpace, 2008.

Aulabaugh, Norman. R. *The Park: Peninsula State Park Histories and Stories.* Orfordville, WI: Valley View Publishing, 2007.

The Boy Scouts of America. *Merit Badge Series: Camping.* Charlotte, NC: BSA, 2012.

The Boy Scouts of America. *Okpik: Cold Weather Camping.* Charlotte, NC: BSA, 1992.

The Coleman Company, Inc. and Outdoor Foundation. 2014 *American Camper Report.* http://www.outdoorfoundation.org/pdf/research. camping.2014.pdf

Curtis, Rick. *The Backpacker's Field Manual: A Comprehensive Guide to Mastering Backcountry Skills.* New York: Three Rivers Press, 2005.

Douglass, Frazier. *Lightweight Camping for Motorcycle Travel: Revised Edition.* New York: iUniverse, 2009.

Douglass, Frazier M. *The Family Camping Guide to Wisconsin, Michigan, Illinois & Indiana*. Boulder, CO: Trails Press, 2014.

_____. *The Tent Camper's Handbook*. New York: iUniverse, 2012.

Duncan, Dayton, and Ken Burns. *The National Parks: America's Best Idea*. New York: Alfred Knopf, 2011.

Flores, Adrian, Tadesse Haileyesus, and Arlene Greenspan. "National Estimates of Outdoor Recreational Injuries Treated in Emergency Departments, United States, 2004–2005." *Wilderness and Environmental Medicine* 19, no 2, p. 91-98, 2008.

Forster, Matt. *The Best in Tent Camping: Michigan*. Birmingham, AL: Menasha Ridge Press, 2011.

Gorman, Stephen. *The Winter Camping Handbook*. Woodstock, VT: Countryman Press, 2007.

Gray, Melissa, and Buck Tilton. *Cooking the One Burner Way*. 2nd ed. Guilford, CT: Globe Pequot Press, 2000.

Harvey, Mark. *The National Outdoor Leadership School's Wilderness Guide*. New York: Fireside, 1999.

Hemmingway, Ernest. "Camping Out." *Toronto Daily Star*, June 1920.

Herod, Lori. *Foil Cookery*. 3rd ed. Arcata, CA: Paradise Cay Publications, 2007.

Holding, Thomas H. *The Camper's Handbook*. London: Simpkin, Marshall, Hamilton, Kent & Co., 1908. Reprint, Whitefish, MT: Kessinger Publishing, 2012.

Holtzman, Bob. *The Camping Bible: The Essential Guide for Outdoor Enthusiasts.* New York: Chartwell Books, 2013.

Hostetter, Kristin. *Backpacker Complete Guide to Outdoor Gear Maintenance and Repair.* Guilford, CT: Falcon Guides, 2012.

Hung, Eric, and David Townes. "Search and Rescue in Yosemite National Park: A 10-Year Review." *Wilderness and Environmental Medicine* 18, no. 2, p. 111-116, 2007.

Jacobson, Cliff. *Basic Essentials: Cooking in the Outdoors.* 2nd ed. Guilford, CT: Globe Pequot Press, 1999.

_____. *Camping's Top Secrets.* 3rd ed. Guilford, CT: Globe Pequot Press, 2006.

_____. *Canoeing and Camping.* 3rd ed. Guilford, CT: Globe Pequot Press, 2007.

Jordan, Ryan, ed. *Lightweight Backpacking and Camping: A Field Guide to Wilderness Hiking Equipment, Technique, and Style.* Bozeman, MT: Beartooth Mountain Press, 2006.

Juckett, Gregory and John G. Hancox. "Venomous Snakebites in the United States: Managemnent Review and Update." *American Family Physician*, April 1, 2002.

Kephart, Horace. *Camping and Woodcraft.* Originally published New York: McMillan, 1917. Reprint, Knoxville, TN: University of Tennessee Press, 1988.

Molloy, Johnny. *The Best in Tent Camping: Kentucky.* Birmingham, AL: Menasha Ridge Press, 2006.

Molloy, Johnny. *The Best in Tent Camping: Tennessee.* Birmingham, AL: Menasha Ridge Press, 2005.

_____. *The Best in Tent Camping: Wisconsin.* 2nd ed. Birmingham, AL: Menasha Ridge Press, 2007.

Mouland, Michael. *The Complete Idiot's Guide to Camping and Hiking.* 2nd ed. New York: Penguin, 2000.

Nickens, T. Edward. *Field & Stream Camping Guide.* New York: Weldon Owen, 2014.

The Mountaineers of Seattle. *Mountaineering: Freedom of the Hills.* 8th ed. Seattle: Mountaineers Books, 2010.

National Geographic. *Guide to National Parks of the United States.* 7th ed. Washington, DC: National Geographic, 2012.

_____. *Guide to State Parks of the United States.* 4th ed. Washington DC: National Geographic, 2012.

Olsson, Helen. *The Down and Dirty Guide to Camping with Kids.* Boston: Roost Books, 2012.

Revolinski, Kevin. *Camping Michigan: A Comprehensive Guide to Public Tent and RV Campgrounds.* Guilford, CT: Falcon Guides, 2013.

Roundabout Publications. *National Park Service Camping Guide.* 4th ed. Lenexa, KS: Roundabout, 2010.

Rutter, Michael. *Camping Made Easy: A Manual for Beginners with Tips for the Experienced.* 2nd ed. Guilford, CT: Globe Pequot Press, 2001.

Schirle, John. *The Best in Tent Camping: Illinois.* Birmingham, AL: Menasha Ridge Press, 2009.

Sears, George W. [Nessmuk]. *Woodcraft and Camping.* New York: Forest and Stream Publishing Company, 1920. Reprint, New York: Dover Publications, 1963.

Seton, Ernest T. *Boy Scouts Handbook.* Originally published by Boy Scouts of America, 1911. Reprinted by Stellar Classics, 2013.

Skurka, Andrew. *The Ultimate Hiker's Guide: Tools and Techniques to Hit the Trail.* Washington, DC: National Geographic, 2012.

St. Clair, Lucas, and Yemaya Maurer. *AMC Guide to Winter Hiking and Camping: Everything You Need to Plan Your Next Cold-Weather Adventure.* Boston, MA: Appalachian Mountain Club Books, 2008.

Stephens, Bradford, Douglas Diekema, and Eileen Klein. "Recreational Injuries in Washington State National Parks." *Wilderness and Environmental Medicine* 16, no. 4, p. 192-197, 2005.

Schultz, Patricia. *1,000 Places to See Before You Die.* New York: Workman, 2007.

Tawrell, Paul. *Camping and Wilderness Survival.* 2nd ed. Lebanon, NH: Tawrell, 2006.

Tilton, Buck. *Backpacker—Tent and Car Camper's Handbook: Advice for Families and First-Timers.* With Kristen Hostetter. Emmaus, PA: Mountaineers Books, 2006.

Townsend, Chris. *The Backpacker's Handbook.* New York: McGraw Hill, 2005.

Waterman, Laura, and Guy Waterman. *Backwoods Ethics.* 2nd ed. Woodstock, VT: Countryman Press, 1993.

Wescott, D. *Camping in the Old Style.* Layton, UT: Gibbs Smith, 2009.

Wisby, Hrolf. "Camping Out with an Automobile." *Outing* 45, p. 739-745, 1905.

Woofter, Bob. *Motorcycle Camping Made Easy.* 2nd ed. North Conway, NH: Whitehorse Press, 2010.

Wood, D. F. *RVs & Campers 1900–2000: An Illustrated History.* Hudson, WI: Iconografix, 2002.

Wright, Micah. *Camping with the Corps of Engineers.* 8th ed. Elkhart, IN: Cottage Publications, 2011.

Printed in the United States
By Bookmasters